Maximizing Quality Performance in Health Care Facilities

Addison C. Bennett
Consultant to Management
Los Angeles, California

Samuel J. Tibbitts
Chairman of the Board
UniHealth America
Los Angeles, California

AN ASPEN PUBLICATION®
Aspen Publishers, Inc.

1989

Rockville, Maryland
Royal Tunbridge Wells

Library of Congress Cataloging-in-Publication Data

Bennett, Addison C.
Maximizing quality performance in health care facilities/ Addison C. Bennett,
Samuel J. Tibbitts.
p. cm.
"An Aspen publication."
Includes bibliographies and index.
ISBN: 0-8342-0025-2
1. Health facilities--Administration. 2. Medical care--Quality control.
3. Personnel Management. 4. Quality Assurance, Health Care. I. Tibbitts, Samuel J.
II. Title. [DNLM: 1. Health Facilities--organization & administration. WX 153 B471m]
RA971.B39 1989 362.1'1'068--dc19
DNLM/DLC
for Library of Congress
88-39437
CIP

Editorial Services: Mary Beth Roesser

Library of Congress Catalog Card Number: 88-39437
ISBN: 0-8342-0025-2

Printed in the United States of America

1 2 3 4 5

Table of Contents

About the Authors

Preface

It seems appropriate that this book was written in 1988, the year of the Olympics—a time when we applaud the athlete's chase of perfection, spirit of competition, and dedication to self-improvement. The athlete's way of experiencing self-fulfillment in his or her physical and mental efforts is to strive ever closer to perfection. While it may be reality that it is impossible to reach total perfection, given enough time the true champion will come close.

John Jerome, in his book: *The Sweet Spot in Time,* makes this observation:

> I don't think we come close to our limits. I don't think we come close to the ultimate limits of human performance in any field. In fact, I think that notion is a contradiction in terms: Human performance implies a lack of limitation. The limit is only to the amount of energy, effort, enterprise that we find worthwhile to expend on exceeding those edges. . . . World records are the curious institution by which we define those edges, these outer limits. The goal, in the record-keeping sports such as track and field, is to go over the edge of what is possible, to venture into unexplored territory, out there beyond the current realm of human experience, where no one has gone before. Imagine the thrill of that.[1]

Drawing the parallel between performance in the sports arena and performance in the arena of the contemporary workplace is believed to be a relevant and useful idea, for just as any well-prepared athlete needs to play the physical limits of the playing surface—to approach the edge of perfection—so must the individual craftsman within the world of work seek the outer limits.

The intent of this book is to seek the outer limits—to approach the edges, to go beyond the current realm of perception—of the quality of human performance. It is written for those holding leadership positions in health care who are ready and willing to replace rhetoric with a replenished commitment to *total* quality.

With a recognition of the centrality of quality assurance programming designed to measure and improve levels of provided care, this book takes the reader beyond the boundary of these essential, time-honored review practices to capture a broader meaning and discernment of the totality of quality that embraces the further dimensions of quality of work itself, quality of life at work, and quality of human conduct. Acting on these extensions brings with it renewed concentration on people-directed affairs not now receiving adequate attentiveness, and gives rise to a more fitting balance between the scientific and human factors of the quality equation.

To maintain excellence in human performance is a condition of managing—managing the technology, the human resources, and the managers themselves. However, to move performance forward to higher levels of human achievement—ever closer to perfection—managers in today's health care institutions need not—must not—accept the world of quality, and its limitations, as it is presented to them. Rather, they must think and act comprehensively—and creatively with respect to the humaneness of quality, and then cause the unequaled essentiality of the human condition of quality to touch the hearts as well as the minds of *all* members of the organizational family. To do less is a mark of failure in understanding the true uniqueness of the mission that sets health care apart from all other fields of human endeavor.

There is, too, a uniqueness about this book that sets it apart from other writings. It is found in the newness of the systemic view of the wholeness of quality that it provides.

- In Part I, a brief glimpse of history is offered as a backdrop to the central task of advancing the *people* side of quality in today's health care organization, which finds its source in its leadership's vision and visualization of a desired state of human affairs.

- Holding to the belief that in every human being there is an artist, Part II gives attention to the actions that will appeal to the craftsmanship of people at work and, in turn, promote honesty of purpose, a spirit of excellence in accomplishment, and the development of human potentialities.

- Part III supports the principle that quality enhancement is a *human* accomplishment, as it centers on the ideas of making human resource management the cornerstone of the quality effort and of reinventing the human resources function to make it capable of providing a wide range of people-directed processes and programs aligned with the quality goals of the institution.

- Part IV offers insight into the essence of quality success experienced in a non-health service organization, as well as the elements of a quality enhancement process considered suitable for adoption by health care management as a blueprint for the revival of quality and of its partnership with employees in making quality *everyone's* business.

- In the closing pages of the Epilogue, the single human being is placed center stage as the basic unit of excellence in every organization, with the underlying notion that the measure of quality enhancement over time is conditioned by the spirit and enlightenment of the individual, who is perceived as the most powerful force in quality achievement.

In keeping with the insistence of inquiry that flows throughout the entire text, it seems appropriate that this key question be asked: How can we best deal with individual differences wisely and humanely, and cause our people, through the uniqueness of their individuality, to be all they can be, and to be the very best they can be? For, indeed, the spirit of individualism and the commitment to excellence are the makings of a champion—and a *winning* organization.

Addison C. Bennett
Samuel J. Tibbitts

NOTES

1. John Jerome, *The Sweet Spot in Time* (New York: Summit Books, 1980), p. 37.

Introduction:
A Time for Quality

> Come, give us a taste of your quality.
> —Shakespeare, *Hamlet,* II, ii.

Let us launch this writing with a statement of the meaning of *quality*:

It means investment of the best skill and effort possible to produce the finest and most admirable result possible. Its presence or absence in some degree characterizes every man-made object, service, skill or unskilled labor—laying bricks, painting a picture, ironing shirts, practicing medicine, shoemaking, scholarship, writing a book. You do it well or you do it half-well. Materials are sound and durable or they are sleazy; method is painstaking or whatever is easiest. Quality is achieving or reaching for the highest standard as against being satisfied with the sloppy or fraudulent. It is honesty of purpose as against catering to cheap or sensational sentiment. It does not allow compromise with the second-rate.[1]

This general impression or feeling about quality is that of Barbara W. Tuchman, historian and twice winner of the Pulitzer Prize. Unquestionably, she is a credible source, since these expressed thoughts capture the personal reflections of an observer with half a century's awareness of and occasional participation in public affairs, supported by the study and writing of history.

The idea of a historical perspective of quality is important to us, whether our horizon time takes us back to the Renaissance period of revival, roughly from the fourteenth through the sixteenth centuries, when the craftsmen and merchants, in their consuming desire for perfection, were challenged by the same requirements as their counterparts are today; or back to the latter part of the eighteenth century, when the social and economic changes brought about by the Industrial Revolution were destined to have profound effects

1

on the way in which things were made and on the quality of these products. Even if our retrospective span is narrowed to cover but a few decades, we cannot turn our backs on the past. This is so because, for us to think about the future, we need a sense of the past.

Looking backward to "the good old days" must not be merely an act of nostalgia, for the rosy filter of nostalgia alone can give rise to a misleading emotion. A more legitimate reason for pondering the past is to determine that part of our past that belongs in our future.

As we contemplate the American values, achievements, and shortcomings belonging to an earlier time, it is hard to deny that the past few decades have been a time of declining quality in our American culture: a time when there evolved a deterioration of standards in craftsmanship designed for excellence; a time when U.S. industry's leadership in quality almost imperceptibly eroded to a deplorable state; a time when we passed into an era of mass mediocrity that cut across "all arts and professions, all layers of society, all politics, law, government, art, science, religion, industry."[2] Indeed, in terms of the vanishing element of quality in product and human effort, it has been a time that might be remembered as "the bad old days."

"The past as a present memory," as St. Augustine once wrote, is made more vivid by the calendar of time that enables us to mark off the decades in neat little packages of ten years each. Putting alternative labels on the decades is also handy.

Let us step back to the "fabulous fifties," a period in which society seemed to have lost touch with itself, as our beginning point in tracking a brief historical account of quality within the business and industrial sectors.

The fifties were glory days, when "made in the U.S.A." proudly stood for the best that industry could turn out. America led Europe and Japan into the post-World War II era, helping to rebuild their industries. The U.S. economy grew to dominate the postwar world, and it was that very dominance that eventually bred complacency and a sense of invincibility. "We got fat and sloppy," says economist Lester C. Thurow, of the Massachusetts Institute of Technology.[3]

It appeared to be a time when certain elements of quality were not of primary concern to many American corporations. In fact, the two quality gurus, W. Edwards Deming and J. M. Juran, were giving lessons to Japanese firms that helped to trigger that country's extraordinary economic rebirth, while our own countrymen rebuffed them. U.S. managers were not against quality, but they were smugly "dozing at the switch" and letting quality slip away.

The fifties yielded to the "soaring sixties," when the innocence of the prior era of a social numbness was lost, and old values for our society were dissolved. Also lost in the sixties was the capacity of top executives in overgrown, bureaucratic corporations to keep in touch with the needs and experiences of their customers. "The sheer size of some companies instilled a sense of superhuman invulnerability among people at the top that weakened their ability to detect and correct mistakes."[4]

Despite an increasing volume of complaints during the sixties, U.S. industries largely ignored the quality issue. The auto firms, for example, possessed with the thought that they were impregnable and unsinkable, were not of the mind to worry if a few customers complained now and then about being stuck with a defective product. The executives at the top had become isolated from contact with the real world of the ordinary consumer.

Added to the loss of the kinds of interests that bound producers and consumers together in preindustrial societies was the problem of alienation and antagonism between labor unions and management, which contributed heavily to America's quality problem during the sixties. Because of the contracts negotiated, "management found it increasingly difficult to discipline workers who botched and bungled their tasks or who stayed home from work on the slightest pretext."[5] It was a time of mediocrity, when buyers would not purchase cars unless they knew on what day of the week they were built, the speculation being that "lemons" were cars that were put together on either Monday or Friday.

The quality atmosphere during the sixties was clearly reflected in the words of the essayist Robert Osborne, who wrote angrily in *The Vulgarians,* "We are settling by default, as no great nation has ever settled, for a conforming, unthreatening, median, massive mediocrity."[6]

The "seething seventies" are best described by the words motion, change, uncertainty, and high pressures. It was a period during which the theme "now nothing works" appeared to prevail, and this widespread sentiment surfaced with clarity as the results of a Louis Harris poll were announced in 1979, a poll

> . . . in which 57 percent of . . . the respondents said they were "deeply worried" about the poor quality of the products they were buying. Seventy-seven percent expressed the feeling that "manufacturers don't care about me." Based on a separate sampling of national opinion, *U.S. News and World Report* concluded "dissatisfaction runs wider and deeper than many experts suspected." Of the people responding to the pollsters' questions, 59 percent said they had returned one or more unsatisfactory products to the place of purchase during the preceding twelve months. A year later the figure had risen to 70 percent. According to a study published in the *Harvard Business Review,* 20 percent of all product purchases on the average lead to some form of dissatisfaction (other than price) among the purchasers.[7]

We are now in the calendar time of the eighties, which has brought with it its own set of trends, values, and association. It has offered the appearances of being a period of "recovery," a promising turning point in the long road back to quality.

A famous teacher once said, "Ye shall know the truth, and the truth shall make you free"—a doctrine that proved to be the genesis of a movement toward making fundamental changes that would ensure better quality in American products and services. There was a growing, terrifying awareness that our whole societal system had become *addicted* to deteriorating quality. Knowing the truth that poor quality was addictive, more and more managements who were losing markets to higher-quality foreign goods were beginning to "get religion" about quality improvement.

While the eighties were becoming susceptible to new forms of addiction (such as that of the poison of material success becoming a kind of free-floating standard of excellence), the industrial sector was busying itself with the task of making quality improvement far more substantial than that suggested by the unsupported exaggerations of rhetoric heard in the seventies.

This time around executives were being more realistic; thus, managing for quality has come to mean nothing less than "a sweeping overhaul in corporate culture, a radical shift in management philosophy, and a permanent commitment at all levels of the organization to seek continuous improvements."[8]

As with any addiction, recovery is very lengthy and difficult, even when the afflicted "are genuinely working and wanting to get well and actively doing the things that are necessary to move along in that process."[9]

The key question is: Is it possible that in this decade or beyond we can look forward to a time when our system will recover? Perhaps. But only if those in high places of management will accept the notion that recovery itself is a process and never an accomplished fact.

Indeed, there are encouraging signs of recovery that spill over into many areas of national life—the concerns being expressed about the quality of schools, from kindergarten through college, for example. There is the demand for a cleaner environment and for higher standards in politics and government, and a search in other arenas in which the contours of the best of our national character can reveal themselves.

Specifically within the business and industrial world we see profound changes in U.S. corporate views about the importance of quality. Here are a few examples of real progress toward making *quality* more than a slogan or declaration:

- Corning Glass shut outmoded plants and won back markets it had lost to highest-quality Japanese products. It now *sells* to Japanese companies.
- GE trimmed 5,600 dishwasher parts to 800, and cracked down on defects.
- Xerox used Japanese methods to boost quality and reduce inventories.
- Ford learned from foreign cars how to make engine repairs easier.

That is the challenge: to design, produce and sell quality goods at competitive prices.[10] Corporate responses to the challenge look hopeful.

THE SERVICE SECTOR

Long waits in banks, stores and restaurants
Now often cause me to fret,
That the closer we move to a service economy
The less we seem to get.
— Edward F. Dempsey[11]

Having moved closer to a service economy for more than half a century, the transition has currently reached the point where fully three-fourths of today's employed persons are classified as working in the service sector, a potpourri of jobs that include dishwashers, store clerks, and nursing home attendants—and also doctors, lawyers, bankers, computer programmers, and even governmental bureaucrats. Essentially everybody who is not in manufacturing, agriculture, construction, or mining is a service worker.

The growth of America's services has been called an "economic miracle," and it shows no signs of slowing down. It is expected that U.S. services will fill nine out of ten jobs created between now and 1995. However, "companies large and small in the service sector are not so much concerned with the spectacular numbers already in the record books, but with prospects for the future."[12] Prospects for the future will depend principally on the fulfillment of the imperative to take a hard look at how services are perceived and how they are managed. Failure to do this could very well dissipate America's broad-based lead in services, as was the case in manufacturing. Unquestionably, there are warning signs appearing which give credence to the idea that such a decline can happen if for no other reason than the service sector's inattentiveness to quality.

Views of Services

The *Harvard Business Review* article by Quinn and Gagnon offers insight into the ways in which many views of services do not agree with the facts.

- Contrary to popular opinion, services are not responses to marginal demands that people satisfy only after they meet their product needs. People value services at least as highly as they do manufactured products and purchase them in much less cyclical patterns than manufacturers.

- Service companies produce value added at comparable or higher rates than do product companies.
- The service sector is at least as capital-intensive as the manufacturing sector, and many industries within it are highly technological.
- Service industries tend to be as concentrated as manufacturing and to have companies of sufficient scale to be sophisticated buyers and even producers of technology.
- Service industries lend themselves to productivity increases great enough to fuel continuing real growth in per capita income.[13]

Quinn and Gagnon go on to say:

> Although they probably know better, many executives still think of the service sector in terms of people making hamburgers or shining shoes. These images belie the complexity, power, technical sophistication, and economic value of activities that now account for more than 68% of the nation's GNP.

Managing Services

Consumers increasingly find themselves paying more for service—and liking it less. The resultant frustrations over poor quality are believed to be attributable to the mismanagement of services, which is being laid open to our vision in the body of written work. For example, the February 2, 1987, issue of *Time* magazine gave us a classic cover story titled, "Pul-eeze! Will Somebody Help Me?," with the subtitle, "Frustrated American consumers wonder where the service went." The article, like so many others, gives a critical review of the mismanagement problem as it focuses attention on corporate failures in managing service workers who are "underpaid, untrained and unmotivated for their jobs, to the chagrin of customers who look to them for help."[14]

To put a stop to deteriorating trends, some companies are scrambling to make amends, and "quality of service" is well on its way to becoming a household phrase. This is particularly obvious in the bylines of airline advertisements. To illustrate, these cogent expressions make frequent appearances.

> Find Out How Good We Really Are.
> Service can get you just about anywhere, with a smile.
> Working to be your choice.
> People expect the world of us.

We Love to Fly and It Shows.
Our low fare comes with more care.
Something special in the air.

These promotional messages of dogmatic certainty lost much of their credence as they moved away from an undeviating attachment to reality. Delta Air Lines, for example, although hit by a string of embarrassing mishaps, including landing a plane in the wrong city, continued to maintain its slogan "Delta gets you there"—an advertisement that ignored the problems.

However, in 1987, which may go down as the year of "the frequently furious flier," there occurred a dramatic turnaround in airline advertisements from that of confidence to that of "confession." The airlines were repenting their sins and starting anew—or at least that is what their advertisements said.

"For an industry frequently criticized as having a consumer-be-damned attitude, such contriteness seems a marked shift in strategy."[15] But is it really that much of a turnabout? Although airline executives say they are genuinely trying to improve the quality of service, their critics tend to believe that many of the moves are primarily cosmetic.

To manifest their regrets for past failures, industry officials are struggling urgently to minimize or eliminate bad air service. "But so far, experts say, most of the measures being developed are short-term remedies for symptoms of a deeply troubled national transportation system."[16] Meanwhile, increasing numbers of airline passengers are the victims of "lost baggage, flight cancellations, mass confusion at ticket counters, rudeness, overbooking, dirty planes and discourteous attendants."[17]

The quality of service conditions within the airlines industry exemplifies what is generally happening in the total U.S. service sector. Recognizably, "The concept of personal service is a difficult quantity to measure precisely, to be sure: the U.S. Government keeps no Courtesy Index on Helpfulness Indicator among its economic statistics. But customers know service when they miss it, and now they want it back."[18] says Thomas Peters, a management consultant and coauthor of *In Search of Excellence*. "In general, service in America stinks."[19]

QUALITY IN HEALTH CARE

As we turn our attention to the quality issue in our American health care system, we readily perceive some differing criteria of quality—the need for a higher intensity of effort and a higher sense of purpose—that set us apart from the business and industrial sectors as well as from other areas of service. We take on a mental and emotional responsiveness to the uniqueness of the mission of today's health care institution that must bring into play a humane quality or action without equal. We become conscious of the need for a very special quality of quality. These eminent distinctions tend to make quality more of a moving target in health care than in other fields of endeavor.

Lagging behind U.S. industry by at least a decade, health care has quickly moved within the past two years to a level of attention that now matches any other arena of human activity. This newly expansive focus on the quality level of health care services has been fueled by the increasing attention being given by such agencies as the Health Care Financing Administration and the Joint Commission on Accreditation of Healthcare Organizations. It, too, has become an issue with politicians, purchasers, and the public, who have placed increasing pressures on providers to establish precise boundaries around this nebulous thing called *quality health care*. Responsiveness to these forces has spotlighted the need for definition, a task already under way in many quarters. For example, the delegates at a convention of the American Medical Association took a stab at defining high-quality care.

> . . . it's treatment that improves patients' physical and emotional status as quickly as possible, promotes health and early treatment, involves patients in decision making, is given by *practitioners* sensitive to illness-related anxiety, is based on accepted medical principles, uses technology and other resources effectively, and is sufficiently documented in medical records.[20]

In the urgency to give definition to the idea of quality, it is very tempting to settle for some brief descriptive statement and then move on to the next topic. "There are many short phrases to choose from, but *the short phrase is a trap*. There is no known short definition that results in a real agreement on what is meant by quality. Yet a real agreement is vital; we cannot plan for quality unless we first agree on what is meant by quality."[21]

The problem of choosing a definition of quality is that there are in reality "several definitions of quality, or several variants of a single definition; and that each definition or variant is legitimate in its appropriate context."[22]

To avoid the trap of establishing a singular, prescribed statement of "What is quality?" as our beginning point and then moving on, there first needs to be an identification and clarity of meaning of *all* elements essential to the quality process, allowing the collectiveness of these elements then to evolve into the context of a final definition that truly reflects the totality of quality.

As expressed by C. Duane Dauner, president, California Hospital Association, "It [quality] can no longer simply be defined by 'what technology is available.' The challenge facing providers is to balance human values, technological resources, quality of life and innovation with economic reality, to provide the best possible care."[23] Joining the broadness of this thought is the need at the same time for the defined meaning of quality to be emphatic because it is individual.

There are other "traps" along with definition that health care executives can avoid if they are wise enough to heed the lessons learned by industrial and other service organizations in their quest for quality improvement over the past several years, traps such as

- emphasizing scale economies rather than customers' concerns
- going for short-term remedies for symptoms of a deeply troubled system
- concentrating on immediate, piecemeal efforts to relieve congestion of the system's pressure points
- looking for instant solutions
- allowing an emphasis on quantification—one of the least frequently noticed features of competition—to get out of balance with qualitative concerns
- placing an emphasis on capturing the consumer rather than producing a better product
- being "cosmetic" about change, rather than recognizing how drastic change needs to be in quality improvement
- letting the issue of quality wane after external overseers become more concerned with other matters
- staying with old concepts too long; not recognizing external change and the need for internal change; not constantly looking at trends and asking, How can we be better, and what do we need to do to facilitate what is happening in this world?
- concentrating on cost-cutting efficiencies that can be quantified, rather than adding to product or service value
- failing to listen carefully and flexibly providing the services customers genuinely want
- falling short of making quality improvement an organizationwide commitment with sufficient investment in time and resources
- talking more about quality improvement than achieving it; top-level executives convincing others, not themselves
- failing to define quality from the consumer's point of view
- failing to support a massive education process needed to cause a major change in attitudes
- giving short shrift to accountability for quality performance
- failing to motivate workers; hiring workers for their hands and forgetting about their heads
- having little or no idea of quality's true dimensions
- failing to make quality improvement a formal part of the business plan; failing to plan for it over a three- to five-year period

- ignoring the critical importance of management preparedness; not knowing that most resistance to quality improvement usually comes from the middle management and supervisory levels, whereas workers are usually eager to assume responsibility for the quality of their work
- failing to involve workers and not communicating well-defined, highly visible goals to the individual employee
- being obsessed with the difficulty, if not the impossibility, of assessing trends and measuring quality

It has been recognized for many years that the quality of health care is highly variable. Economist Walter McClure, president of the Center for Policy Studies, Minneapolis, notes that "at its best, health care in the United States is the best in the world, but there are plenty of places [in this country] where health care has *not* been at its best."[24] Perhaps in these places administrations already have fallen into some of these traps.

With a commitment to avoiding these ensnarements, and with the belief that quality has no limitations, it would seem evident that we must reexamine our ideas about the nature and significance of quality, how we think about quality, and how we manage it. In so doing, we can bring about needed changes in understanding, definition, and perception. The changes that need to occur are believed to be these:

- to leave behind the prevailing tendency to "circle around" quality with the vagueness of rhetoric, and to penetrate more deeply into its inner significance, which will give meaning beyond immediate impressions
- to sharpen our sights and insights regarding quality through organized and continuous self-assessment
- to move from conventional assumptions about quality to considerably more realistic judgments about it based on increasing measurement and preciseness of definition
- to bring into being a more purposeful connectedness between quality and the central organizational elements of performance, cost effectiveness, productivity, and innovation
- to view quality enhancement as a concept that goes beyond the boundaries of a planned process to that of "a way of life" that makes quality part of everyday thinking in all corners of the institution
- to grasp fully the obviousness of the fact that quality is never the problem, rather it is the solution to the problem; it does not come free, for it demands a high investment in resources and human energy
- to perceive quality systemically so that our view and understanding embrace dimensions beyond quality assurance programming, including the quality of work itself wherever it is performed; the quality of a life-at-

work environment in which work is performed, and the quality of human
conduct at all levels, and in all areas, of the enterprise

It is essential that we strengthen our capacity to come to grips with the
human complexities that pervade the whole idea of quality as we broaden
our sights to embrace the three additional dimensions of quality of work,
quality of work life, and quality of human demeanor, which this text is all
about.

Achievement of quality is essentially a human accomplishment, and it is
the quality of people—more than advancement in technology—that gives the
health care institution its reputation for excellence as perceived by consumers
of health care services. This thesis was substantiated by the results of a survey
conducted for Voluntary Hospitals of America by the National Research Corporation. Of attributes associated with high-quality care, patient relations or
employees' caring attitudes were mentioned by 52 percent of the four thousand consumers surveyed. A highly qualified medical staff was mentioned
by 30 percent of consumers. Some 20 percent said high-quality hospitals
featuring advanced technological services and a wide range of services. A
hospital's reputation for quality was mentioned by 14 percent of consumers.[25]

The fate of quality enhancement hangs upon the human condition; upon
the power of people to remain united for the leadership and purposes they
respect; upon their spirit of interest and enthusiasm; and upon their feelings
of trust, self-esteem, and satisfaction at work. These are the conditions of
high quality. They are the root of the matter, and they become the measure
of progress over time. They need to be nurtured by all members of management as the custodians of quality. This they can do most effectively if they
give conscious attention to developing the conceptual habits required to influence and handle human behavior and actions within the service-giving environment where people make the difference.

Progress toward perfection does not come automatically with the passage
of time, nor will it show itself if we fail to free ourselves from a tendency
to concernment rather than commitment, to passivity rather than action, to
assumptions rather than the good sense of reality, to fixed habits and attitudes
rather than continuous renewal. In short, it is a time for definitiveness in the
meaning and significance of quality, for more challenging standards of human
conduct, and for self-reform and renovation where needed. Altogether, it is
a time for the quest of a new sense of quality.

NOTES

1. Barbara W. Tuchman, "The Decline of Quality," *New York Times Magazine,* Nov. 2, 1980,
p. 38.

2. Norman Corwin, *Trivializing America: The Triumph of Mediocrity* (Secaucus, N.J.: Lyle
Stuart Inc., 1986), p. 150.

3. "The Push for Quality," *Business Week,* Jun. 8, 1987, pp. 130–144.

4. Marvin Harris, *Why Nothing Works* (New York: Simon & Schuster, 1981), p. 131.

5. Harris, *Why Nothing Works,* p. 27.

6. Corwin, *Trivializing America,* p. 151.

7. Harris, *Why Nothing Works,* pp. 18, 19.

8. *Business Week,* "Push for Quality," p. 132.

9. Anne Wilson Schaef, *When Society Becomes an Addict* (San Francisco: Harper & Row, 1987), p. 138.

10. Extracted from *Kiplinger Washington Letter,* Jan. 8, 1988, p. 4.

11. Edward F. Dempsey, "Pepper . . . and Salt," *Wall Street Journal,* Dec. 4, 1986, p. 15.

12. Steven K. Beckner, "The Boom That Won't Quit," *Nation's Business,* Apr. 1986, p. 26.

13. James B. Quinn and Christopher E. Gagnon, "Will Services Follow Manufacturing into Decline?" *Harvard Business Review,* Nov.–Dec. 1986, pp. 95–96.

14. "Pul-eeze! Will Somebody Help Me?" *Time,* Feb. 2, 1987, pp. 48–57.

15. Francis C. Brown III, "Airlines Come to the Aid of Consumers—Sort of," *Wall Street Journal,* Nov. 9, 1987, p. 31.

16. Francis C. Brown III, "Air Travel Remedies Sound Good but May Not Treat Deeper Illness," *Wall Street Journal,* Dec. 2, 1987, p. 32.

17. Clemens P. Work, with Evelyn Bankhead, "Can This Airline Be Saved?" *U.S. News & World Report,* Aug. 3, 1987, pp. 37–38.

18. *Time,* Feb. 2, 1987. p. 49.

19. Ibid.

20. *Hospitals,* Jul. 5, 1986, p. 18.

21. J.M. Juran, *Juran on Planning for Quality* (New York: The Free Press, 1988), p. 4.

22. Avedis Donabedian, *The Definition of Quality and Approaches to Its Assessment* (Ann Arbor: Health Administration Press, 1980), p. 27.

23. "News," California Hospital Association, Sacramento, Vol. 18, no. 21, Sept. 12, 1986.

24. *Hospitals,* Jul. 5, 1986, p. 54.

25. Michael D. Hays, "Consumers Base Quality Perceptions on Patient Relations, Staff Qualifications," *Modern Healthcare,* Feb. 27, 1987, p. 33.

Part I

Influences

Chapter 1

Humanizing Health Care in a Technologized Society

> The real danger of our technological age is not so much that machines will begin
> to think like men, but that men will begin to think like machines.
> —Sydney J. Harris, Publishers Newspaper Syndicate

"The genius of the modern American hospital is that, in its best light, it has become one of the most remarkable concentrations of science, technology, and medical art ever amassed under one roof."[1] This is the opening sentence of an article appearing in the November 16, 1979, issue of *Hospitals*. It fortuitously captures the very essence of this chapter, which centers on the concern for a harmonious alliance and arrangement between science and technology and the art of humanized care and service.

Naturally, this concern takes on new meaning and intensity as we extend our view of the totality of quality to embrace not only quality assurance programming but quality of work itself, quality of work life, and quality of human conduct as well.

A disunion between human values and technological needs has resulted from a continuum of unbalanced growth in the sciences and the humanities. Scientists and technologists, over time, have responded to the challenge of rapid change more effectively and easily than have the humanists and sociologists. While the scientists have been the forerunners of change, oriented to the future, the social scientists, who scarcely have a past, are primarily oriented to the present; and the humanists, who have been lingering on several fronts, have remained largely past-oriented, seldom turning their attention to the present, much less to the future.

In the interest of providing continuing enhancement in the "totality of quality" and in terms of the implications of scientific and technological discoveries on our daily lives, it is believed that the greatest need for change in our health care environment today is *to advance the role of humanism in the organizational life of our health care institutions and to bring the humanistic dimensions of work, which are at the very core of our business of people-*

serving-people, to a formative position that is more in balance with the medical technologies of our day.

It is difficult for even those of us so close to the health service scene to grasp fully the brilliant growth and progress in medical sciences and technology within a comparatively short span of time, although daily many of us are witness to the beneficiaries of medical science. In our attentiveness, however, to the marvelous results of modern technological medicine, our sights tend to become clouded to the fact that modern medicine is unable to alter, in a positive mode, the basic patterns of behavior of people at work in our institutions. Technology and expertise in the science of medicine are not quite enough. They must be coupled with a response to the call for reform in human activity within the health care organization.

In our pursuit of change in the future that will bring us closer to perfection in the complementary union of technology and the art of human effort, we must look to the past. This is so because for us to think about the future, we need a sense of the past—a sense of history.

The history of science and technology enlightens us to their increasing intersection.

> Science leads to, and supports, technological advance. Once applied, technology demands that science help solve its practical problems; it demonstrates phenomenological regularities that beg for scientific explanation; and, fiscally and otherwise, often it "carries" science within institutions. Technologies become instrumentation for scientific advancement.[2]

Within the field of pharmacology, for example, the overlap between technology and science is substantial.

A historical view of science also offers revealing insight into the fact that "the fascination with nature, the search for its theoretical and practical mastery, the intellectual or esthetic appeal of scientific inquiry, had been an integral part of virtually all earlier cultures . . . with each culture coloring science with its own characteristic hues.[3]

Of particular interest in our retrospective look at science as a unique historical phenomenon is the beginning of a development—without doubt a most momentous phase in the entire history of science—that occurred within the Renaissance culture, roughly from the fourteenth through the sixteenth centuries.

A RENAISSANCE

While influenced by the earlier medieval phase, the Renaissance was a revolt of the entire human personality against everything in the medieval tradition that tended to stifle elementary human needs. It was during the Renaissance that art and science converged so closely that they often became almost interchangeable. Many great Renaissance artists and architects excelled in the sciences of their time, to which they made outstanding contributions. Leonardo da Vinci was perhaps the most spectacular master in a long line of Renaissance scientists-artists.

Virtually all empirical sciences profited immensely from this new unity with art.

> The close affinity between art and science was not only due to the discovery of the earth, the fascination with a world that had in effect been forbidden; it also had to do with one of the most central features of the Renaissance, *l'uomo universale*. The artists' easy switching from an esthetic to a scientific approach and back was part of the phenomenal versatility that the Renaissance released through its appeal to the creative potential. After all, what could be more stimulating for the unfolding of one's talents than a cultural climate that called for uncovering the beauty and the hidden mysteries of this earth? A person's whole potential found itself pitted against the adventure of the world. Everything—art, science, technical skill, the mastery of different media, and a broad range of intellectual abilities—were called into action by this total challenge to the creative personality.[4]

Science as knowledge advanced very rapidly throughout the seventeenth and eighteenth centuries. The seventeenth century "is the one century which consistently, and throughout the whole range of human activities, provided intellectual genius adequate for the greatness of its occasions."[5] It has been referred to as the "century of genius," represented by the likes of Francis Bacon, Galileo, Descartes, Newton, Locke, and Spinoza, all of whom published to the world important work. There, too, was Harvey, the discoverer of the circulation of blood, who was associated with great advances in biological science within the century. Science was becoming quantitative; by the end of the century physics had been founded on a satisfactory basis of measurement, and advances in mathematics appeared among the achievements of scientific thought.

The eighteenth century continued the work of its predecessor in clearing the world of muddled thought, and it did so with ruthless efficiency. "In this century the notion of the mechanical explanation of all the processes of nature finally hardened into a dogma of science."[6] In technology, it produced the steam engine, and thereby ushered in a new era of civilization. Undoubtedly, as a practical age, the eighteenth century was a success.

Peculiar and new to the nineteenth century, distinguishing it from all previous centuries, was its technology. Its greatest invention was the *method* of invention, which broke up the foundations of the old civilization. This new attitude, developed from science, concerned not so much with principles as with results, providing an abundant source of ideas for utilization.

> There have always been people who devoted their lives to definite regions of thought. In particular, lawyers and the clergy of the Christian churches form obvious examples of such specialism. But the full self-conscious realisation of the power of professionalism in knowledge in all its departments, and of the way to produce the professionals, and of the importance of knowledge to the advance of technology, and of the methods by which abstract knowledge can be connected with technology, and of the boundless possibilities of technological advance—the realization of all these things was first completely attained in the nineteenth century.[7]

It was the century in which the possibilities of modern technology were first realized in practice.

Science and science-based technologies have become a pervasive dimension of human experience in the twentieth century. There are more scientists alive now than have lived in all of history. Both the amount of new knowledge and the kind of new knowledge produced in the twentieth century overshadow the work of earlier times. And if it were just a matter of counting up the scientific accomplishments of each century, the twentieth would win the title hands down.

At the very beginning of this century, Andrew Carnegie provided the funds to build the Carnegie Institute of Technology. It was the harbinger of an abounding growth of large laboratories and other centers of scientific advance devoted to specified technological goals, even in some of our universities. Carnegie's technical institute was envisioned "as the apotheosis of the machine and, by extension, the glory of the nation's technology and industry and of the nation itself."[8]

The invention and application of technology to help humans become more productive, while beginning some two hundred years ago, greatly accelerated during the twentieth century. "Today there is no area of human endeavor including every facet of art and music that does not seek to exploit technology in some manner."[9]

The rate of growth of U.S. technological research, development, and trade had faltered since the postwar era, signaling the imperativeness of a major response to the challenge of the nation's technological leadership. As a result, since the deepest point of the 1982 recession, a reevaluation and overhauling of American industry have occurred and continue. In short, a great new race has begun toward unprecedented technological-industrial advances that are laying the foundation for a whole array of future astonishing technological accomplishments in emerging fields such as microprocessing, fiber optics, superconductivity, space technology, and recombinant DNA, along with almost equally spectacular gains in conventional medical techniques.

As we look back at the achievements of science during the twentieth century, we see "a mixed bag: control of disease, new labor-saving devices, rapid transportation—and nuclear weapons, industrial pollution, carcinogenic chemicals."[10] Our glance at technological innovations reveals that virtually every industry in the U.S. today is developing and utilizing a high-tech array in efforts to improve productivity and quality, increase efficiency, enhance profitability, and ensure long-term viability.

High technology is reshaping the U.S. industrial scene and reinventing today's factory.

> Gone are the oil stains on the floor and the rags smeared with grease from calloused hands. No longer does the clomp of sturdy high-top work shoes echo down the aisles. In the locker room, soiled denim overalls slung over pegs have given way to pristine laboratory smocks on hangers. The trappings familiar to generations of blue-collar workers may be missing, but this is still a real-life factory. Despite the antiseptic veneer, metal gets ground and drilled and stamped. Small parts still get bolted or soldered or welded to other parts to make bigger components. Only now it's done by robots and other computer-controlled machinery that humans watch from glass booths.[11]

As a result of this new manufacturing technology, the factory has reemerged as the focal point of corporate strategy after two decades of neglect. Some two to three dozen U.S. companies —primarily the giants of the aerospace, appliance, automotive, computer, and heavy-equipment industries—have been the vanguard of this revolution. And now that the giants have blazed the trail, and learned some expensive lessons in the process, the push to high technology has cascaded down to smaller companies.

One of the giants, General Motors, in one of its advertisements, concludes, "Putting people in charge of technology in a new method of production is the competitive edge."[12] This statement implies a central imperative of our time—the need to *manage* technology effectively. Indeed, the future will be brighter if we learn how to manage it well.

The computer is undoubtedly the most visible example of modern technology, and it is proliferating beyond most people's imaginings. "As a calculating engine, a machine that controls machines, the computer does occupy a special place in our cultural landscape. It is the technology that more than any other defines our age."[13]

Not only has computer technology begun to change how science progresses, it has emerged from the laboratory as an indispensable amplifier of human intellect within an information-based society. Its implications for the typical large business twenty years hence have been conjectured by Peter Drucker in a *Harvard Business Review* article in which he envisions the shift to the information-based organization, the organization of knowledge specialists. Drucker states:

> We can perceive, though perhaps only dimly, what this organization will look like. We can identify some of its main characteristics and requirements. We can point to central problems of values, structure, and behavior. But the job of actually building the information-based organization is still ahead of us—it is the managerial challenge of the future.[14]

Computers that have maximum power capability—termed "super computers"—have assumed a significant role in several industries, opening "the door to improved product performance and to major savings in the design and development phases of industrial products."[15] For example, they have been adopted by

- the aircraft industry, in which the super computer now stands alongside the wind tunnel in its importance;
- virtually all of the major automobile manufacturers in the design of aerodynamic cars;
- the petrochemical industry for both oil exploration and recovery;
- the construction industry for use in modeling stress and earthquake resilience on major projects such as bridges, nuclear-reactor containment vessels, large spectator arenas, and skyscrapers.

SERVICE TECHNOLOGY

Since the early 1970s the American service sector has committed massive expenditures—six hundred to eight hundred billion dollars—to the installation of automated equipment, according to government and industry statistics. Some segments of the service economy, particularly telecommunications and finance, have been reaping the rewards of the electronic advances for several years. Other arenas in the corporate world of service—namely banks, supermarkets, hotels, and department stores—also are making claims of gaining a competitive edge in speed, efficiency, and accuracy as a result of customer interface with user-friendly technology. To illustrate:

- In the business of banking, computerization is bringing innovation to cash management, providing customers with new, sophisticated ways to monitor account balances and transactions.

- When a business executive checks into a luxury hotel these days, the desk clerk is ready for him. She knows the names of his wife and children, and even the name of his personal secretary. She is well aware that he expects *The Wall Street Journal* and *The New York Times* delivered to his door each morning. The clerk also knows he demands a microwave oven and a full-sized refrigerator in his suite. She even knows that he will not accept phone calls in his room from Saturday at sunset until Sunday at sunset. The desk clerk has not memorized the habits of this executive, but the hotel's $250,000 computer has.

  This is just one example of how high technology is helping to personalize—and improve—hotel guest service. "Intense competition among first-class hotels is forcing hotel operators to try to out-automate each other with technological gadgetry that not only dazzles customers, but in some cases, saves hotels money. Some of the technologies speed up reservations and track marketing information. Others assume greater guest safety and comfort. Some save energy and others give traveling executives the use of modern office equipment outside the office."[16]

- At large self-service retail food stores, exiting through the checkout stand is made easier for consumers by bar-code scanning. Locating desired food items also is aided by technology. For example, "at Stop & Shop's new superstore in Medford, Mass. (three times the size of a football field), customers can use three touch-sensitive computers to help them find what they're looking for. To find artichoke hearts, press 'A' on the 14-inch screen—a directory of all items beginning with 'A' is displayed, everything from abalone to azalea. Then touch the screen again for the item you want—a map of the store appears with a flashing trail directing you to the right aisle."[17]

- As shoppers enter their favorite department stores, many are encountering a new phase of technology as "thousands of retail clerks are learning to wave magnetic wands, answer electronic questionnaires and use laser guns to record sales in much the same way as supermarkets have been ringing up grocery sales for more than a decade."[18] It is a technology that makes purchases faster and tallies stock. And it does it by having a laser scanner "read" each item's Universal Product Code, after which the computer

  1. prepares sales slip, registers payment, and indicates correct change if the transaction involves cash;
  2. obtains credit authorization within seconds by communicating with other computers, if the purchase involves a credit card;
  3. adjusts inventory to reflect sale; in some cases, the sale triggers an electronic order for replacement goods;

4. extracts information about credit-card purchases for consumer pro-
files; this information helps target promotions and it may also be
sold to other businesses.

All of these tasks are performed at the incredible speed of 30 to 60
seconds for a single purchase.

Like human workers, robots are moving into the service industry in increasing numbers as well. Having been stuck on the factory floor for a long time,
they are breaking loose.

> For several years service robots have been at work in nuclear plants,
> where people risk exposure to radiation, and under the sea, where
> human divers require cumbersome and costly life-support systems.
> Today, the protean machines are embarking on a multitude of new
> activities: taking care of the handicapped and elderly, picking
> oranges, cleaning office buildings and hotel rooms, guarding com-
> mercial buildings, even helping cops and brain surgeons.[19]

The visionary boosters of robotizing service jobs see a much bigger market
than that in manufacturing.

In light of these examples of technological advancements, it would appear
that the future holds high promise of lifting quality within the service industry. Unfortunately, this is not quite so, since in spite of the industry's quest
for "the best," customers continue to view services as still falling far short
of what they could or should be. In fact, in many instances, "the best" of
services now offered by service organizations may not be as good as it used
to be.

Although companies in every part of the economy have been experiencing
difficulties with the applications of technology, no sector appears to be having more trouble than businesses that sell services. During the 1980s, the
average yearly rate of growth in the productivity of businesses that do not
produce goods—from transportation and banking to retail stores and business
services—has fallen to more than a third of what it was before the advent
of the computer and electronic technology in the early 1970s, according to
the U.S. Labor Department. Contributing to this anemic increase in the efficiency of service companies are two factors: (1) human problems at the
workplace as millions of workers are being relegated to stifling, equally bor-
ing work at computer terminals, or who are discovering that their computers
open the door to an unwelcome presence—an electronic supervisor "capable
of tracking an employee's every move"[20]; (2) the many organizational and
operational problems of modern work that are merely being disguised or
created by new technologies. Problems such as these, as yet unrecognized,
let alone understood, are even more difficult to address.

Considered to be of importance equal to, or even greater than, these conditions are the growing dissatisfactions among consumers about their impersonal, technologized experiences within a supposed high customer-service environment. Among the same fields of service focused on earlier, we find an ongoing commentary of service deficiencies and dissatisfactions in our daily newpapers and business magazines. Here are but a few accounts.

Department Stores

In the good old days, you shopped at Sears to buy a bolt of cloth, paid your money and off you went. A couple of times a year, the store would close for an afternoon to take inventory.

Things have advanced considerably since then. Stores don't need to close because they keep a running inventory. Computers have brought to the salesclerks' fingertips the ability to do a lot of what the stores used to handle in the back office.

There's just one problem. What's good for the store may not be so good for the customer. Go buy that bolt of cloth now, in a hurry to get to the next department, and you stand there while the salesperson punches buttons.

Pretty soon you're looking at your watch. It probably doesn't take as long as it seems, but it takes a lot longer than it should.[21]

Banks

. . . it was not the Grinch who stole a piece of Christmas, but a computer. It's tough enough to find humans willing to work on Christmas Eve, but now the bank has to wonder about machines as well.

All day long, thousands of bank customers rushed to automated teller machines for last minute Christmas cash only to find that many of the contraptions were shut down. The problem, Security Pacific said, was that the huge computer that runs the bank's 235 machines around the state inexplicably kept turning off and on throughout the day.

"Computers do these things, although I must admit it's not the best day for it to happen," said James Griffith, a Security Pacific Senior Vice President. "Needless to say, people are not too happy about it."[22]

Bank of America acknowledged that it has abandoned a computerized accounting program after spending $60 million over several months in an unsuccessful attempt to fix the system.

The system was supposed to provide the most advanced accounting and reporting services to the bank's lucrative institutional trust division. Instead, recurring problems meant months of delays in issuing account statements and a system that was supposed to attract customers wound up driving away some and angering others.

[Customer] departures may have run into the billions of dollars.[23]

Hotels

Some hotels offer guests a choice of computer or human contact. Two years ago, the Hyatt Regency in Chicago was the first hotel in the country to install automated check-in and check-out machines. Guests in a hurry can come and go without stopping at the front desk. They simply slip their credit cards into one of these $30,000 machines, and presto, they're checked out. But only 15% of the Chicago Hyatt Regency's guests use the machines. . . . (What seems to have surfaced is a remaining preference for human contact.)

But not all hotels have greeted the computer with open arms. . . . The 400-room Westin South Coast Plaza in Costa Mesa, is one of the few hotels in Orange County that has consciously avoided computers. . . . "It isn't high costs or computer phobia that has kept computers out of the hotel," said Robert Seddelmeyer, general manager, "We just don't want our desk clerks so busy looking down at computers that they forget to smile at the guests," he said.[24]

Retail Food Stores

Ending up on a lighter side, one of the authors of this book observed a sign posted at the entrance to a food store: "Customers who think our clerks are rude, should see the manager."

THE HUMAN FACTOR IN THE HEALTH CARE WORKPLACE

In our discussion of technology in the realm of industrial effort, we gain a sense of the power of its force and influence. Even in the service sector, but perhaps to a lesser degree, we acquire the uneasy feeling that there is a general tendency to accept technology as an irresistible force rather than as a tool—a force that exercises an ultimate power over the minds and lives of people at work. What seems to have evolved as a reality is that technology has produced a paradox. It has greatly increased the power of human beings, but, at the same time, it has reduced the impression of their importance.

More than ever, other industries are pinning their hopes on high technology. According to Thomas G. Gunn of Arthur Young, "The real issue is quality,"[25] because of the quantum leaps in product quality that are possible through automation.

In turning our attention to *quality*—which indeed is the real issue in health care—we are deeply conscious of the "quantum leaps" that need to be made in our understanding as we differentiate health care from all other sectors of human effort, and as we perceive the imperatives that these distinctions place upon us.

In our unique environment of human compassion and caring, the positioning of technology needs to be directed to *values,* as opposed to *things.* If it is found that encouragement in the use of technology is based on materialistic purposes or intended for the sake of progress alone, it must be rebuked by a humanistic attitude, an attitude that views technology as an instrument created for no other purpose than to serve humankind. There needs, too, to be a sensitivity to the balanced growth of individuality so as to ensure human control over technology and sustenance of the creative spirit and activities of the professional who works side by side with technology.

In health care, we need to hold a special concern for placing science and technology on a human scale by tapering their capacity to diminish man's image of himself, thus preventing dehumanizing care.

> Under certain conditions, the technological imperative in health care does tend to be dehumanizing; When it inhibits communication between patients and staff; when it exaggerates the mystique and power of health professionals; when it pressures patients to accept surgical and pharmacologic solutions to their problems rather than psychosocial therapies; when it fragments the care of whole persons; when it denies patients a choice between extreme measures and palliative treatment; when it exacerbates inequities in the distribution of health resources; when it compels hospitals to acquire hardware for its own sake; and when it mandates the aggregation of services into larger and larger structures.[26]

To block the threat to humanity in the health care environment, we must be quick to perceive or apprehend the absence of balance in the scientific and human dimensions of work. Imbalances made visible by

- the practice of medicine based on hard science and high technology without the oldest and most effective act of doctors, that of humane touching. As Mr. Rothman, of Columbia's Center for the Study of Society and Medicine, states, "The message to future physicians is quite clear—the mastery of technology is not the beginning and end of medical education. The practice of medicine will require you to navigate in the realm of values and ultimately to respond to more than what is on the chart."[27]

- the exercise of roles and responsibilities by managers through knowledge of scientific principles and technological requirements without an accompanying understanding of the human needs and expectations of their people.

- the behavior of technicians who may tend to lessen their attentiveness to patients as they interface with the oppressive power of technological machinery.

- the intervention of the computer at the nursing station, which potentially may be a restraining influence on the closeness of bedside care.

- the obstructive placement of computers in the admitting office that may cause reception clerks to be "so busy looking down at computers that they forget to smile at the guests."

- the preoccupation on the part of human resources department staff members with computer input and output, preempting an adequate devotion of time and energy to visiting with the "troops" or to introducing new "people policies" and practices deemed desirable in the use of technological assistance.

- the job performance of other "staff" service personnel, including those trained in accounting, whose scientific instruments are the computers that can very well blind them to the human-capital side of the institution's bottom line; or the management engineer whose technical creativity is not supported by an extension of interest in human relations, psychology, and the social sciences.

- the placement and operation of sizable, computerized word-processing machines that may interfere with the administrative secretaries' ability to provide emotional responsiveness to the public.

- decision making at any level, and in any area, that is based on signs and numbers conveying information to the exclusion of an adequate *knowledge* of their meaning.

Erasing dehumanizing practices in the health care workplace will undoubtedly become increasingly difficult as the promise of future advancements in technology becomes a reality. Consider, as a single example, the human impact of a new robotic invention being tested in a Connecticut hospital. The robot is called HelpMate, a nurse's aide that will deliver meal trays to bedridden hospital patients. "Along the way, the wheeled robot will take elevators and negotiate hallways by itself, doubtless startling unwary visitors."[28] If it startles visitors, what will be the feelings of patients regarding this added hiatus of human contact?

The challenge to humanize tomorrow's work environment in health care will not be an easy one. We will have a rugged time of it to keep our sense of balance in capturing the benefits of technology as well as the creative acts of men and women in the workplace. We will have a rugged time of it, all of us, in keeping this balance flourishing in all places remote and unfamiliar within the complexities of organizational life. But this is a matter of highest urgency, that of improving the human condition, which requires the active participation and contribution of *all* professionals and nonprofessionals working inside the walls of our health care institutions. This is so because there is the need to extend our perception of "total quality" to embrace not only the central element of quality assurance programming, but also the interrelated components of quality of work itself, quality of work life, and quality of human behavior.

Throughout history there has been a slow separation of science and the arts evolving out of a growing tendency to think of them as fundamentally separate. What is required, in essence, is a present-day renaissance that will bring to the health care workplace a more intimate linkage of technology with human activities. Like the artists and scientists of the Renaissance, we have it in our power to make improvements in the human estate. And like those artists and scientists, all of us in health care today, both in our scientific endeavors and in the artistry of our work, need to share the fundamental belief: man is the measure of all things.

William Barrett, in his book *The Illusion of Technique,* helps us to rationalize the value of this belief: "Technical requirements have led us to quantify and calculate a great many more parts of life; but preoccupied as we may be with objects and data, the human subject is still there, restless and unappeased, haunting the edges of the technical world."[29]

NOTES

1. Jan Howard and Robert A. Derzon, "Prospects for Humane Care Are Hopeful," *Hospitals,* Nov. 16, 1979, p. 76.

2. William W. Lawrance, *Modern Science and Human Values* (New York: Oxford University Press, 1985), pp. 34–35.

3. Thomas Goldstein, *Dawn of Modern Science* (Boston: Houghton Mifflin, 1980), p. xi.

4. Thomas Goldstein,*Dawn of Modern Science,* pp. 219–20.

5. Alfred North Whitehead, *Science and the Modern World* (New York: The Free Press, 1953) pp. 39–40.

6. Alfred North Whitehead, *Science and the Modern World,* p. 60.

7. Alfred North Whitehead, *Science and the Modern World,* p. 97.

8. William Stockton, "The Technology Race," *New York Times Magazine,* Jun. 28, 1981, p. 14.

9. *The Impacts of Technology,* Futures Research Division, Los Angeles: Security Pacific Corporation, 1987. p. 1.

10. Jeffry V. Mallow, *Science Anxiety* (New York: Thomond Press, 1981) p. 207.

11. Special Report: "High Tech to the Rescue," *Business Week,* Jun. 16, 1986, p. 100.

12. *Wall Street Journal,* Apr. 20, 1987, p. 32.

13. J. David Bolter, *Turing's Man* (Chapel Hill: University of North Carolina Press, 1984) p. 8.

14. Peter F. Drucker, "The Coming of the New Organization," *Harvard Business Review,* Jan.–Feb. 1988. p. 45.

15. Albert M. Erisman and Kenneth W. Neves, "Advanced Computing for Manufacturing," *Scientific American,* Oct. 1987, p. 163.

16. Bruce Horovitz, "Luxury Hotels Go High Tech in Bid to Pamper Guests," *Los Angeles Times,* Mar. 23, 1986, p. 23.

17. *Future Scan,* Los Angeles: Security Pacific Corporation, Futures Research Division, Mar. 31, 1986.

18. Michael de Courcy Hinds, "Stores Rush to Automate for Holidays," *The New York Times,* Nov. 28, 1987, p. 16.

19. Gene Bylinsky, "Invasion of the Service Robots," *Fortune,* Sept. 14, 1987, p. 81.

20. Harley Shaiken, "When the Computer Runs the Office," The *New York Times,* Mar. 22, 1987, p. 21.

21. John F. Lawrence, "Computers Are Running Us, Not Vice Versa," *Los Angeles Times,* Aug. 10, 1986, p. 19.

22. Robert Magnuson, "Bank's Automated Tellers Take Unscheduled Holiday," *Los Angeles Times,* Dec. 25, 1981, p. 16.

23. Douglas Frantz, "B of A Abandons Costly Computer for Trust Clients," *Los Angeles Times,* Jan. 26, 1988, p. 18.

24. Horovitz, "Luxury Hotels," p. 23.

25. "High Tech to the Rescue," *Business Week,* p. 102.

26. Jan Howard and Robert Derzon, "Prospects for Humane Care," p. 77.

27. Amy Wallace, "Teaching the Human Touch," *The New York Times Magazine,* Dec. 21, 1986, p. 72.

28. Gene Bylinsky, "Invasion of the Service Robots," p. 82.

29. William Barrett, *The Illusion of Technique* (Garden City, NY: Anchor Press, 1976) p. 218.

Chapter 2

The Corporate Heart

People want to be who's and not what's.
—Roscoe Pound

Humanity has always had a difficult time coming to terms with its place in the natural world. Human history has been characterized for the most part by conflict rather than compassion. And in today's social and cultural environment we see clear signs of being further divested of the deeper human meaning that traditionally has been affixed to human life.

The basic quality of life for the peoples of this nation has been greatly diluted and demeaned since the founding of the republic. James Madison, the Constitution's chief architect, warned in the *Federalist Papers* that "the public good, the real welfare of the great body of the people, is the supreme object to be pursued; and that no form of government whatever has any other value than as it may be fitted for the attainment of this object."[1] The understanding of this Madisonian idea, "so important through most of our history, has begun to slip from our grasp. As we unthinkably use the oxymoron 'private citizen,' the very meaning of citizenship escapes us. And with Ronald Reagan's assertion that 'we the people' are 'a special interest group,' our concern for the economy being the only thing that holds us together, we have reached a kind of end of the line. The citizen has been swallowed up in 'economic man.' "[2]

When economics is the main model for our common life, there is the increasing temptation to put ourselves in the hands of the experts, experts themselves who do not know how to deal with the big human questions. "Nobody knows how to deal with them," says Saul Bellow, one of America's greatest novelists who was cited for the human understanding and subtle analysis of contemporary culture that are combined in his work. "And now methods have become so professionalized," Bellow continues, "that there is no room any more for normal human understanding—and without such understanding, solutions become absolutely impossible."[3]

Our humanity is at risk in other ways as our society becomes daily more complex, more powerful, and more affluent, and its individual members find it difficult to reconcile themselves with the remorseless problems of a mass society that will be increasingly with us. Dr. John A. Logan Jr., president, Hollins College, in perceiving the dilemma, stated that, "Never before has there been so much scope and opportunity for development of the individual, but paradoxically, never have so many individuals in our society felt so alienated, alone, frustrated, and depersonalized. . . . The sense of purposelessness, the crisis of identity, and the rebellious frustration which is everywhere reflected in our literature and our political life are systems of a deep-seated malaise . . . for which remedies must be found."[4]

The central role of technology already has been recognized in Chapter 1 with regard to its impact as it interacts with the culture and values of our environment. Technology has provided the solution to many of society's problems. It also is often blamed for them. Most discussions about technology and its influence on change produce a whole set of contradictions. Notwithstanding these differing viewpoints, there persists a concern among the historians of technology about the separation of technology and the humanities.

Bellow laments the fact that "There's no sacred space around human beings any more. It's not necessary to approach them with the tentativeness and respect that civilization always accorded them. People now are out there in the open. They're fair game."[5] The potential danger in all of this is that people may stop putting up a struggle for "the human part of themselves."

THE IMPERATIVE OF A CORPORATE HEART

It seems logical to believe that our most successful social invention, the modern organization, can bring to bear remedies that will correct some of our social disorders. After all, the modern organization, with its mighty source of power and control, has become a force capable of shaping values in the contemporary environment. However, the bad news is that the organizational community itself has caught something of the infection, and its general health is in need of repair.

Scott and Hart remind us that "at one time, organizational health meant adjusting organizational inputs so that they were minimized relative to outputs. Success in this endeavor was called *efficiency,* and the object of management was to increase it . . . [in more recent times] growth and adaptability have been added to the older notion of efficiency as criteria for organizational health. The sum of these factors is now expressed by a new term, *organizational effectiveness,* a new ideal for managerial success. Unfortunately, few people are sure what the term means, let alone how to measure it."[6]

There does exist, however, a popular belief that "organizational effectiveness" equates to such factors as technological advances, higher productivity, abundance of product, cost reduction, and realization of short-term gains, which in the process, according to Scott and Hart,[7] tend to displace the more individualistic values of the past. More specifically the change is

from the values of:	*to* the values of:
innate human nature	malleability
individuality	obedience
indispensability	dispensability
community	specialization
spontaneity	planning
voluntarism	paternalism

Regrettably, the major value changes seen as having produced organizational America do not champion the values central to the American tradition, since they are considered to be poor prescriptions for the societal maladies affecting the wellness of the human spirit.

When we focus our attention on the health care organizations of today, those of us concerned with the human condition are quick to be offended by anything less than an all-out commitment on the part of administrations to make their institutional systems responsive to human needs—not a commitment that speaks boldly of intentions, but rather actions that speak louder than the words.

Roger M. D'Aprix, who has had extensive experience as a corporate manager, states,

> My experience tells me that significant numbers of people are coming to believe that institutional renewal of any kind is so frustrating and so bewildering that it's either futile or not worth the personal pain. Their answer is either to drift with the tide or to do their best to turn inward on their own lives and problems.
>
> If they are right (and I believe most emphatically that they are not), then twentieth-century man has rendered himself personally irrelevant and hopeless through the construction of his organization.
>
> That may sound like too somber a conclusion. I don't think so. I believe that if we turn our backs on the task of institutional reform in this highly organized society, we are digging our own graves. Our best hope—our only hope—is for each one of us to dedicate himself or herself to the frustrating and never-ending task of reforming and renewing our organizations to make them fit for human habitation, and to direct them in such a way that they make their human resources productive in doing the work society needs to have done.[8]

D'Aprix gives voice to a challenge that is being taken up by increasing numbers of health care executives who not only are cognizant of the fact that "We are living in one of those rare times in history when the two crucial elements for social change are present—new values and economic necessity"[9] but, more important, have the wisdom to understand that they must have both, since neither force is powerful enough to produce social change on its own. There must be a balanced blending of both new humanistic values and economic necessity.

Yet, at the same time, if we call to account the state of humanistic inadequacies currently remaining within most health care organizations today, it becomes quite comprehensible that these very failings are perverting the institutions' essential purpose of providing *quality* in their care and services.

In this chapter we discuss some of the basic requirements for renewing our health care organizations by making them more responsive to human values and needs believed indispensable to enhancing qualitative outcomes—the task we call *the quest for a corporate heart.* In this discussion the center of concern and interest is the human condition of the institutional system, embracing its principles and values; professional integration; key processes; interdependent functions; and organizational responsibilities, relationships, and structure.

THE ESSENTIALITY OF PRINCIPLES

"In culture there is strength" is the proposed new law of business life set forth by Deal and Kennedy in their book *Corporate Culture.*[10]

> They go on to express the belief that people are a company's greatest resource, and the way to manage them is not directly by computer reports, but by the subtle cues of a culture. A strong culture is a powerful lever for guiding behavior; it helps employees do their jobs a little better, especially in two ways:
>
> A strong culture is a system of informal rules that spells out how people are to behave most of the time.
>
> A strong culture enables people to feel better about what they do, so they are more likely to work harder.

While the notion that much of an organization's success is tied to its culture has been around for more than two thousand years, it has been within the present decade that we have witnessed a resurgence of interest in culture as man's medium. What appears to be running rampant is the hiring of gurus to change corporate cultures.[11] Dozens of major U.S. companies—including

Ford Motor Company, Procter & Gamble Company, TRW Inc., Polaroid Corporation, and Pacific Telesis Group, Inc.—are spending millions of dollars on training designed to foster teamwork, company loyalty, and self-esteem. Several health care organizations have followed suit in engaging outside consultants to conduct similar attitudinal training.

Employees, however, have had decidedly mixed reactions to their organizations' efforts to transform their cultures. Many workers say that the training and management are simply paying lip service to serious concerns in the workplace. Others claim that in the seminars and exercises they attend they hear for the first and the last time about improvements on the job. "It's too bad," says Harley Shaiken, professor of work and technology at the University of California at San Diego, "because efforts at manipulation today will only create resistance to more legitimate reorganization tomorrow."[12]

As competition grows, Ford Motor Company's leaders continue to push for a shift in culture. "Ford is putting people throughout the company through an array of development programs, some of which are downright touchy-feely although company executives bristle at the term."[13] "What we're trying to do is make this place the most loving, caring group of people in Ford," Joseph Kordick, the general manager of parts and service, says of the workshops held in his division. On the other hand, those going through the program say that it all sounds a bit flakey.

In our own industry, emergency room nurses coming out of a series of such behavior-directed seminars sponsored by the hospital described the new experience as "scary" and "eerie."

Culture-changing programs using the advice and expertise of consulting firms, each with its own diagrams, buzz words, and theories about how organizations can change their work environments *may* prompt people to change their habits and behavior, but these "packaged programs" often can backfire in the long run. As Dr. Lawrence W. Green, of the Texas Health Science Center in Houston, has stated, "If people make behavior changes without changing their internal values, beliefs, and attitudes, the new behaviors are less likely to stick when the external supports disappear."[14] He adds this comment: "I'm developing a growing concern about the gimmickry used in a lot of programs."

When are we in health care going to be concerned and committed to the point where we will begin to withdraw from the bad habit of thinking that changes in culture, and in individual and group behavior, can be truly impacted by such faddish and fashionable approaches? Just when will the leadership of our health care institutions begin to think comprehensively rather than linearly about corporate culture and values so that events will be considered comprehensively and priorities weighed according to a system of common good, all of which can be positioned in their proper place and time?

In the words of Edward T. Hall,

> There is not one aspect of human life that is not touched and altered by culture. . . . This means personality, how people express themselves (including shows of emotion), the way they think, how they move, how problems are solved, how their cities are planned and laid out, how transportation systems function and are organized, as well as how economic and government systems are put together and function.[15]

A consciousness of the pervasive role of culture throughout the human process causes us to believe that it is worthy of a good beginning. And that beginning is found in matters of philosophy.

The idea that people perform with high levels of quality when they know the ideals toward which they are striving has long been supported by social scientists and managers themselves who have learned this lesson through practical experiences. The late Thomas J. Watson, head of IBM for a half-century, for example, knew the value of declaring the philosophical posture of the firm. The word "think" was a piece of that philosophy which Watson promulgated through his many plants. Add to Watson's, the names Alfred P. Sloan, Jr., Cyrus S. Eaton, Nat Cummings, and Jim Connel—all headmen whose statements embodied a basic offering of beliefs designed to guide the destinies of their organizations and managements.

For whatever reasons, we do not seem to find as many expressions of philosophical thinking among the contemporary crop of corporate leaders as we used to. (And this also is true in the health care industry.) There appears to be all too little inclination and assertiveness to take on the battle of principles and to commit to words a definite statement of mission and goals that characterize the value system of the enterprise. In essence, this is a statement of the organization's commitments to its various "publics," embracing its customers, its employees, and its shareholders. These commitments can be redeemed only through the quality of performance that the declaration of beliefs itself can help bring about. The very presence of a documented set of overriding principles brings with it

- a unifying philosophy, a common culture, a set of values;
- a vision of the future, a sense of uplift;
- a more creative and productive community of workers;
- a consistency, coherence, and harmony in the organizational process;
- organizational reform and renewal.

The corporate deed of dealing explicitly with the values of the enterprise and of declaring these values (with an avoidance of lofty generalities) is "a good beginning" and unquestionably the most important of all serious things the board and the chief executive officer must accomplish.

Just as there cannot be a decent philosophy without humanity, there cannot be the human condition without a philosophy. In sum, it is through the articulation of philosophy that people symbolically reflect answers to inevitable and uniquely human questions concerning their place in the order of things, and in the order of being, as well as their relationship to their fellow human beings in the general society and within the work environment itself.

The notion of philosophy as the system of values by which the organization lives and by which its leadership questions and understands very common ideas related to the quality of the human condition has been exercised as a doctrine of centrality by Ancilla Systems, Inc., of Chicago, a Catholic health system with institutions and services in the states of Illinois and Indiana. The principles expressed in the Systems' statement of philosophy guided Katherine Kasper, founder of the congregation of the Poor Handmaids of Jesus Christ, and attracted other women to serve the poor and the sick in the village of Dernbach, Germany, in 1851. While circumstances of today are different, the initial principles are perpetuated as the congregation calls on all who work in this health ministry to reflect on and follow these principles and the actions that flow from them. The congregation exercises accountability for promotion of the philosophy by delegating the task of implementation to the Ancilla Systems boards and managements and requires evidence of progress through periodic verbal and annual written reports.

Four principles guide the Ancilla congregation in continuing sponsorship of health services.

Dignity of the Person
We believe that each person is created in God's image, having equal worth and dignity regardless of social standing, race, sex, age, religion, or mental and physical capacity.

Stewardship
We believe that the resources and gifts that have been entrusted to us call us to be responsible servants as we use and share these gifts. These include:

- the mission of Jesus continued by the Church
- the history and spirit of our religious congregation, Poor Handmaids of Jesus Christ
- the gifts and talents of those who share in health services
- the material and financial resources that we administer.

Community
We believe that God calls us to love and serve each person as brother

or sister. We join with Jesus to make whole what is disunited. Together we work for unity and harmony, wholeness and healing.

Caring Quality

We believe that continuing the mission of Jesus calls us to provide compassionate and skillful attention to the needs of others so they may attain their highest potential.[16]

This statement outlines the values and expectations for those who fulfill the health care ministry within Ancilla Systems. It defines what the corporate culture should be. It provides its individual and group activators with the conception of what it is to think philosophically about things. Indeed, this in itself is an exceptionally worthy achievement in our busy, unphilosophical age.

To ensure the transition from philosophy to practice, Ancilla Systems' long-range strategic direction includes a set of nine standards based on those principles embraced by the Systems' philosophy statement. The standards that describe the manner in which Ancilla Systems carries out its mission and expresses its values are referred to as the characteristics of service. They are:

Principle: Dignity of the Person

1. Respect for Dignity of the Person. Evidence that patients, families, personnel, physicians, volunteers and the general public are recognized as individuals who are physical, social, psychological and spiritual beings, and who are esteemed in word and action, assuring individualized relationships, while balancing the rights of groups and living with realistic constraints of time, money, and other resources.

Principle: Stewardship

2. Research and Development of Innovative Approaches to Health Care. Evidence of stewardship of talents and diversity of human resources throughout the organization by encouragement of new ideas, willingness to take risks after appropriate investigation and a dedication to learning from mistakes rather than drawing away from risk taking.

3. Faithfulness to Catholic Identity through Close Relationships with Church and Congregation Resources. Evidence of stewardship in imaging Catholic, Christian identity through attention to Church and congregation tradition and teachings and willingness to use Church and congregation representatives as sounding boards to achieve this result.

Principle: Community

4. Orientation to the Family Unit. Evidence of recognition that the family is the basic unit of society and community, and of attempts to develop, maintain, or heal the family relationships and wholeness during its contacts with the health services or facility.

5. Formal and Informal Relationships with Physicians. Evidence of recognition of the physician as an individual, as well as a key person in the health facility, not only in the care of the physician's own patient but as an important participant in the entire healing ministry of the health facility or service.

6. Local Health Systems Providing a Spectrum of Services Responsive to Community Need. Evidence of "system orientation," rather than one that is individual, departmental, or hospital limited, while emphasizing the mission of meeting the needs of the community of immediate service.

7. Collaboration with Community Agencies and Other Health Care Providers. Evidence of activity to bring about synergistic results in the health of the community served by participating actively in community projects and with other health services and facilities in the community.

8. Political Advocacy through Education. Evidence of awareness of the need to speak for justice and for those who have no voice, especially the poor, through educational efforts within and outside the health service or facility and by fostering responsible citizenship on public issues.

Principle: Caring Quality

9. Quality and Personalized Services. Evidence of offering quality of care to all individuals and in all areas of service in a compassionate and caring manner.

Expressed in the terminology of day-to-day business operations, these characteristics are an effort to "bring our mission and philosophy off paper and into life,"[17] according to Systems' chairperson, Sr. Judian Breitenbach.

With the standards set and expressed in concrete, measurable terms, the next step is to evaluate how all parts of the system are meeting them. A multifaceted methodology involving both a written survey and on-site observation has been developed by Ancilla. The evaluation process comprises data collection, analysis, and a final report to the Systems board. It is scheduled to take place at each system affiliate and service agency once every three years.

Written reports are only one part of the characteristics of service evaluation. A site survey at each institution allows for a more subjective observation of the environment in which services are provided. The intent of the surveys is to help hospitals conform to the characteristics of services, not police what they are doing. According to Sr. Stephen Brueggerman, vice president of mission effectiveness, "The process enhances awareness of health care as ministry and raises consciousness of how the health services philosophy is expressed in everyday actions and behaviors."[18]

While more exact measures and fixed standards are to be developed over time, the establishment of beginning measurement tools and flexible performance standards and expectations is a major step in actualizing the corporate culture described in the sponsor's health services philosophy statement.

Together, the philosophy *and* characteristics of service accomplish the overriding deed of providing inner strength to the vital center of the institutional being—the corporate heart. Mutually, they create an organizational culture designed for people; they offer the utterance of a set of beliefs conceived to relate man to his environment; they match corporate culture and business strategy, and they define success through the articulation and encouragement of positive values essential for higher achievement.

THE EVER-PRESENCE OF VALUES

Pivotal to advancements in total quality is the concept of value. A value is "a belief upon which a person acts by preference; an enduring belief that a specific mode of conduct or end-state of existence is personally or socially preferable to an opposite or converse mode of conduct or end-state of existence."[19]

As the heart of organizational culture, values have a powerful influence on an organization's climate. We can readily appreciate the significance of pervasive values as we examine closely some of the inhibiting human features of the climate in today's health care workplace.

As we continue our discussion of the work of the professional, along with the processes, functions, and structure of organization, certain specific values tend to surface—values thought to be essential to the cause of quality as they provide the foundation for the purpose of the enterprise, "silently give direction to the hundreds of decisions made at all levels of the organization every day,"[20] and bring their force to bear on the workplace of the health care institution as it continues to be afflicted with the ills of traditional organization. Parenthetically, these values are thought to be essential within the Ancilla Systems.

PROFESSIONAL INTEGRATION

To begin with, we need to make the initial distinction that hospitals and other health care organizations are *professional* organizations, since they are formed primarily for the accomplishment and extension of professional objectives, rather than to facilitate commercial or industrial objectives. As professional organizations, we find existing within them inherent conflicts common to nearly all professional institutions. The presence of these conflicts works against the overall pursuit of quality.

The characteristics of professionals are troublesome to many managers: they have allegiances to other, diffuse organizations; they are not completely "organization men"; and they cannot be controlled completely by the interior rules and sanctions of the immediate institution. When one examines the composite profile of productive professionals that emerges from many studies of their personalities, it is quickly acknowledged that "controlling" and "managing" them is a most difficult, if not impossible, task.

In truth, hospitals and other types of health care organizations are formed, in part, for physicians, nurses, researchers, and teachers, and not just for patients alone. Because of this truth, they differ from nonprofessional organizations in that people who are not necessarily positioned in any particular line of authority are able to impose their defenses onto the stage of corporate life. The authority they exercise is not vested in a designated position or bestowed by the organization, but rather is arrogated on the basis of expertise and a reputation for competence. Such behavior on the part of professionals brings into being an accumulation of power as a vehicle for transforming individual interest into activities that influence other people, and negatively impacts the quality of their life at work. The most vivid of examples is the continuing deterioration of physician-nurse relationships.

While power is an innate right of the organization, it is not really a necessary attribute of the professional; when it is self-appointed in an accumulative sense, administration and its key executive players experience the frustrations of not being able to withdraw into the safety of organizational and managerial logic. The difficulties accompanying these circumstances are antithetical in nature, since they tend away from the overall professional image and status the organization wishes to evidence, the patient desires to experience, and the employee feels good about.

Beyond the issue of fostering humanistic approaches to doctoring within the medical community itself, there is the need for much repair in professional relationships within the organizational community of today's hospital. The remedy begins with the presence of a corporate culture to which physicians can relate, a culture that embraces a set of values capable of bringing the physician into a logical and natural association.

A value seen as essential to professional integration is *balance*—first, the balance of past and present. An organization's history contains its heritage and traditions. It is a record of human behavior and experiences that provides the organization's membership and affiliates a qualitative sense of the institution's history of human achievement, offering a vitalizing link between past precepts and the current corporate culture.

Growing numbers of companies going through periods of change are searching for a more historical perspective. Companies such as Citicorp, Hewlett-Packard, General Motors, Texas Instruments, Citibank, and Deere and Company have experienced the benefits of their historical accounts as an aid in training and educating their people and as a way to learn more about why important strategic decisions were made in the past. What these organizations recognize—and what we in health care need to be more cognizant of—is that applying the past to the present holds significant implications for the fidelity of individual performance evolving out of a strengthened integration of loyalties to the corporate system.

For physicians there prevails an unfulfilled sensibility to the history of the institution in which their professional skills are exercised. Without this understanding of the institution's heritage and traditions, physicians do not see the present as part of an organizational process "rather than as a collection of accidental happenings."[21]

Within the meaning of the value of balance, there, too, is the need to strike a proper balance *between differentiation and integration.* In a highly differentiated system, such as a hospital, the parts are more individualized and have a greater relative autonomy, a greater independence from the whole. This is highly characteristic of the medical subsystem within the total hospital system. What results from this state of differentiation, of course, is the distinct tendency toward the breaking up of the harmony of the whole, which brings with it the danger of disintegration of the system. The system must exert its influence not by opposing differentiation but by *coordinating* the differentiated parts of the whole under the general systems principle of *reintegration.* This organizational process commands keen discrimination of perception and needs to be understood equally by trustees, administration, and physicians. Movement in the direction of disintegration, rather than reintegration, is unquestionably a counterproductive happening for the total institutional system. It is a devastator of the organization's good health that can often cause permanent impairment. Unfortunately, in dealing with *differences* among functions, we are, at the same time, dealing with the *indifferences* of man.

In keeping with the value of balance, there, too, is a criticalness in attaining an intellectual, acute balance between the exercise of ordained power and the sharing of power. It is regrettable that too many individuals in positions of power either do not comprehend or are not willing to accept the basic thought that the most effective way for one to gain power is to *share* one's power—a rather simple lesson to be learned and applied by all who desire to join together in a relationship of unrivaled strength, diversity, and stability.

Finally, there is the idea of *reciprocity* that needs to be positioned within the value of balance. It is an idea that will not go away in the competitive arena, and much has already been done by hospitals to meet the requirement of reciprocation through joint venturing with physicians in various ways.

There still remains, however, much that needs to be done in furthering mutual or cooperative interchange of privileges involving the physician population, including

- increasing participation in planning, goal setting, budgeting, and other activities that hold people together;
- the placement of greater emphasis on establishing a problem-solving environment that strengthens the bonds of common problem-solving projects and group participation in common situations—and the adoption of organizational flexibility that accommodates the creation of such an environment;
- the effective management of information so that it is available wherever and whenever needed to make decisions, to solve problems, to respond to new demands, or to create meaningful change.

In all of these proposed actions, the physician must have a good, solid piece of the coordinative action.

THE QUALITY OF TRUST

Before moving on to a discussion of organizational processes, it is important that we focus briefly on the value of trust. It is not only the purest essence of an organization's value system, it is the first link in the series of values and processes by which an organization proceeds toward its quest for a corporate heart that beats with a concern and love for its people. Trust remains, as it always will, as a fundamental requirement of human life. A corporate culture in which people aspire to truth and trust is a fundamental requirement of a healthy organization.

"Trust is a social good to be protected just as much as the air we breathe or the water we drink."[22] So argues Sissela Bok, a lecturer on medical ethics at Harvard Medical School, in her book *Lying.* Most Americans would readily agree. Yet American workers are finding it ever more risky to trust the world about them, including their world of work. Within their individual workplaces, they have witnessed a deterioration of organizational integrity and mutual respect between themselves and management.

Managing trust is a most difficult task. Trust is not easy either to develop or to maintain, yet it is all too easy to destroy. A powerful story that illustrates the truth of these notions is to be found in the U.S. auto industry. During the thirties and forties relationships between workers and management were at an all-time low. "Workers openly *defied* management by putting in as few hours as possible. And management demonstrated its open contempt for workers by promulgating one humiliating work practice after another."[23]

Under such conditions, it would be the height of folly for either party to trust the other. Indeed, lack of trust contributed to the eventual long-term decline of the American auto industry. General Motors and others have learned that, if there is to be even a hope of a chance of producing a quality car that is competitive in cost, the work force must be totally involved in participating in the design and maintenance of the entire manufacturing process. They also have learned that a turnaround in trust does not happen hurriedly. Slowly, distrust of the past has been replaced by cooperation and mutual respect. Employees who formerly regarded work as nothing but a purely economical, contractual arrangement have added a perception of working as a deeply feeling, emotional activity. "Any view of work that stresses one [of these views] to the detriment of the other is not only naive but actually dangerous because of the complexity of today's world. We need to function as total human beings, not as fragmented robots."[24]

COMMUNICATION AS A CENTRAL PROCESS

Human communication, as the saying goes, is a clash of symbols; and it covers a multitude of signs. But it is more than media and messages, information and persuasion; it also meets a deeper need and serves a higher purpose. Whether clear or garbled, tumultuous or silent, deliberate or fatally inadvertent, communication is the ground of meeting and the foundation of community. It is, in short, the essential human connection.[25]

Human communication is the very essence of all organization. Its clear and open channels, following different directional paths, are the "arteries" and "capillaries" that carry the lifeblood of the institution from the corporate heart to all employees in all corners of the enterprise. They too are the "veins" that return to the heart, completing the cycle of the human connection.

Human communication as an organizational process is central to the task of creating trust. If the process is defective, mistrust will be fueled. If effective, in the following sense, trust will be elevated.

Communication Is Appropriately Perceived. Communication is appropriately perceived as a process that involves the sending and receiving not only of information but of attitudes and feelings. There needs to be an awareness that knowledge alone is not enough. We must also seek understanding. What also needs to be grasped is the thesis that more effective communication—that is, a more effective sharing of ideas, feelings, and attitudes for the benefit of the organization and its people—can get work done better and problems solved more efficiently, and therefore can affect both quality and cost.

A Meaningful Communication Policy Is Established. All too many health care organizations do not have a written communication policy, yet such a document provides a purposeful beginning for improving the communication process. A communication policy explains, as explicitly as possible, *why* management believes in the importance of communication and of communications improvement. It also describes the methodologies and procedures that management wants followed for the organization's different kinds of communications, such as annual meetings of all employees, department director meetings, small group meetings, departmental and work unit meetings, and hotlines. A documented communication policy (including sanctioned methodologies) offers two main benefits: first, it removes the evaluation of messages from the area of personal and arbitrary taste, and offers (at least to some degree) specific standards that a communication must meet; second, it not only acts as a guide to action, it also convinces superiors and subordinates alike that communication is an important activity in the organization.

Human Communication Tells It Like It Is. In reality, human communication is a trusty process in which differences and feelings of encouragement or of disappointment are openly expressed; a reliable process in which people share all relevant information and freely explore ideas and feelings that may be in or out of their defined responsibility; an honest process that fosters "a high level of give and take and mutual confidence in each other's support and ability."[26]

There Is Continuity in the Sponsorship of Training in Communication. Basic training in communication principles and skills—writing, reading, listening, speaking—needs to be sustained over time. Training in improvement of attitudes also is essential, although it is more difficult to characterize. It involves more than a training course—generally designed to make participants aware of the effects of motivation and attitudes on communication performance. The methods employed to impart new knowledge and understanding need to combine both a rational and an emotional understanding of human relations principles as they apply in an actual work situation. Attitude training generally focuses on the superior-subordinate relationship, and generally concentrates on oral as opposed to written communications.

It Is Recognized That There Is the Need To Make People Better at Listening to Each Other. The bad news is that listening is undoubtedly the weakest link in an organization's communication system, and no administration can afford the price of poor listening—costly work and deterioration of quality. The good news is that listening *can* be taught. All of us can be made better listeners, and in the process we can become even more aware of how essential good listening is, an awareness we can then bring to the people with whom we work and to the patients we serve.

There Is In Place a Planned "Feedback" System. Human communication does not function well if all of it is in the "telling." To get feedback is, of course, to add another dimension to "telling" communication—to discern to what extent communication has been achieved and to learn just how effective it has been. It is "knowledge of results," and it tells management (1) whether employees have understood and acted upon a message; (2) what employees can contribute to the solution of a problem, and (3) what remains to be said to reconcile the needs of management, employees, and the organization.

> Without feedback, many executives tend to overrate the effectiveness of their communications. They are too remote from supervisory and non-supervisory personnel to directly observe the frustrations, tensions, and inefficiency resulting from poor communication, and may consequently often be unaware of the very real relationship between communication, morale, turnover, etc. Through feedback, evaluation can be more objective and realistic. Problem areas can be more easily and accurately detected. In addition, properly emphasizing feedback can convince employees of management's interest in their ideas, and attitudes, with consequent effects on morale, as well as on communication and job performance.[27]

The communication process of the enterprise not only functions as the circulatory system connected to the corporate heart, it also serves the needs of all other organizational processes as they execute their series of actions, changes and functions designed to bring about desirable results.

ACHIEVING EXCELLENCE THROUGH ORGANIZATIONAL PROCESSES

The human heart beats at the rate of about seventy to eighty times a minute. Like the human heart, the "heart" of the health care institution increases its pace when the system is active, when it provides a place where the spirit soars every working day. Similar to the human heart, it also is perceived as the vital center of the system's being, emotions, and sensibilities. It is the innermost aspect of organization: its inner strength, its character. And it is the repository of compassion, sympathy, generosity, love, and affection.

As we turn our attention to the internal processes of the organization, we recognize the consequence of these processes, giving evidence to the soundness of the corporate heart. We also acknowledge the significance and influence of the standard of *excellence* as a deep-seated, pervasive value that needs to give guidance to fashioning the purposes and design of the institutional processes.

> The quest for excellence is an idea that the human race has honored over time. At any given time in a society, the idea of what constitutes excellence tends to be limited, just as it also tends to be limited in organizational life. However, at this point in the history of work, a point at which we find ourselves in a period of fundamental change rather than modification, we need to move beyond honoring mere portions of the full range of excellence. All members of management must put forth some hard questions about their own practices in honoring the excellences that are most fruitful for continued vitality of the organization.[28]

Employees, too, need to be vigilantly attentive to their own contributions to the corporate value of excellence.

The uncompromising quality of health care and service delivery outcomes demands at all times a standard of excellence and precludes any thought or action whatsoever related to doing less than the best. Yet, today's health care institution as a workplace very often reflects an element of less than the best in the ways in which internal processes are designed, implemented, and maintained. All too often, the processes are fashioned to serve the needs of the organization rather than to serve the needs of people. This inappropriate happening is more often than not the consequence of not connecting the design of the processes with the value system of the organization.

Management needs to take stock continuously of its organizational processes to discern the extent to which they mirror the sensibility of the corporate heart to the critical concern of excellence in performance. With an eye on opportunities for enhancement, management must view its processes from the high ground of quality so that it will know what path to take to improve the human condition. For example:

- The *assessment process* needs to be founded on the belief that what is essential is intelligent questioning if assessment is to work. Intelligent questioning means having concern for the individual being questioned and for the human factors contained in the surrounding environment.
- The *strategic planning process* requires the matching of corporate culture and business strategy, bringing into play the delicate art of balancing social and business values. Beyond the integration of financial and strategic planning, there is the imperative of introducing more effective ways to integrate human resource considerations and perspectives into the strategy-development process.

- The *goal-setting process* should be conceived as a philosophy and approach of management directed toward positioning the institution to the needs of patients and the community; giving emphasis to the significance of quality-directed goals; enhancing teamwork and unity of purpose among employees through the sharing of goals, and responding to the values of people at work as they relate to their desire for self-direction and participation in decision making.

- The *human resource management process* needs to go beyond the fundamental activities of hiring, processing, and record keeping. It needs to affect the total human condition within the organization, beginning with the effectual entry of the brand-new employee into the corporate culture and continuing throughout the tenure of the employee with the exercise of creative programming directed toward advancing the fulfillment of the individual's expectations and aspirations. Key to this process is the ongoing human connection between management and staff, either collectively or individually, on any matters concerning employee job satisfaction and general well-being.

- The *performance appraisal process* needs to be an evaluative experience in which "performance" takes on a new meaning. Its essentialities include clear expectations, equality of participants, freedom of discussion, focus on goals, objective measurement, accountability for outcomes, deserved rewards, and a positive and challenging climate. Above all, it needs to be a humanistic process centered on stimulating motivation and fostering increased competence and growth, thus serving the needs and welfare of the individual.

- The *facilities management process* represents another vehicle through which the organization may both communicate to and serve its constituencies. The design of the interior of the facility, along with its comfort, cleanliness, appearance, and repair, are major ingredients of quality in the eyes of the patient. A well-designed functional area or cafeteria speaks volumes to the employees about how the organization feels about them.

A SYSTEM OF INTERDEPENDENT FUNCTIONS

"Together we work for unity and harmony, wholeness and healing" are the words found in the Ancilla Systems' statement of philosophy—unquestionably, an indispensable value in the cultural framework of a health care institution. Yet, as one attempts to describe today's hospital organization as a workplace, there appears to be a gap between the way in which we think about the *system* of health care—the whole idea of systematism in the practice of medicine—and the way that many of us think about the hospital itself as a systemic organism.

In studying the problems of hospital organization, it is found that non-systems viewpoints remain all too common among members of the hospital staff at all levels of organization. Nursing staff members perceive themselves as the "lonely crowd"; department managers tend to operate in isolation; members of the administrative staff often fail to help guide the organization as a whole system of activity; and the department of human resources more than not is organized as a special function disengaged from the mainstream of the central management process.

To this falling-short of capturing an interdependency that enhances the organization as an instrumentality of *collective* action toward common goals and outcomes add the intricate aggregation of a multicultural populace whose attitudes, perceptions, and resulting behavior bridge the full spectrum of possibilities. There are the technologists, the intellectuals, the highly skilled, and the inexperienced—who, as a total admixture of human beings, reveal the difficulties inherent in the heterogeneity of value systems existing within the work environment. In essence, the effectiveness of the health care institution, as a patient-directed organization, in serving the diversified care needs of those in the *outside* community is not always matched by its successes in attending the workplace "maladies" being endured among the citizenry of the organization's *internal* community. Regrettably, this occurrence tends to counterpoise the corporate value of *systems* orientation.

Along with their inseparable companion—communication—coordination and collaboration are among the most common organizational ills. Today's organization (in any field of endeavor) as a system of simultaneous and mutually interdependent interactions among multiple components is often wanting and hard to come by.

At almost any point in time, the literature carries many stories about the importance of unity, which apparently is very much on the minds of management. "Let us have unity!" was a cry increasingly heard over two hundred years ago, when Thomas Jefferson helped to set in motion the machinery that created our nation, the Committees of Correspondence. Today, given the reality of superiority and distance (rather than connection and membership) that tend to hold firmly within the complex organizational structures that dominate the contemporary workplace, the watchword that has come into vogue is "All power to the fragments!"[29] The scattering of "fragments" needs to be given a new direction of getting it all together, since "any act done in such a way as to disrupt cooperation destroys the capacity of organization."[30]

Disharmony and disunity are not conditions that mankind has ever sought deliberately. Rather, these conditions are believed to be regarded with disapproval in light of more people being actively concerned about goals, priorities, achievement and meaningful involvement. The problem is that the community of effort within the organization has eluded formulation.

Some Coordinative Principles And Practices

To move toward the realization of unity and harmony, it is essential for management to take note of certain recommended principles and practices of mutual coordination and teamwork. The first five of these were emphasized in an earlier writing.[31]

- Managers should increase their efforts to develop goals that will focus on the values that hold employees together. A system's approach would help managers to set goals that would allow them to concentrate their commitments on the needs and welfare of patients.
- Greater emphasis should be placed on problem solving and attaining measured results. The main task here is to strengthen the bonds among the individuals working within the enterprise so that the organization and its goals become the axle on which the agglutination of operational efforts evolve. Very simply, the objective is to move managers and their employees from being part of the problem to being a party to the solution. This is attempted specifically by strengthening the bonds of common problem-solving projects and group participation in common situations.
- Managers should undertake the kinds of reform in the organizational and management structure that will better meet the needs of people working together toward some common goals.
- Effective management of information and knowledge is required. Solid, real-world information and knowledge about what is needed, what is happening and what is about to happen must be communicated to achieve coordination. Doing this effectively calls for communication that crosses artificial boundaries of divisions, departments, and units to help solve problems detrimental to the common cause of the enterprise.
- Effective coordination also requires the placing of a new priority on the function of management. This means developing management resources to the fullest through more effective training and educational programs and through organizational arrangements that are conducive to managerial growth.
- The driving force for unity needs to be the idea of systems—the notion of wholeness. People within the organization need to know and understand that the answer is complicated not so much by any one problem but by interrelationships; that the problems hidden between the boundaries of functional departments often are more significant than those found within each single department, and that no single change for improvement is either good or bad until its effect on the total organizational system is understood.

- Collaborative behavior depends not on isolated decisions and solutions but on the clarity of the mission and goals of the organizational system as well as its value structure and the policies that govern the multiple decision-making points. "In such systems, interrelationships between parts are usually more significant than characteristics of the parts separately."[32]

- "Engendering teamwork requires more than stable team membership. Managers have to be willing to work at building successful teams. Workers have to be willing to work at building successful teams. Workers have to be convinced that they are considered an important part of the team. Individuals with different personalities and skills have to be carefully fit together as a workable team."[33]

- Individual employees need time to learn how to work together effectively and to refine the precise skills they will need to use as team members. They need to be taught reciprocity and to care about the welfare of others.

- Cooperation and team play need to be considerations in the organization's recognition and reward system. Employees have to learn that cooperative behavior will have a payoff based on objective performance appraisal criteria.

- Beyond the barrier of a shortage of necessary skills in cooperative problem solving, there is the influence of an environment that favors immediate improvements offering short-term advantage at the expense of long-term satisfaction. What must be avoided is the exclusion of projects with a more distant time horizon capable of producing significant improvements in organizational performance.

- When moving toward greater coordination and teamwork, it is essential to accept the fundamental proposition that conflict and differences, if properly managed, can contribute to organizational effectiveness.

In the search for unity we must avoid the danger of producing conformity that in the end will prove to be more deadly than the trauma of confrontation. An ancient Greek philosopher once declared, "That which opposes also fits." Even if our coordinative efforts do not always make for a good fit, we need to be mindful that the organization is large enough to encompass managed conflict and difference.

The philosophy of Benedictus de Spinoza, one of Europe's greatest thinkers, is quite germane to this principle: "Only with such a vision of unity can we have our beliefs and let others have theirs, confident that our understanding is a crucial part of the whole but at the same time humble in our recognition that others' convictions are crucial, too. We are all a part of a single grand concern—and our differences and disagreements are not cause for antagonism or suspicion but rather the bonds of concern that draw us together."[34]

- One way to encourage mutual, cooperation is to make the interactions more durable for extended periods of time. "The prolonged interaction allows patterns of cooperation which are based on reciprocity to be worth trying and allows them to became established."[35] Another way to promote cooperation is to make the interactions more frequent.
- There is the need for greater coordination and teamwork at the higher management levels of health care institutions. While the top management membership may be expected to operate as a single team, team play should extend to embrace the department directors so that these two upper levels of management function more closely as a *total* team.

  This new direction would call for more frequent meetings of the total group; collaborative approaches to solving macro-problems, and some significant changes in the management performance evaluation process that would provide *all* members of top management with a broader view of the entire department director level, knowing more about each manager at that level, and having the benefit of other administrative members' opinions and input regarding individual and group performance at the directors' level.
- Managers and other employees who lack direct contact with patients still have opportunities to contribute to "customer" satisfaction. Every employee is part of a chain of internal "customers" and "suppliers" that ultimately extends to the patient. "The manager's job is to process work through the internal customer-supplier chain, helping employees play their part in ensuring that the end product or service fully satisfies the end user."[36] This is an excellent way to help people think and act together.
- The concluding thought is that behind the coordinative and teamwork process stands the central value of *quality* that is doubly affected by the process: (1) an increase in the solving of quality problems stretching across the organizational system, and (2) a more superior quality in the solutions of problems.

  Thurow, in drawing an analogy, asks us to "Think of the quintessential American game—professional football. The Pro-Bowl team, the all-stars, has individual players who are superior to the players on the Super Bowl, the league champions, yet no one doubts that the Super Bowl team could easily beat the Pro-Bowl team. A team of inferior individuals who have played together is simply better than a team of superior individuals who have not.[37] What is true in sports is equally true in organizational teamwork.

RESPONSIBILITIES, RELATIONSHIPS, AND STRUCTURE

Responsibilities

Another characteristic of the hospital as a workplace is stress, for while the business of a hospital is to make sick people well, its working environment does not always tend to provide an atmosphere conducive to the health of its own people. "Stress can be good, stress can be bad. Most people need some form of stress to bring out their best performance, but if the stress is of the wrong form, or too much, it becomes damaging. One of the major tasks of management in organizations is to control the level of stress."[38] This is so because stress at work can prove to be detrimental to the health of the organization and to the health of its people.

A factor contributing to the problem of organizational stress requiring our attention is *role ambiguity,* which past studies have shown to cause individuals to experience lower job satisfaction, higher job-related tension, greater futility, and lower self-confidence—conditions that assuredly can affect the human condition and the quality of human performance within the institution.

One of the most frequently cited instances of role ambiguity in a work situation is the uncertainty about scope of responsibility and accountability.

In a study by Norman Maier and two colleagues, vice-president of several organizations were each asked to select an immediate subordinate with whose work they were thoroughly familiar, and to define his or her role (including major responsibilities, priorities among these, and qualifications required by the job). The subordinates were then requested to define their own roles independently but with respect to the same variables. The agreement between the members of the pairs was of the order of *35 percent.*[39] Surely, this would appear to be a reasonable and insightful exercise for any hospital executive to conduct.

Role ambiguity is viewed as a problem serious enough in terms of its potential impact on the quality of work to warrant a sense of urgency in getting solution strategies under way. One recommended strategy worth pursuing is to launch the clarification of expectations at the supervisory level, where uncertainty in the minds of these management members is generally of the greatest severity.

Utilizing the job of the "supervisor" as the pivotal point of the analysis process allows management to examine at the same time the "spilling over" effects on both higher and lower hierarchical levels as it moves closer to a definition of "supervisor" unique to its own institution. This is believed to be a novel idea, since it is somewhat apparent that most health care organizations have not as yet defined with any adequate degree of specificity the role of the supervisor. They have not as yet dealt effectively with the problem of role ambiguity within the largest segment of their management population, where the heart of motivation for achieving increased quality in human performance and behavior prevails.

Relationships

One of the great payoffs of implementing solution strategies designed to deal with role ambiguity, such as the approach described above, is the opening up of new opportunities for pushing greater responsibility, authority, accountability, and *ownership* further down to the lower rungs of the organizational ladder. Currently, the workplace of the majority of health care organizations is not being sufficiently responsive to staff employees, who are increasingly demanding some freedom to perform their jobs outside the traditional top-down lines of control imposed on them by the organization and members of its management. The organization and its management team need to take up the unending challenge of ensuring that the collective intellect, experience, creativity, and energies of its people (its "human capital") will be more effectively and efficiently utilized in the workplace.

A bureaucratic culture resounds with maxims of self-protection: never complain; don't make waves; don't take risks. As an enlightened contrast, a democratic culture designed in the interest of people promulgates the values of treating all human beings with respect, properly using the gifts and talents with which they have been endowed, and of helping them to attain their fullest potential. It is these corporate values that are served by a renewed environment for personal growth engendered by the extension of responsibilities and the establishment of new relationships at the bottom of the organization. In other words, changes that will change the shape of work by putting to productive use such concepts as task teams of employees, "entrepreneurial" opportunities, institutionalizing networking, committee or council membership, special project assignments, closer connection to the locus of decisions, partner relationships with managers, and objective compensation systems based on performance.

We are in a period in which the values of trust, justice, freedom, personal autonomy, and respect for the individual need to be expressed and evidenced in the nature of work so that those placed in nonmanagement positions may discover new depth and quality in their work experience that are truly meaningful. This means pushing down to the lowest levels of the organization a greater sense of control over work activity.

It is almost impossible to think of what it means to be human without thinking of work. Indeed, it is through work, as a provider of useful services, that the individual employed in health care or in any other field of work carries out those roles and responsibilities that define him or her as a full and valued member not only of the organization but also of society.

Structure

The workplaces of health care institutions continue to be afflicted with the ills of traditional organization. People problems are not respecters of traditional organizational forms. An effective organization must be designed and structured to fit its values, its strategies, its tasks, and its people. Yet we find ourselves attempting to get the task done in an organizational setting that is constraining in its familiar pyramid-shaped, hierarchical diagram of interconnected boxes and lines that all too often proves to be a formidable barrier to gaining the advantages of systemic arrangements. While the traditional organizational chart is being reshaped in today's climate of mergers, acquisitions, and restructurings, there is much structured repair still to be done in the interest of people and their quality of life at work.

The health care field at large has always actively fostered career opportunities in a more global sense; however, the workplaces of the hospital and other types of health care facilities have shown a less than adequate unshackling of employees from just working at a job to growing in a career position. Notwithstanding the limited opportunities in smaller institutions, the hospital as a workplace does not always reflect an air of high interest in the intriguing and promising concept of organizational restructure designed for individual growth, of withdrawing from the rigidities we have about jobs and our addiction toward specialization.

"Grow with us" needs to be the theme of an administration that holds a healthy suspicion of traditional ways of structuring and is committed to the value of innovation. "Grow with us" is a proposition not aimed at making people "happy," but rather to be more useful, to be responsible, to be more satisfied and productive. "Grow with us" is an idea that comes not only from the mind of a resourceful organization but from its heart and soul as well. It is an idea that represents a special affirmation of the human condition.

NOTES

1. Theodore Draper, quoted from, "Hume and Madison: The Secrets of *Federalist Paper* No. 10," *Encounter* 58 (February 1982):47.

2. Robert N. Bellah et al., *Habits of the Heart* (Berkeley: University of California Press, 1985), p. 271.

3. Saul Bellow, " 'Matters Have Gotten Out of Hand' in a Violent Society," *U.S. News and World Report,* Jun. 28, 1982, p. 49.

4. John A. Logan, Jr. "Problems of an Age of Change," *Hollins College Bulletin,* date unknown.

5. Bellow, " 'Matters Have Gotten out of Hand,' " p. 49.

6. William G. Scott and David K. Hart, *Organizational America* (Boston: Houghton Mifflin, 1979), pp. 36, 37.

7. Scott and Hart, *Organizational America,* p. 54.

8. Roger M. D'Aprix, *In Search of a Corporate Soul* (New York: AMACOM, 1976), pp. 2, 3.

9. John Naisbitt and Patricia Aburdene, *Re-inventing the Corporation* (New York: Warner Books, 1985), p. 2.

10. Terrence E. Deal and Allan A. Kennedy, *Corporate Cultures* (Reading, Mass: Addison-Wesley Publishing Co., Inc., 1982), p. 19.

11. "Motivate or Alienate? Firms Hire Gurus To Change Their 'Cultures,' " *Wall Street Journal,* Jul. 24, 1987, p. 19.

12. "Motivate or Alienate?," p. 19.

13. "Ford's Leaders Push Radical Shift in Culture as Competition Grows," *Wall Street Journal,* Dec. 3, 1985, p. 1.

14. Jane E. Brody, "Why Many Efforts Fail To Change Unhealthy Habits," *New York Times,* Apr. 28, 1987, p. 31.

15. Edward T. Hall, *Beyond Culture* (Garden City, N.Y.: Anchor Press/Doubleday, 1976), p. 14.

16. Poor Handmaids of Jesus Christ, *Health Services Philosophy* (Elk Grove Village, Il.: Ancilla Systems, Inc., revised 1986).

17. "Characteristics of Service," *Linden Leaf* 3, No. 1 (Spring 1987).

18. "Characteristics of Service."

19. Warren H. Schmidt and Barry Z. Posner, *Managerial Values and Expectations,* (New York: American Management Associations, 1982), p. 14.

20. Schmidt and Posner, *Managerial Values and Expectations,* p. 14.

21. George David Smith and Lawrence E. Steadman, "Present Value of Corporate History," *Harvard Business Review,* Nov.-Dec. 1981, p. 164.

22. Frank Trippett, "The Busting of American Trust," *Time,* Oct. 20, 1980, p. 106.

23. Ian I. Mitroff, "Mutual Trust Helps Produce Quality Goods," *Los Angeles Times,* Nov. 24, 1985, part V, p. 3.

24. Mitroff, p. 3.

25. Ashley Montagu and Floyd Watson, *The Human Connection* (New York: McGraw-Hill Book Co., 1979), p. ix.

26. Louis B. Barnes, "Managing the Paradox of Organizational Trust," *Harvard Business Review,* Mar.-Apr. 1981, p. 107.

27. Addison C. Bennett, *Improving Management Performance in Health Care Institutions* (Chicago: American Hospital Association, 1978), p. 55.

28. Addison C. Bennett and Samuel J. Tibbitts, *Making Innovation Practical* (Chicago: Pluribus Press, Inc., 1986), p. 14.

29. John H. Schaar, "Getting Us All Together," *New York Times,* date unknown.

30. Chester I. Barnard, "The Nature of Leadership," in *Organization and Management* (Cambridge: Harvard University Press, 1948), pp. 88–9.

31. Bennett, *Improving Management Performance,* pp. 66–9.

32. Jay W. Forrester, "Decison-Makers Seek More Scope," *New York Times,* date unknown.

33. Lester C. Thurow, "Where's America's Old Team Spirit?" *New York Times,* Jul. 26, 1981, p. 31.

34. Robert C. Solomon, "Spinoza Didn't *Do* Anything Except Inspire," *Los Angeles Times,* Nov. 24, 1981, p. 21.

35. Robert Axelrod, *The Evolution of Cooperation* (New York: Basic Books, Inc., 1984), p. 129.

36. George H. Labovitz, "Keeping Your Internal Customers Satisfied," *Wall Street Journal,* Jul. 6, 1987, p. 30.

37. Thurow, "Where's America's Old Team Spirit?," p. 31.

38. Charles B. Handy, *Understanding Organization* (Middlesex, England: Penguin Books Ltd., 1986), p. 65.

39. Charles B. Handy, *Understanding Organization,* adapted from Maier et al., "Breakdowns in Boss-Subordinate Communication," (Foundation for Research on Human Behavior, 1959).

Chapter 3

Quality of Leadership

It is time for a new generation of leadership to cope with new problems and new opportunities. For there is a new world to be won.

—John F. Kennedy

Dr. John W. Gardner, former Secretary of Health, Education and Welfare, in addressing the National Massachusetts Institute of Technology Alumni Officers Conference on the subject of leadership, said that the principal task of leadership is to "make values live in the acts of men." During his appearance, Gardner described these five guideposts for leadership: a change in the framework of order that must be responsive to human needs, since "there is no freedom or justice without order"; equal access to opportunity; a renewed quality of life that emphasizes the importance of the individual to society and prevents the smothering of individualism; the embedding of values in the laws of the nation; and "ways of living together."[1] While Gardner's views were intended for the national scene, their transference to institutional renewal and development is most appropriate in terms of the obvious relevancy of these five guideposts to creating the corporate heart.

Another example of transference is found in the writings of Walter Lippman, who expressed the thought that "Those in high places are more than the administrators of government bureaus. They are more than the writers of laws. They are the custodians of a nation's [an organization's] ideals, of the beliefs it cherishes, of its permanent hopes, of the faith which makes a nation [an organization] out of a mere aggregation of individuals. They are unfaithful to that trust when by word and example they promote a spirit that is complacent, evasive, and acquisitive."[2]

UNDERSTANDING LEADERSHIP

In 1974, *Time* magazine asked several historians, philosophers, writers, military men, businessmen, and others the question, "What makes a great leader?"[3]

Mortimer Adler, U.S. philosopher, replied in Aristotelian terms, "The good leader must have *ethos*, *pathos*, and *logos*. The *ethos* is his moral character, the source of his ability to persuade. The *pathos* is his ability to touch feelings, to move people emotionally. The *logos* is his ability to give solid reasons for an action, to move people intellectually."

Alexander Heard, U.S. educator, expressed the belief that "No concept of leadership is complete without the element of zeal and fervor, an almost spiritual element."

Jules Masserman, U.S. psychoanalyst, stated that "Leaders must fulfill three functions—provide for the well-being of the led, provide a social organization in which people feel relatively secure, and provide them with one set of beliefs."

These respondents, and others who have thought about the idea of leadership, cite innumerable definitions and distinctions involving character, moral force and intellectual power, good and evil. Most definitions emphasize honesty, candor, and vision combined with sheer physical stamina and courage.

In the collectiveness of the array of answers, the nature of their contents appears to support the thought of one of those queried, Henry Steele Commager, U.S. historian, who replied that "Leadership is intangible. You can't define all the parts." Also supported was the notion of the French critic, Henri Peyre, that "leaders are indeed mystery men born in paradise or some devil's pit."

While apparently no one is quite sure just what leadership is, there are things we *do* know about it with some certainty. For example, we are aware that

- There is some truth to the observation that leadership is one of those things you don't know you need until you don't have it.
- Leaders *do* matter. "Much depends on how they view themselves, what they say and whether they appeal to the best or the worst in the people."[4]
- There is a need for leadership for a new social character that has been transformed by three interweaving currents since the craft and entrepreneurial eras: (1) technology, which requires "new adaptive traits and abilities, and since it replaces physical with brain work, it requires a schooled work force and schooling develops habits of learning and openness to new ideas"; (2) the movement to "an organizational society with new definitions of work . . . Individuals are raised to be flexible and mobile, to be at the same time more autonomous and more cooperative with strangers in organizations"; and (3) more confident employees—"A new sense of security emboldens employees who feel entitled to rather than grateful to the employer for their job and its benefits."[5]
- There are some old myths about leadership that have been discredited, including:

1. Leadership is a rare skill. "The truth is that leadership opportunities are plentiful and within the reach of most people."[6]
2. There is one best leadership style, or that there are leaders who excel under all circumstances.
3. There are some men and women who are born leaders, and training, experience, or conditions cannot materially affect leadership skills. "Leadership can be developed and improved by study and training," General Omar Bradley once told a class at the Army Command and General Staff College in Fort Leavenworth, Kansas. "But don't discount experience. Someone may remind you that Napoleon led armies before he was 30 and Alexander the Great died at 33. Alexander might have been even greater if he had lived to an older age and had had more experience. In this respect, I especially like the theory that 'judgment comes from experience and experience comes from bad judgment.'"[7]

- Leadership "is the pivotal force behind successful organizations and that to create vital and viable organizations, leadership is necessary to help organizations develop a new vision of what they can be, then mobilize the organization change toward the new vision."[8]
- The fundamental process of leadership is the ability to "make conscious what lies unconscious" in the minds and hearts of others.[9] Whether the others are many or few is almost immaterial. Defined this way, the essence of leadership becomes qualitative, not quantitative, although numbers can provide an indication of effectiveness.
- Leadership in the health care institution is a difficult role, yet its difficulty tends to be underrated by those outside the field. As of now we know far too little about leadership in the health care environment; it is simply too recent a phenomenon.
- Leadership differs from managing, and it is needed at every level and in every single unit in which managing is exercised. However, if leadership is to flourish there must be conditions in which it can emerge. The bureaucracies of large organizations have a suppressive effect.

In this chapter we examine the leadership role (and the actions it requires) as it needs to be generated by the board, the chief executive officer (CEO), and the top administrative team, and the middle management group of department directors and supervisors to make the minds and hearts of the organizational membership conscious of the centrality of quality.

THE BOARD

"Every good and excellent thing stands moment by moment on the razor's edge of danger and must be fought for." That quote hangs on the right-hand wall just before you enter Ross Perot's office in downtown Dallas. Mr. Perot, the Texas billionaire, does not know where the quote comes from, but he does know how to offend tradition when it comes to the manner in which boards on which he sits run their affairs, particularly when the issue of quality is the focus of discussion.

In February 1986, when the Winston Churchill Foundation bestowed its leadership award on him, Henry Ross Perot searched for an appropriate summation of just what he was. He told the audience that he once dreamed of being a pretty pearl, but with his jug ears and crooked nose that seemed unlikely. Then he realized that his lot was to be the grain of sand that irritates the oyster enough to make the pretty pearl. "That's what I am," he said, "an irritant. I stir things up." A recent oyster he rubbed up against was the world's largest auto maker, General Motors.[10]

An "irritant" is defined as that which provokes; stirs up; urges on; incites to action—a characteristic that is well-intended, in a positive sense; a disposition that needs to show itself in the makeup of more boards. The nature of all too many governing boards in hospitals today is typified by an inadequacy in the delicate art of asking hard, tough questions—questions that are provocative and penetrating, and perhaps irritating to the CEO.

The attribute of curiosity needs to be exercised by members of the board as they gain increasing knowledge of the institutional environment. The peril is that their skill of inquiry and desire for understanding will become blunted unless they are successfully transferred to intellectual interests and involvement in the boardroom. Merely asking "Why?," for example, is a useful stimulus toward imagining what the cause or purpose of a proposed plan of action may be. "How?" also is a useful question in provoking thought about the mechanism of a process embraced by the plan. Whatever the queries might be, there exists a potential risk in their short supply, for with each advance in our curiosity "we reach a higher level from which a wider field of vision is open to us, and from which we see events previously out of range."[11] *The asking of insightful questions as an incentive to thinking about quality is believed to be in less-than-adequate supply in today's hospital board rooms.*

The governing body has no greater responsibility than that of providing quality oversight. Yet, in spite of having a substantial responsibility for quality of care and service, "most trustees," according to William Jesse, M.D., Vice-President, Joint Commission on Accreditation of Healthcare Organizations, Chicago, "are less comfortable dealing with their quality of care responsibilities than they are with their financial responsibilities."[12] Dr. Jesse attributes that reluctance to trustees' perception of quality as the "province of the medical staff." He contends that trustees can feel comfortable with the quality in their institutions if "all health care professionals are performing appropriately, patient risk is kept to a minimum, and there is efficient use of resources." According to Jesse, there are four areas in which trustees can fulfill that goal: credentials/privileges, quality assurance, risk management, and employee performance evaluation.

Beyond Quality Assurance

The prime mechanism present within health care institutions today is an organized quality assurance program designed to enhance patient care through the ongoing objective assessment of important aspects of patient care and the correction of identified problems. It is the board's responsibility to establish, monitor, and support, through administration and medical staff, this program which converges on the very essence of our concern—patient care. While, indisputably, this single issue will always remain at the center of our attention, there are, at the same time, other interacting and interrelated elements of the institutional system that also require concomitant attention in terms of quality improvement. These added elements include quality of work itself, which embraces all of the actions that involve doing jobs right the first time, and in turn, affect costs all along the line. There, too, is the quality of a life-at-work environment that nurtures caring and collaboration while negating conflict, stress, dissatisfactions, and inappropriate behavior at the workplace. These extensions of concern fall in line with Dr. Jesse's reference to employee performance.

Making Total Quality a Reality

Nothing short of top-level leadership will do the job of quality enhancement. The board, administration, and medical staff principals—vanguards of the continuing endeavor—need to sense the broader context of the quality system and take action accordingly: actions along these lines, for example.

- Make clear the meaning and import of quality and quality enhancement. To pervade the corporate culture with a sense of quality, there is no better starting point than the institution's mission statement.

    Other central documents that also need to furnish resolute evidence of commitment are the bylaws of the organization and attending staff, in which the expressions of quality are all too often conspicuously deficient in their fullness and richness.

- Set and approve policies designed to ensure conformance to high-quality standards and long-range strategic plans that contain quality targets.

- Initiate massive educational programming beginning with the board and flowing down through all institutional levels. Quality begins with the performance of people, not things, and it is the quality awareness and understanding of the organizational membership that must be gained.

- Embrace a *systemic* perception of quality in all of the board's thoughtfulness in decision or action.

- Devote adequate time to the cause of quality improvement through the receipt of substantive accounts of the quest for quality presented by medical staff members as well as by the administrator and his or her management representatives. Insistence not only on substance but on measurability, where possible, of the information imparted needs to be defended and sustained.

- Establish decisively a cooperative tie with administration and the medical staff. The quality of these working relationships improves the quality of the work of all.

- Imbue the management system with a consciousness of quality. The expectation of superior levels of manager performance coming from sound management practices, in both a quantitative and qualitative sense, needs to be continuous.

- Open up a communication network with business and industry so as to capture the quality control techniques and practices utilized by outside organizations that are known to have long-operated in the tradition of excellence.

This sampling of actions is centered on the idea that there is a wholeness to quality when viewed as going beyond the core of commitment to the organization's assurance program.

The governing members need to make the corporate message very clear that "good is never good enough." They need to become an unwavering source of making quality certain throughout the institution. They also need to make it evident to the "mind" of the organization that quality is everyone's business, and comes only to those who work hard to achieve it.[13]

The Human Side of Trusteeship

The health care field today is not faced with a single, isolable crisis situation; rather, it is moving through an unprecedented period of transition that cannot be responded to by intermittent peaks of board performance. It requires, instead, reforms in the fundamentals of board structure, membership, agenda, and modes of performance warranted by the multitude and magnitude of the issues at hand: the thrust toward marketplace competition; the tenacity of government legislation and regulation; the surging growth of alternative delivery systems; the quickening pace of organizational systems networking, both vertically and horizontally; the continued focus on cost containment and reduction; deep difficulties in the accessibility of resources; and the growing problems embedded in human performance and productivity. Any one of these impacting issues alone can cause dire distress; all together, collectively, they can spell misadventure for any governing body (and its management) that has not left behind an "agenda" of a more simplistic and customary process of thought because of its failure to conceive the need for a systemic agenda that views, in totality, the whole institution and the surrounding external environment with which it interrelates.

A hospital is a socioeconomic enterprise, and, as such, it demands that its corporate governance, beyond economic deliberations, give full recognition to socially related purposes and constituencies. High in order of importance, value, and urgency is the quintessential issue of the quality of human performance. In reality, quality and economics are indeed inseparable concepts.

According to the Nobel Prize-winning economist, Theodore W. Schultz, the most important economic resource consists of the acquired abilities of people—their education, experience, skills, and health.[14] This "human capital"—not space, energy, land or other physical properties of the work environment—is decisive in enhancing the vitality and success of today's and tomorrow's health care organization. Yet, "the absence of an agendum dealing with human capital characterizes too many board meetings,"[15] as does the infrequency of questions posed by individual governing board members about the human side of enterprise—queries along these lines: What is the predominant mood or spirit within the organization? How is it perceived and evaluated? What is the true level of employee morale within the hospital? How do the attitudes within our hospital compare with the attitudes of similar groups of workers in other organizations? How do we generally rate the satisfaction of work and the performance of our people at different organizational levels? What is our responsiveness to the human needs of our people as these needs relate to the quality of their life at work? These expressions of inquiry, all of which are variations of the underlying theme of human resource management, do not tend to surface with any degree of regularity within the context of most board discussions.

How is a pervasive consciousness and sensibility to the human affairs of the organization captured and sustained at the corporate leadership level? Here are some selected and succinct thoughts for possible action.

- Call for the board's direct participation in the development and documentation of the philosophical stance of the enterprise that clearly articulates its commitment to respond to its various constituencies, including the employee population.
- Develop specific written descriptions of the responsibilities and work methods of the board and of individual members in a context that brings balance to the qualitative and quantitative dimensions of their missions, all in keeping with the philosophical posture and credo of the corporation.

- Fashion the makeup of initial orientation so that it is designed to sensitize and inform the newly elected members about the need to accommodate both economic and social objectives, and about the values of maintaining a systemic recognition of the impact of organizational actions and activities on all of the constituent parties.

- Work diligently toward bringing into being a balanced board of working members whose careers, experiences, and interests qualify and motivate them to contribute a high diversity of fresh points of view, under the conductorship of a chairperson who encourages free and independent expression.

- Create at the board level a human resource committee (or restore the vitality of an already existing "personnel committee"), and assign to it the responsibility of sensitizing the board to trends in the societal environment affecting peoples' attitudes toward work and their quality-of-work-life expectations. Adjunct to this is the task of providing guidance in placing evaluative judgments on the appropriateness of existing personnel policies and practices.

- Examine anew the character and programmed details of the board's agenda for possible departure from time-honored custom and practice that have tended to give less-than-adequate attention to qualitative considerations.

- Broaden the perspective of board membership to embrace an "arithmetic of quality" when focusing on purely economic issues, since traditional balance sheets and profit-and-loss statements are unquestionably too narrow to measure true growth.

- Commit to a continuing process of self-assessment systematically structured to take a fresh and uncluttered view of "the world" within the total enterprise and to involve individual trustees in this self-examining and -assessment process.

- Give key staff members (human resource executive, nursing administrator, educational director) visibility and voice through scheduled appearances before the board for purposes of sharing observations and insights about conditions at the workplace as they *actually* exist.

- Activate an effective, ongoing educational process to assure that the members of the board are kept abreast of trends and happenings (both within and outside the organization) having relevancy to their humanistic mission and responsibilities.

Obviously, there is the need to give renewed recognition and response to a major challenge that has arrived as a "sign of entitlement," a challenge that holds all indications of remaining with us for some time to come. It is a challenge given voice to by today's workers who have been affected by new social values and life styles and, as a result, have brought a whole new set of beliefs, attitudes, and behavior to their performance at work. As suggested by social analyst Daniel Yankelovich, we are increasingly encountering among all groups a tendency to hold back, to bargain harder, to demand and expect more without necessarily giving anything more in return.

"Holding back" cannot be the disposition of hospital boards of trustees. To the contrary, their behavior must be characterized by a persistent search for better ways of conducting every humanistic and qualitative aspect of corporate activity.

THE CEO AND TOP MANAGEMENT TEAM

Leadership at the apex of the health care organization demands the kind of quality that can turn effort into accomplishment. It is a tough job, not to be measured by the "hard" facts of revenue and earnings alone, for to view the operations of an institution as essentially a material process is to undervalue the human mind and heart. With increasing importance, the leadership task at the top must also be valued for the "softness" of its artistry as it influences the advancement of the human condition throughout the total organizational system.

Evaluating the CEO, too, is a tough job. It represents one of the more significant contributions of the board to the quality of organizational performance, "Yet often when the subject of evaluation is raised, an uncomfortable look appears on the CEO's face that usually means either the board has not done any kind of a performance evaluation or the job it *has* done has not been done well."[16]

To be effective and meaningful, the evaluation process should cover the full range of the functions and responsibilities of the CEO. However, our interest here is to consider certain aspects of the process having a direct relationship to the advancement of quality that both the evaluation committee of the board and the CEO should consider as they work together to establish performance objectives and criteria.

The importance of these quality-directed dimensions is supported by a key finding of a Sibson & Company survey of board members and senior human resource executives in 345 U.S. companies. The finding: "Quantitative results take second place to qualitative aspects of performance, such as leadership ability, when assessing CEO performance."[17]

Agreement between the board and the CEO as to what is to be evaluated from a qualitative standpoint can be made easier by asking these kinds of questions: What do you think the business and societal environment will be five or ten years from now? What particular problems do these environments pose for this organization? What problems has the organization had in the past that are likely to recur? How would you describe the culture, character, or style of the organization? Does the organization provide a positive work atmosphere that recognizes the vital importance of human resources? What is the current state of human affairs within the organization? What issues do we identify as our priorities? What issue will have to take a secondary place? What trade-offs are you making? What are the crucial factors about the organization that influence your deliberation? At what stage is this organization in its growth and development? What then are its pressing developmental tasks?[18]

Answers to these questions, among others, should find their way onto the CEO's position description or be translated into accompanying criteria. They, too, should bring greater fullness to an understanding of, and a sensibility to, standards of leadership impacting on quality that provide a means for judging the CEO's performance. Standards such as the following make the task meaningful.

The Ability To Communicate. The CEO should have the ability to communicate and to advance, on a continuing basis, the organization's total communication system to a better state of quality.

Communication is the most humanly imperfect process in which any CEO engages, yet it potentially offers the CEO a reliable avenue for disseminating a conveyed sense of integrity, character, and justice in the leader. Unquestionably, it is a dependable road to managing the paradox of organizational trust.

People in the organization cry for reflective and objective modes of communication. They believe it unacceptable for the leader at the top to carry on his or her role in isolation. The leader must come in contact with the eyes of his or her people if their minds and hearts are to be reached. The leader also needs to be a listener, a distinctive feature of a high achiever and an indispensable characteristic of one's humanity. In communications, there is a place for the use of humor, which shows that the leader is at ease with himself or herself.

The Skill of Crafting Strategy. The CEO should have the skill of crafting strategy as an artist who has a vision of the organization as it can become; a craftsman who possesses a "feeling of intimacy and harmony with the materials at hand, developed through long experience and commitment,"[19] and who senses a link between a past of corporate capabilities and a future of opportunities for serving the "customer."

Leaders at the top may have to "live strategy in the future, but they must understand it through the past." As Mintzberg states:

> Like potters at the wheel, organizations must make sense of the past
> if they hope to manage the future. Only by coming to understand

the patterns that form in their own behavior do they get to know their capabilities and their potential. Thus crafting strategy, like managing craft, requires a natural synthesis of the future, present, and past.[20]

The Talent To Orchestrate the Activities of People. The orchestra is an elegant metaphor because organizations are indeed too complex to be left without direction. A symphony orchestra, functioning perfectly, represents utopia.

> Many people, doing their best at the quite different things for which they happen to be qualified, work smoothly together toward the common goal of producing beautiful music. They need a conductor (a leader) to bring their various voices into harmony and appropriate rhythm, but he can achieve nothing without their confidence.[21]

It is no use turning away and trying to settle for a simple old tune. The people have learned their skills and know the score. It all comes down to the matter of playing together with honest, able direction coming from the CEO of the organization.

The Ability to Help Others To See What Is Possible. What needs to be witnessed is a continuing quest for excellence in which goals are set a little higher and performance takes on new meaning as the organization's culture provides consistency in developing performance enhancement strategies. The leader at the top needs to enlighten the "mind" of the organization as to these thoughts and beliefs about the concept of excellence.

- Excellence needs to be viewed as a goal.
- While excellence cannot really be seen or touched, it has presence, sustained by achievement.
- Excellence abhors the static. It demands movement toward perfection, knowing we cannot be perfect.
- Excellence can be experienced everywhere, but we must demand it everywhere.
- Excellence is more than competence. It is a spirit. It flourishes on energetic desire—on trying, not repose. It is essentially invulnerable and inexhaustible.
- Excellence is attitude.[22]

Donald Peterson, Chairman, Ford Motor Company, had this to say about the pursuit of the best: "The principle by which we will live and die is that once we can do something well, we have to figure out how to do it even better."[23]

The Ability To Make a Team Work. The quality of being able to make a team work at the very top of the organization is essential to the CEO. Success in getting the senior executive group to set goals, accept responsibilities, and create a real team can have an impact of great intensity on the total organizational system. Deficiencies such as

- damaging conflicts between or among team members
- confusion about responsibilities or unclear roles and relationships among team members
- absence of clarity in goals or low commitment to goals
- communication deficiencies: group members do not speak up, do not understand how important it is to listen, and have not captured the art of conversation in business situations
- lack of trust—the quintessential ingredient of it all

if allowed to happen, will surface and be readily detected by managers and staff employees alike at all levels of the organization. As we have known for a long time, workers' perceptions of those at the top, as individuals or as a group, can influence their morale, attitudes, and job satisfaction.

The Capacity To Think Comprehensively. "In making their day-to-day and minute-by-minute tactical maneuvers, senior executives tend to rely on several general thought processes such as using intuition; managing a network of interrelated problems; dealing with ambiguity, inconsistency, novelty, and surprise; and integrating action into the process of thinking."[24] Is the CEO effective in thinking about how to do things? Does he or she focus on process? Tolerate ambiquity? Maintain and sharpen intellectual skills? See problems as interrelated, and then move on to ask these kinds of connective questions: How does quality relate to marketing strategy? To capital expenditure guidelines? To research and development? To the new performance-appraisal system? To management preparedness? To goal-setting? To recent efforts in human resource planning?

Obviously, what is being looked at and evaluated here is what the CEO thinks about and how he or she thinks. Also, how far and how successfully does the CEO take the organization beyond the classical rational model of approaching problems, making decisions, taking action, and implementing change?

The Creativeness and Willingness To Innovate. Routine and predictable courses of action will no longer suffice, nor will caretaking as one's customary manner of management, nor will comfortableness with the idea of preserving the familiar.

The CEO sets the tone and spirit of innovation, and, by example, needs to bring into being a winning team of individuals at the top with the experience, vision, and ingenuity to develop fresh approaches to large and complex problems; to establish a philosophy about where the corporate culture should be heading; to nurture a substantially new manner of thinking throughout the organization; and to develop the environment and resources essential to encouraging experimentation and generation of new ideas.[25]

Over time, it is the CEO and members of the senior executive group who preserve the continuity and vitality of the organization while ensuring its renewal day by day.

Commitment To People Development. The CEO and the top management team must give emphasis to "people development" as a way to increase the organization's pool of potential leaders and to perpetuating good leadership at all levels. Andrall Pearson states that

> most top managers know they should be doing a better job of building the superior organization they want. They may not, however, know what more successful managers are doing—or how to do it themselves. And while most would agree that their business's success hinges on the quality of its people, very few executives are willing to adopt the tough, aggressive approach to managing people that's required to produce a dynamic organization.[26]

These kinds of criteria for judging the performance of the CEO, as well as the members of the top management team, are considered desirable because they are directed toward serving the organization's need to adapt to changing competitive conditions while adhering to basic corporate values believed suitable to the cause of quality.

LEADERSHIP AT THE MIDDLE OF THE ORGANIZATION

Leadership at the top is primary, but there is no way for a chief executive officer and his or her administrative staff to do the job of quality improvement alone. With an awareness of their limitations, together they need to build a team at the middle of the organization to help with the quality agenda—a team of a new breed of managers at the department director, assistant director, and supervisory levels who are not merely *managers* in the traditional sense but, more important, *leaders* in a new qualitative sense, a cadre of managerial leaders who evidence striking dissimilarities to many of the time-honored practices of "managing." If today's health care institution is to be truly successful in the quality arena, it needs to pay more attention to producing a new breed of managers at the middle of the organization who combine the skills required by both an action-oriented cerebral process and an action-oriented interpersonal process. Negligence or failure in this regard is perhaps the single greatest factor blocking a renaissance of total quality in the health care workplace.

In contrast with typically hard-working, analytical, tolerant, and fair-minded managership, it is imperative that there be managerial leaders at the middle who can create superior quality because they

- give greater attention to the role, mission, philosophy, and overall culture of the organization
- reflect new value systems in the way they evaluate themselves and their people
- renew the organization day by day by questioning established procedures and creating new concepts
- can cope innovatively with the rapid movement of change and have the creativity for introducing a climate of experimentation
- have the sensibility of an artist to perceive and think globally as they act locally
- have the ability to temper the natural competitive spirit with a human touch that builds the work environment to human scale
- understand the forces that are shaping the new workplace
- possess a flexible mentality that enables them to adopt new approaches to the management of people
- seek, and are able to alter profoundly, human relationships
- are able to convince people that their needs and desires are the same as one's own
- have the ability to communicate effectively and to instill cooperation, loyalty, and teamwork in their employees
- nurture freedom by giving people as much responsibility as they can handle
- promote the ultimate goal of personal growth
- recognize that the limitations of their specialization must be illuminated by the light of other disciplines

Managers at the Middle: A Mismanaged Resource

In most health care institutions today, there is more quantity than quality in the middle ranks of management; more technical skills than managerial talent; more management expertise than leadership competence. The key target is *not* to move toward less managing for the sake of more leadership, but rather to create a different style of managing by blending the managerial focus on process with a leadership concentration on substance.

In an increasingly competitive climate, a successful organization needs good, solid management at the middle, for it is truly the backbone of the enterprise. It is the level at which ideas for quality performance are translated into action through the energies, competencies, and enthusiasm of those providing leadership in the various operating components. But the problem is that fewer and fewer managers at the middle have good things to say about their organizations, while the top bosses appear to be insulated from reality, as they see few problems at the middle and really think that the morale of department managers and supervisors is strong. Indeed, this is a sad commentary on a set of human conditions that comes at a time when more and more managements are talking about trying to effect quality, costs, and productivity through joint efforts of people from various management and non-management levels.[27]

As Emanuel Kay puts it in his book *The Crisis in Middle Management*

> The middle managers . . . operate the management systems which make the organization work. The impact of this five percent is multiplied, for better or worse, on the other 95 percent (and this includes the one percent of the organization which is top management). If we can provide an environment in which our middle managers are more effective, then we can multiply the effectiveness of the entire organization.[28]

The meaning of "environment" in this sense is the complex of individual competency and cultural conditions affecting the qualitative nature of the manager-leader and of the organization upon which the manager-leader impacts.

How do we penetrate the health care organization with such an environment, and move the five percent to "a good, solid middle management" group that can effect changes in the other 95 percent? By top management doing the things that it is not doing in the majority of our health care institutions today.

Past experiences soundly support the significance of the following sixteen imperatives if the "new breed" of managers-leaders is to come into being.[29]

Assess, Assess, Assess. The act of assessing is the province of every manager. What is required, however, is the application of an organized, structured, and purposeful approach to the discovery of innovative improvements. In fact, what is required is a "perpetual inventory" of needs and opportunities in all sixteen imperative areas, demanding a substantially new manner of thinking, and a change in the attitudes of managers who ask the questions and those who answer them.

Think Systems. Absence of systems thinking remains a damaging deficiency in efforts to develop managers. For example, there persists the popular tendency to give attention to developing only certain segments of the institution's management populace. This practice continues at a time when it is so essential to plan for the enhancement of *all* managers (from administration to supervision) in an *interdependent* development process designed to interlock levels of responsibility so that growth and expansion of potentialities will take hold as the process cascades down through the entire management mainstream.

Focus on Performance. To avoid the wastefulness and bewilderment of faddish and fragmented efforts aimed at isolated areas of development such as productivity, cost, and quality, it is believed sensible to give direction toward the central thrust of *performance.* As the overriding concept of concentration, the idea of performance provides a highly acceptable framework within which all elements of a total development effort can find a comfortable and contributory position. Surely, performance as the quintessential theme offers an appropriate focus as the process of development moves through the management ranks and beyond.

Formalize Management Resource Planning. The discipline of a management resource planning process is the only way to go if an organization wishes to control its managerial destiny, if it wishes to ensure the placement of the right people in the right places at the right time for the right reasons. As one CEO put it, "I feel that without a management resource planning process program that was followed in a disciplined manner, our organization would not be where it is today, primarily because we would not have the management we have, as well as the trained reserves."

Bring in the Best. One of the most underpaid positions in today's health care organization has to be that of the recruiter/interviewer who sits at the entry point of employment. Indeed, the position demands a professional who can bring in "superstars"—the best—for it is at this initial engagement that the beginnings of productivity, cost containment, innovation, and quality are launched. It, too, is a time when dynamic and creative energies need to be put to work toward enhancing organizational performance and obtaining greater fulfillment of managers' expectations and aspirations.

Clarify Expectations in Advance. "What should a manager look like for our organization?" "What qualities should an effective manager at our hospital possess?" These queries need asking by top management if it is to develop and implement a measurable and meaningful management performance improvement process. Why are these questions important? Because once they receive suitable responses, other elements of manager development fall into place: assessment of development needs, goal effectiveness, job enrichment, program design improvement, objective-based evaluation of performance, and reward systems.

Design Development as a Process. Here are two additional questions to which the CEO should have the answer: "How many *total* dollars did our organization spend during the past fiscal year on developing our managers?" and "Are our managers better managers this year than they were a year ago?" Responding to these basic inquiries not only provides one with a sense of investment but, more important, offers insight into the key concept of *return on investment.* There is but one reason for training and development: observable and measurable change for improvement in skills, attitudes, and behavior. The barometer of success is not numbers of management trainees or how they feel about it, but rather, whether they are truly moving toward becoming effective agents of change.

The fervid imperative is to replace training *programs* with a development *process* fitting to the unique needs and resources of the individual institution and its managers. This process should be planned systemically over time in a sequential, building-block fashion, with each learning experience calling for manager accountability for the fulfillment of specific expectations and outcomes linked to performance appraisal and rewards. When sending managers off to external seminars and workshops, their respective "bosses" must do their homework in seeing to it that change occurs both in the manager returning from a new learning situation and within the organizational context through the transferability of at least one novel idea gained by networking with the outside world.

Let Managers Manage. Letting managers manage provides the real payoff in advancing management performance. In all too many hospitals today, there is the appearance of highly active manager-development programs taking place, yet the reality is that managers truly are not allowed to manage, to exercise newly learned skills, to strengthen capabilities, to realize their untapped potential, to engage in creative efforts. At the *department director* level, responsibilities, authority, decision making, risk taking, and accountability are often soft areas of allowance. At the *supervisor* level, we find excessive extensions of former nonmanagement tasks being performed by these so-called "members of management."

What needs to be done? Define what a "supervisor" is in terms of managerial responsibilities; push down delegated decision making, tolerate risk taking, firm up the organization's support system, and loosen up the organization to make time for managing. What will come out of all this? Without question, higher levels of manager performance.

Perceive Appraisal with Newness. The act of evaluating the performance of others is viewed perhaps as the most difficult and discomforting event in the life of a manager. This is so because of the manner in which appraisal is fundamentally perceived and designed. For the key process of performance management to be both effective and efficient, the conduct of appraisal needs to move

- from a negative to a positive experience
- from a purely subjective to an increasingly objective process
- from a "court of judgment" to a partnership in development
- from an inequality of status to an equality of freedom of discussion
- from a singular responsibility to a joint accountability
- from a retrospective domination to a progressive view to the future
- from a once-a-year ritual to a continuing process of development
- from ambiguous or noncommunicated expectations to a planned design for development
- from attention to dollars first to a concentration on performance first
- from a preoccupation with form to a primary concern with principles, values, and policy

All in all, the conduct of appraisal needs to move from a state of stability to a search for newness in how performance is appraised and the manager is developed, in the total sense.

Reward Performance. In today's world of work, we need the best of the new breed of managers. And we must reward them well. It is no longer affordable to provide long-term shelter for underproductive managers. Loyalty to the organization is rewarded by meaningful work, not by ignoring less-than-acceptable levels of performance.

Pay linked to performance is an expectation of more than three-fourths of those employed in today's workplace, whether they are of short or long tenure. "Don't compare me to others; compare me to myself in terms of my own individual performance" is what they are voicing. "If I'm a superior performer, set me apart from those who are merely satisfactory or less; be discriminate; reward me for *my* accomplishments and contributions" is the clear message of managers that needs to be heeded.

Organize with Flexibility. A central task is to realign and simplify structure, operating with fewer levels of management. This requirement needs to be met not only at the middle level but also at the administrative level, where top-heavy staff has been put into place, using familiar forms of structure, and very often because of prevailing weaknesses below. There also is the need to dismiss the tendency within the industry to disparage lateral moves as a meaningful avenue to revitalizing the ambitious managers at the middle, to providing new job challenges, and to changing the present system of promoting members of management.

Create a Cross-Functional Environment. Administrations need to move closer to the Japanese system of rotating management (and nonmanagement) employees through various departments in their careers. Widespread absence of vision and value given to this cross-functional concept has deprived all too many health care organizations of opportunities to gain greater teamwork among managers; to build organizational flexibility; and to minimize difficulties stemming from the rival reluctance of divisions, departments, and work units to share their expertise and experiences.

Open Up Two-Way Communication. The right to know is an expectation of people at work today. Open, two-way communication needs to characterize the organizational climate. Managers at the middle are at the axis of the information network. They need to have maximal access to those above them and the skills to impart information effectively to those below.

Find Better Ways To Manage Information. Managers at the middle who succeed in the years ahead will understand and know how to use information. Thus, the organization, in its efforts to find better ways to manage information, must assign greater significance to the capability of the support system to transform data into information, and to improve the manager's ability to utilize existing data and information.

Develop New Practices. The organization should actively engage in a continuing research program that reaches out to business and industry for possible adaptation and development of new, innovative management practices.

Move to Truly Human Resource Management. All of the above imperatives need to be served by an organizational function that goes far beyond the time-honored practices of personnel administration. Merely a semantic change in the function's identity to "human resource management" will deprive the organization in its efforts to gain a return on its investments in management. What is required is recognition that the boundaries of developing human capital must reach beyond recruitment and selection, position descriptions, and salaries and benefits to a whole new array of quality-of-work-life actions and activities that respond to the personal needs and expectations of people at work. As top management takes on the task of giving meaning to the concept of "human resource management" for its own organization, its definition needs to mirror *all* of the above imperatives. None can be ignored or discounted if there is present a belief in the primary thought that organizational performance is, in essence, management performance—that is, the performance of a new breed of managers.

These are ideas that will not go away. They are ideas that CEOs and their senior executive staffs need to subscribe to if there is a desire to change the organizational waistline from fat to muscle. All too many hospitals continue to be overmanaged quantitatively and underled qualitatively. Without question, the executives at the top are going to have to think harder and smarter about the whole middle populace of department managers and supervisors; to think how to push greater responsibility, authority, and ownership farther down to lower rungs of the organizational ladder; to stay lean by structuring the middle along "small is beautiful" lines; to spend fewer dollars by demanaging at the middle; to pay to those who are truly combination leader-managers better salaries than the levels that now prevail, and to get, in return, not only high levels of quality performance, but *exceptionally* high levels of quality performance; and finally, how to best build on the middle managers' strengths and eliminate their weaknesses.

We are still not at the end of this chapter on the quality of leadership, since, as the saying goes, "quality is a journey, not a destination." The journey takes us to the nonmanagement employee levels of the organization.

From the start, management must recognize that the worker, if permitted, can provide an important impetus for quality improvement. On the surface, this may sound almost routine to health care organizations that pride themselves on progressive human resource practices. There is evidence, however, that health institutions generally are *not* moving quickly enough on worker involvement.

In a recent Gallup Poll on quality practices in American industry, workers were singled out as the primary source of quality problems by a majority of surveyed executives. "This is pure bunk," says James Houghton, chairman of Corning Glass Works. He goes on to say,

> If there is one thing our company and others like us have learned from our efforts to enhance quality, it is that the person on the job knows more about that job and how to improve it than anyone in the organization. For too long we managers have worn blinders when looking at our workers. We have underestimated their creativity and failed to tap their resourcefulness. They want to do a good job. They want to be an integral part of the quality process. . . . Listening to the workers, placing more faith in their capabilities, can often produce dramatic results.[30]

Interestingly enough, it can also produce "leadership" in the pursuit of quality enhancement at the bottom of the organization.

NOTES

1. *New York Times*, Sept. 7, 1968, p. 24.
2. James Reston, "Private Behavior, Public Responsibility," *New York Times*, Dec. 25, 1987, p. 21.

3. "In Quest of Leadership," *Time,* Jul. 15, 1974, pp. 21–36.

4. James Reston, "Do Leaders Matter?" *New York Times,* Aug. 31, 1983, p. 6.

5. Michael Maccoby, *The Leader* (New York: Ballantine Books, 1981), p. 39.

6. Warren Bennis and Burt Nanus, *Leaders: The Strategies for Taking Charge* (New York: Harper & Row, 1985), p. 222.

7. "In Quest of Leadership," p. 28.

8. Bennis and Nanus, Leaders, pp. 2, 3.

9. James M. Burns, *Leadership* (New York: Harper & Row, 1978), p. 40.

10. N. R. Kleinfield, "The 'Irritant' They Call Perot," *New York Times,* Apr. 27, 1986, sec. 3.

11. W.I.B. Beveridge, *The Art of Scientific Investigation* (New York: Vintage Books, 1957), p. 84.

12. *Trustee,* Aug. 1986, p. 26.

13. *Trustee,* Oct. 1984, pp. 29–32.

14. Theodore W. Schultz, *Investing in People* (Berkeley: University of California Press, 1981), p. 6.

15. *Trustee,* Aug. 1983, p. 12.

16. Richard P. Moses. *Evaluation of the Hospital Board and the Chief Executive Officer* (Chicago: American Hospital Publishing, Inc., 1986), p. 28.

17. "Mini Trends," (Los Angeles: LHS Corp., 1986), p. 5.

18. Harry Levinson, "Criteria for Choosing Chief Executives," *Harvard Business Review,* Jul.-Aug., 1980, p. 113.

19. Henry Mintzberg. "Crafting Strategy," *Harvard Business Review,* Jul.-Aug. 1987, p. 66.

20. Mintzberg, "Crafting Strategy," p. 66.

21. Flora Lewis, "Orchestra as Metaphor," *New York Times,* Jan. 26, 1981, p. 21.

22. Addison C. Bennett and Samuel J. Tibbitts, *Making Innovation Practical,* (Chicago: Pluribus Press, Inc., 1986), p. 14.

23. *Fortune,* Jan. 4, 1988, p. 24.

24. Daniel J. Isenberg, "How Senior Managers Think," *Harvard Business Review,* Nov.-Dec., 1984, pp. 81–90.

25. Bennett and Tibbitts, *Making Innovation Practical,* pp. 125–127.

26. Andrall Pearson, "Muscle-Build the Organization," *Harvard Business Review,* Jul.-Aug., 1987, p. 49.

27. Addison C. Bennett, "Administrators Must Share Authority," *Modern Healthcare,* Feb., 1980, p. 90.

28. Emanuel Kay, *The Crisis in Middle Management* (New York: AMACOM, 1974), p. 8.

29. Appearing in part in *Hospitals,* Sept. 20, 1987, p. 88.

30. James Houghton, "For Better Quality, Listen to the Workers," *New York Times,* Oct. 18, 1987, p. 33.

Part II

Systems Triad

Chapter 4

The Artistry of Workmanship

> The artist has a special task and duty: the task of reminding men of their humanity, and the promise of their creativity.
>
> —Lewis Mumford

We live in a time when past concepts of human behavior capable of creating enduring excellence are dwindling away or have already disappeared from the environment in which work is performed. One such concept is the "instinct of workmanship"—the pride of doing something well.

Haydn Pearson in a *Treasury of Vermont Life,* tells of a personal involvement in workmanship:

> Years ago as a young lad I was helping an old man build a section of wall of a sidehill slope of a farmyard. For almost two centuries Old Ben's family had been famous dry-wall builders. Old Ben was the last of the line. We had dug the trench wide and deep, three feet or more, so that the big foundation stones would be below the frostline. Slowly the wall rose. The old man was very particular about each rock and chinking piece. To an impatient lad the old craftsman was unconsciously slow. The idea of chinking rocks below the soil surface was particularly irksome. "Who's going to know if these are chinked or not?" was a boy's question. The old man's astonishment was genuine as he peered over his spectacles. "Why," he said, "I will—and so will you."[1]

A real craftsman, like Old Ben, has always demanded a lot of himself—and of others—and has always viewed every job as having the quality of a calling. In fact, the shorter Oxford English Dictionary defines the word "craft" as "a calling requiring special skill and knowledge."

In retrospect, we can identify the passing of craft through three historical stages, beginning with a time when everything was craft and then proceeding to a stage when there evolved during the Renaissance and beyond an intellectual separation between the concept of craft and that of fine art. The third stage arrived much later, during the Industrial Revolution, when there occurred the division between the products of craft and the products of machine.

While craftsmanship remains with us today, although in diminishing dimensions, it is the central characteristic of the true craftsman (such as that illustrated in the narrated account of Old Ben's quality-mindedness of his product and the display of pride in himself) that has almost vanished as the essence of human activity and behavior at work. Yet, in spite of the fact that within recent times we have lost much of the instinct of workmanship to the methods and machines of technology, today's workers can still take pride in themselves. After all, through their own human efforts, they are their own product. Quite simply, it is work itself that not only makes them who they are, but also takes them beyond self by connecting them to the human community.

While we may be justified in passing unfavorable judgment about the absence of workmanship in today's world of work, we must, at the same time, be optimistic in the knowledge that an American tradition—craftsmanship—still shows some glimmering signs of life. It may not abound, and the human heart from which good work proceeds may not be beating strongly; however, there appears to be some scattered signs of support for its survival. Take, for example, the following full-page testimony of United Technologies Corporation to the value of the pride of doing a job well.

I TAKE PRIDE
IN MY WORK

I'm a little fed up with
the constant criticism
of American workmanship.
How other people do their
jobs is their business.
But I do good work and I
know it. I have perfected
my skills. I make each
minute count. When I make
a mistake I correct it. I
would gladly sign my name to
every piece of work I do.
I'm going to hang this
message over my work area
to let my employer, my
customers, my co-workers

know that I take pride in
my work.*

How many people in our contemporary work force would eagerly and voluntarily "hang this message" over their work area? Perhaps not sufficient numbers, it is feared, if we attach any continued significance to the findings of a Public Agenda study conducted in 1983 that clearly surfaced the deterioration of American workers' behavior.

> Fewer than one out of four (22%) say they are performing to their full capacities. Nearly half of the workforce (44%) say they do not put a great deal of effort into their jobs over and above what is required. A majority feel that, under the right conditions, they could significantly increase their performance. Moreover, there are indications that effectiveness is actually *decreasing*. Several surveys reveal, for example, a widespread impression that people aren't working as hard as they used to.[2]

As we approach the threshold of the nineties, we are made conscious of the prevalence of slipshod performance all about us. In Part I we focused briefly on the lessening quality of work performance within the service industry. Airlines, for example, remind us of their commitment to "Doing what we do best"; yet frequent flyers know very well that the best they do is not good enough. Add to the airlines the services of hotels, restaurants, retailing stores, banks—and hospitals—and we continue to witness second-best standards and shoddy workmanship running rampart as increasing numbers of customers find their experiences with less than the best ranging from the troublesome to downright appalling. Apparently evident in all of this is the weakening of the American work ethic.

While the sociologists may have been disturbed over the years by the fact that "the Protestant ethic of work" has lost its grip and "the gospel of hard work" has lessened its power on the behavior of man, it must be recognized that our hope for a revival of quality in human effort at work is not to be found in the rebirth of the hallmarks of work standards pronounced by Luther, Calvin, and other reformers of the sixteenth century who raised the work ethic to the pinnacle it seemed to hold for the next 450 years. Nor is it considered constructive to draw comparisons between today's workers and their counterparts in times past. Rather, the immutable principle that needs to be acknowledged and served is the single idea that work for most people has

---

*Source: A message as published in the *Wall Street Journal* by United Technologies Corporation, Hartford, Connecticut 06101. © 1988 United Technologies Corporation.

always remained, both in yesteryear and in the present, an important part of their lives. Allied to this principle is Albert Camus' warning: "Without work all life goes rotten. But when work is soulless, life stifles and dies."[3]

As we deliberate upon the centrality of work in human life, it is troublesome to realize that workers in all fields of human effort are suffering a loss of purpose; not thinking greatly of their function; deeply distrusting their motives; and feeling the absence of the value, merits, and satisfaction of work itself.

"Work seems synonymous with promise," states Robert Howard in *Brave New Workplace*.

> It is the means by which we nourish a sense of mastery and achievement in the world. It is the major activity through which we shape our ambitions and our talents and, thus, come to know ourselves. Work also takes us beyond the self. It is our link to society, our chief (and, for many, only) collective activity. Through our work, we dedicate ourselves to an end—a product or service, a professional or occupational group, a human community. In its inherently double nature—simultaneously personal and social—work quite simply makes us who we are. [4]

Howard's concluding note is that "if the idea of work contains a promise, then the obligations of working life, for many, signify a promise rarely kept."[4]

THE PURSUIT OF MEANING

It is human to hunger for fullness of being, and to find dignity, identity, and emotional rewards in what one does. This pursuit of meaning is common to both working and living, for "What is the difference between living and working?" asks Mary Caroline Richards, poet, teacher, and seeker. "If working is not living, what is it?" "If living is not work, I miss my guess," she adds.[5]

Can we integrate into our form of living and working a new spirit and sense of quality that can move us into areas where people at work are deprived, and would, in turn, help build a defense against the assault on high standards; against shoddy workmanship; and against meaningless, prideless workdays? Can we establish the identity of the source of new beginnings for the collective hearts and minds of today's work force? Can we better serve the inner needs of the three out of four workers (according to the Public Agenda study findings) who believe that they could be helpful in improving the quality of their work?

Indeed we can, through *the act of advancing the art of living by instilling a life of art into the total human experience at work*. It is believed that the idea of an artful work ethic holds the promise not only of reawakening the calling of a craft but also of creating a resurgence in bringing pride and dignity back into the workplace by allowing people at work to be fully human.

THE ARTISTRY OF WORK

Of all man's inventions, art has perhaps proved the most enduring. Yet art is fragile in nature and requires continuing attention and nurturing for it to make a difference in putting quality and goodness into work.

E. F. Schumacher, in his book *Good Work*, quotes Ananda Coomaraswamy as saying: "Industry without art is brutality." "Why?" Schumacher asks. "Because it damages the soul and spirit of the worker."[6] Surely, without the unification of art with the science and technology of work, we fall short of attaining a comprehensive approach to human experience in the modern workplace. Art and science are distinct in their nature, each with a long and discrete history, yet they are mutually supportive and sustaining in the pursuit of quality and effectiveness of work. At present there is a clear imbalance between the two in that the scientific and technical dimensions of work activity—namely, the scientific knowledge and skills of the individual gained through experience or study, along with applications of technological advancements to improving functional processes—are at center stage, with art proving to be a lesser contributor. The time has come for bringing art to a higher plane of attachment.

To arrive at insights into the significance of the contributions the concept of artistry can make to both living and working, as well as the manner in which the concept itself can be carried into effect, let us, for the remainder of this chapter, consider these three dimensions: (1) how those who create works of art relate to their craft; (2) the motivations, drives, and desires of the artist; and (3) the kinds of responses that are inclined to nourish those who will perform their work as if it were an art.

Relating to Art

First, let us gain an understanding of how artists relate to their art by citing a selected few of their expressions of personal thought and perception.

> I think if I weren't an artist, I would be dead. To me, being an artist is life.[7]
>
> —Carole Jeane Fenerman

> There's no doubt in my mind that I will always make art. I do it the way I live my life, so I can't imagine being and feeling alive and

not doing it. And when I say alive, I don't mean that if I am dead I can't do it. I'm talking about having the feeling of life in me. I feel that the art is coming from somewhere inside me where life is. As long as I feel alive, I will do art.[8]

—Michael Steiner

Art is the medium between me and the world. It fits me into the world.[9]

—Julian Schnabel

Art is a state of caring—there is no place for indifference. . . .[10]

—Vicci Sperry

Art is truly an expression of one's own individuality and is created without dependence on another. The depth of art is a universal language that speaks to the universal quality in man. . . .[11]

—Vicci Sperry

The more we know about the true nature of art, the more we know about our own abilities and feelings.[12]

—Vicci Sperry

Art by its nature expresses the deepest and best in man.[13]

—Jacques Barzun

Art is the result of the creative urge of life consciousness. It is the graphics of ideas. . . .[14]

—Ernst Fischer

Art . . . creates a moment of humanity, promising constant development. . . .[15]

—Ernst Fischer

. . . unless it wants to break faith with its social function, art must show the world as changeable. And help to change it. . . .[16]

—Ernst Fischer

It is not the function of art to break down open doors but rather to open locked ones. . . .[17]

—Ernst Fischer

All true art has always invoked a humanity that did not yet exist. . . .[18]

—Ernst Fischer

. . . .the permanent function of art is to re-create *as every* individual's experience the fullness of all that he is not, the fullness
of humanity at large. . . .[19]

—Ernst Fischer

Art is the indispensable means for . . . merging of the individual
with the whole.[20]

—Ernst Fischer

These quotations enhance our grasp of the inner significance of penetrating
the modern workplace with the spirit and manifestation of art as a means
of capturing "the deepest and best in man," thus advancing the pursuit of
aesthetic excellence (quality) for its own sake.

The notion of making art an essential organizational element of the highest
order is believed to be a rational thought, for two reasons:

1. Art in the organizational community has a refining influence, offering a multiplicity of advantages for the enterprise as a result of
   human expression and action that mirror the spirit of life; the constructive force of caring; the promise of constant growth and newness;
   and a real understanding of the relative importance of things, order,
   and balance.

2. Art is the province of *every human being*. To some degree, every individual is an artist. This was a central belief of a great teacher and
   American artist, Robert Henri, who expressed it so eloquently in his
   book *The Art Spirit*.

   I have no sympathy with the belief that art is the restricted province
   of those who paint, sculpt, make music, and verse. I hope we will
   come to an understanding that the material used is only incidental,
   that there is artist in every man; and that to him the possibility of
   development and of expression and the happiness of creation is as
   much a right and as much a duty to himself, as to any of those who
   work in the especially ticketed ways.
       When the artist is alive in any person, whatever his kind of work
   may be, he becomes an inventive, searching, daring, self-expressing
   creature. He becomes interesting to other people. He disturbs, upsets,
   enlightens, and he opens ways for a better understanding. Where
   those who are not artists are trying to close the book, he opens it,
   shows there are still more pages possible.[21]

Motivations of the Artist

If the idea that "there is artist in every man" is an acceptable notion (and indeed it needs to be), then it follows that to think or reason by analogy, too, is a reasonable act. Thus, if we were to reveal the particular motivations, drives, and desires of those who are engaged in the art professions, we may then, as a logical consequence, grasp an understanding of the parallel characterizations of the "artists" employed in the human activities of today's workplace.

A review of the literature on art and artists brings to view these dominant attributes among artists.

- Artists keep their principal attention fixed upon the highest excellencies. They form themselves upon great principles and great models.
- They excel in their art because they not only possess a love for it, but also an enthusiastic ambition to excel in it.
- It is the *attitude* of artists that is the one great essential.
- Artists enjoy the challenge of undertaking matters above their strength which holds the advantage of discovering their own deficiencies, and this discovery alone is viewed as a very considerable acquisition.
- Artists desire to express the deepest freedom and to experience the expression of individuality.
- The great business of artists is to form a mind adapted and adequate to all times and all occasions.
- Artists avoid the narrowness and poverty of conception. Their works transcend traditional boundaries.
- Emotion for artists is not everything; they must also know their trade and enjoy it.
- Artists seek new forms—go new ways—let their imagination take its course, until the solution fulfills their expectations.
- Artists are deeply involved in the understanding of their fellow man.
- In the works of artists there is a continuing process from idea to technical expression and back to idea.
- The performance of artists is not a solo virtuosity, but an expansive, embracing unfoldment.
- Artists communicate through the product of their work so as to raise the thoughts, and extend the views of others, as well as to bestow a refinement of taste.
- Artists are ever conscious of the need to get acquainted with themselves just as much as they can. And they know it is no easy

job, for it is not a present-day habit of humanity. This is what the artists call self-development, self-education.[22]

The Act of Responding

The expression of the foregoing characteristics is intended to expand our experience and knowledge of artists and to explore more deeply the sense of being an artist. As these distinctive features emerge, we become more conscious of the nature of responsive actions necessary in our organizational environments to make the "artist" come alive in people at work so that there will be greater meaning in what they do and high levels of quality in how they perform.

Let us examine these responses as we state them in the form of a set of principles.

- There is an essentiality in helping each individual toward a "fullness" that he or she senses and demands; toward a fullness of all that he or she is not; toward a fullness of life; toward a more comprehensive world—a world that makes sense.

- There is the persevering imperative to abhor and prevent dehumanization and depersonalization so that people in a world in which *things* have greater value do not become objects among objects.

- What is required in all organization life is a philosophy that gives insight into human nature and relates to the manners and affections.

- To do a thing in style is to set for oneself standards of behavior in the belief that the manner of doing anything has a certain aesthetic and qualitative importance of its own, independent of the importance of what is done.

- Consciousness is not a vacuum; therefore fill it with that which is positive rather than that which robs one of inspiration.

- Talents want to be expressed; therefore sustain and support the idea that individuals are bigger than anything they do, and continue in the efforts to expand and extend work fitting to the human potentials.

- Touch people with grace, not as a stranger to gaiety, for the joy they bring to work releases their capacities.

- Bridge the contradiction that individuals face, that of being a limited "I" and at the same time part of the world.

- Excellence in work proceeds from the whole man: heart, head, and hand, in proper balance.

- Trust must be freely at work in the mind when anything excels in its accomplishment. One gains insight into good work by open trust rather than by attempts at intellectual understanding.

- It is the human right of individuals not to allow others to tell them what they feel.
- Controlled freedom in workmanship—being free from impediments—will contribute more to the quality of the environment by way of diversification than will any other means.
- Different experiences need to happen in the workplace not as a privilege but as the normal gifts of free and active human beings.
- Every activity is accomplished through form; form is striving toward a goal which is the original source of excellence. What is required, then, is forwarding the idea of direction in which people act for the sake of an ultimate purpose.
- Human beings need belief, free play of imagination, and intuition in their workplace or they become starved. They can only take pleasure in their work if they are allowed to invent, to exercise thought: that is to say, to design as well as to make.
- Without an outlet of expression, the products of work are heartless.
- There is always present the requirement to advance unity—to turn away from the fragmentation of people and their narrowing field of vision.
- Work must not be considered in isolation but in the context of the history of work as a whole, as a moment in historical development. It is a legitimate and desirable idea to carry on from a point already attained.
- In the absence of appropriate recognition, even the greatest artists cannot do sufficient work.
- Change or variety is as much a necessity to the human heart and brain in work as in other aspects of life. Thus, it would appear not only reasonable but beneficial as well to import into the unnatural work environment that we have made some of the quality of unmonotonous unexpectedness that the human race was born to live with.
- There is the imperative to prevent the concentration of power, which can be so great that many people are inclined to think that their personal decision does not matter and, therefore, they surrender to "fate."
- Work advances in value if the excitement of the future runs through it.
- It is necessary for people to honor and nourish their own gifts. To help them begin consciously to build their own new maps of reality, it is the obligation of the organization to inform them, to get them to inform themselves, and to contribute to the development of their innate abilities and talents.
- Artisans of the future need to be concerned with the problems, aims, desires, and requirements of people around them. They need to grasp an awakened respect for what they contribute to a larger purpose, since the extent to which they contribute to society determines their values.[23]

Obviously, these principles of thought offer little simplicity of action for the reader, yet they are abounding in value for those who hold true commitment to the cause of gaining greater quality in the work performed by their organizational membership. For those lacking in resolution, the principles may seem too distant and thus have the appearance of not being useful because of their philosophical nature. Unquestionably, by themselves, they can be all too disappointing to those who look for a quick and easy answer to the question: "What can I do?" In E. F. Schumacher's book *Good Work*, this precise problem is found in this paragraph:

> Frequently people at his lectures seemed disappointed with Schumacher's answer to their "What can I do?" They appear to want something quicker and easier and more painless. . . . What I fear they have not yet realized is the degree to which good work is an inner program. There is no outer prescription, course, or exercise that will bring a person to good work. We find it from the inside out.[24]

Most ideas of workmanship now current in the West have been influenced by the doctrines of the Arts and Crafts movement. The ideas that launched the movement seem to have been John Ruskin's. They were written down by 1850, and appeared in the second volume of his *Stones of Venice*. In his words, he eloquently condemns the evils that resulted from the industrial practices of his day. He says that "in our manufacturing cities we manufacture everything except men"; that "to brighten, to strengthen, to refine, or to form a single living spirit, never enters into our estimate of advantages."[25]

The degradation of the worker was Ruskin's concern, as it should be ours today in our contemporary work environment. This "evil" of human debasement can be met only by a right understanding of what kind of labor is good for people. It is the very intent of the previously cited principles to penetrate the inner dimensions of good work and thus provide a philosophical framework in which these principles can be converted into strategies of greatest leverage that will yield the most worthy results in terms of furthering the quality of human accomplishment at work, strategies that will enter into and permeate the organizational system, effecting a whole series of events in all areas of the enterprise ranging from the declaration of new corporate beliefs to novel modes of action at the operating level.

The Artistry of Management

Whatever the organizational initiatives might be, naturally, they begin with management, which has the responsibility of leadership, guidance, and protection of artisans in the divisions and departments of the institution. As leaders, managers help their people to feel their own strengths. As teachers, they help to bring forth the natural endowments of their workers through inspirational approaches that deepen understanding and stimulate interest in the quality of work. To do such things, and to do them well, members of management, too, need to be artists of the highest distinction. Said another way, they need to be highly skilled in the art of managing people.

Without artistry in management, we are left with its science, which by itself is inadequate to the task of creating a quality environment. With the absence of the art experience in leadership ranks comes the risk of "closing the book" on new and good ideas for improving quality. But when we allow the arts to enter the senses and intellect of management, we open up the organization to innovative experiences that go beyond what was thought possible in the total arena of quality.

Since the attainment of higher levels of quality is a human achievement, its nurturing depends greatly on the emphasis given to the continuing development of artistry in management designed to recreate for each of its members, as an individual experience, the fullness of all that he or she is not, the fullness of humanity at large. More specifically, the development of artistry in management should be designed to promote such qualities as these:

- *Comprehensive view*. The artistic manager keeps the whole picture in mind; maintains sight of the whole, and helps establish unity. As the manager keeps sensing the totality, nothing is isolated; all is integrated. A oneness is seen within which everything is related; as the whole is surveyed, the manager helps others to such a comprehensive view.

- *Human sensitivity and understanding*. The artistic manager is an individual of maximum sensitivity to humanization, which requires compassion, cooperation, and altruism. He or she is one who possesses human character, human feelings, and great love for people, and who has an interest in the search for and analysis of values and exercises his or her skills as a cultural mediator.

- *Creative consciousness*. Artistic managers imagine intensely and comprehensively, are visionaries of the possible, have a sense of wonder and humor, and explore open-mindedly. Their desire for inquiry and exploration causes them to break through the limited reality around them.

- *Intellectual dignity*. The artistic manager displays good balance between intellectual ability and intuitive insight. Surely, a thinker from the heart and spirit, bringing harmony between emotion and idea. The product of his or her thinking is not petty demands and notions but rather ideas of substance.

- *Capacity for renewal.* The attention of artistic managers is fixed on the higher excellence of performance. With a willingness to renew themselves, they are always in the process of self-development and self-education in pursuit of knowledge of themselves and the world around them. In competition with themselves, artistic managers never stand pat. They build on experiences to gain individual growth.[26]

The Evidence of Individuality

"The gap between art and commerce is far less than you might imagine," was the theme of the General Electric Company's advertisement appearing in the *Wall Street Journal*.[27] The role of art in the business of service has also been made obvious by the printed advertisements of other companies as well, such as First Los Angeles Bank and Singapore Airlines. However, as art has entered the mainstream of American life, it has not edged its way deeply enough into the world of work. In its widest possible definition, it has not been generally acknowledged as providing a practical, as well as an aesthetic, function of human effort within an organizational context.

The proposition advanced in this chapter is that art appears in many forms. In viewing and accepting art in its broadest sense, there is embraced the arts of engagement in new concerns and perspectives; the arts' contagion of discovery; and the arts of the human condition that give attention to the needs, aspirations, talents, and creativity of people at work. All of these arts are relevant to the furthering of the quality of product or service and of the world in which work is performed.

The thought also is put forward that to some degree every human being is an artist, possessing the capacity to wield a refining influence on the qualitative manner in which work is done. But to exert such effectiveness, the great cry of Walt Whitman needs to be heeded—that is, for man to find himself, to understand the fine thing he really is. As Robert Henri states it: ". . . in everyone there is the great mystery; every single person in the world has evidence to give of his [or her] own individuality, providing he [or she] has acquired the full power to make clear this evidence."[28]

The challenge is to enlarge individuality, and to move continuously toward expanding corporate strategies fitting to the particular organization and designed to provide opportunities for individual fulfillment. Only through helping people at work to find the best in themselves as "artists" will the world of work experience those unique benefits that art can provide.

NOTES

1. Haydn Pearson. *Treasury of Vermont Life*, (Countryman Press, date unknown).

2. D. Yankelovich and J Immerwahr, "Let's Put the Work Ethic to Work," *Industry Week*, Sept. 5, 1983, p. 33.

3. E. F. Schumacher, *Good Work* (New York: Harper & Row, 1979), pp. 120–1.

4. Robert Howard, *Brave New Workplace* (New York: Viking Penquin, Inc, 1985), p. 1.

5. M. C. Richards, *The Crossing Point* (Middletown, Conn.: Wesleyan University Press, 1974), p. 125.

6. Schumacher, *Good Work*.

7. Harvey Stein, *Artists Observed* (New York: Harry N. Abrams, Inc., 1986), p. 77.

8. Stein, *Artists Observed*, p. 104.

9. Stein, *Artists Observed*, p. 132.

10. Vicci Sperry, *The Art Experience* (Los Angeles: Hennessy & Ingalls, Inc., 1969), p. 17.

11. Ibid.

12. Ibid.

13. Jacques Barzun, *The Use and Abuse of Art* (Princeton, N.J.: Princeton University Press, 1974), p. 84.

14. Ernst Fischer, *The Necessity of Art* (New York: Penquin Books, 1963) chap. 5, p. 150.

15. Ibid.

16. Ibid, p. 12.

17. Ibid, p. 15.

18. Ibid, p. 210.

19. Ibid, p. 219.

20. Ibid, p. 223.

21. Robert Henri. *The Art Spirit* (New York: Harper & Row, 1984), p. 15.

22. Barzun, *The Use and Abuse of Art*; Benthall, *Science and Technology in Art Today* (New York: Praeger Publishers, Inc., 1972); Clark, *What Is a Masterpiece?* (New York: Thames and Hudson, Inc., 1979); Dewey, *Art as Experience* (New York: G.P. Putnam, 1979); Fischer, *The Necessity of Art* (New York: Penquin Books, 1963); Henri, *The Art Spirit* (New York: Harper & Row, 1984); Kumar, *The Schumacher Lectures* (New York: Harper & Row, 1981); Lucie-Smith, *The Story of Craft* (New York: Van Nostrand Reinhold Co., 1984); Pye, *The Nature and Art of Workmanship* (New York, Cambridge University Press, 1968); Reynolds, *Discourses on Art* (New York: Collier Books, 1961); Richards, *The Crossing Point* (Middletown, Conn.: Weslyan University Press, 1973); Sloan, *Gist of Art* (New York: Dover Publications, 1977); Sperry, *The Art Experience* (Los Angeles: Hennessy & Ingalls, 1969); Yanagi, *The Unknown Craftsman* (New York: Kodansha International Ltd., 1972).

23. See n. 22 above.

24. Schumacher, *Good Work,* p. 215.

25. David Pye, *The Nature and Art of Workmanship* (New York: Cambridge University Press, 1968), p. 65.

26. Addison C. Bennett and Samuel J. Tibbitts, *Making Innovation Practical* (Chicago: Pluribus Press, Inc. 1986), pp. 186–7.

27. *Wall Street Journal*, Feb. 26, 1985, p. 8.

28. Henri, *The Art Spirit*, p. 135.

Chapter 5

The Quality Environment

Pleasure in the job puts perfection in the work.
—Aristotle

Quality of product or service demands quality people: people who not only have mastered their craft through the application of knowledge and skill and who have the intelligence, personality traits, and other individual characteristics fitting to their job assignments; but, more important, who possess the will to work. It is this central ownership of sustained interest and positive attitude, when added to the knowledge, skill, and potential of the individual, that provides the quantum jump to attaining the quality standards we are seeking.

"New attitudes change the very experience of daily work," states Marilyn Ferguson in her book *The Aquarian Conspiracy*. In her words,

> Work becomes a ritual, a game, a discipline, an adventure, learning, even an *art*, as our perceptions change. The stress of tedium and the stress of the unknown, the two causes of work-related suffering, are transformed. A more fluent *quality* of attention allows us to move through tasks that once seemed repetitive and distasteful. We make fewer judgments about what we're doing ("I hate this," "I like this"). Boredom diminishes, just as pain abates when we drop our futile resistance to it."[1]

The will to work rests on acquiring new attitudes toward the idea and motives of work. Surely, for the "artist" at work, attitude toward his or her subject is the one great essential. It is on this attitude that the "quality of attention" to the task at hand, its significance, and distinction of technique, depend. It is on this attitude, too, that the artist's feelings of *self* evolve.

In more recent times, the waning of positive attitudes and good feelings about life at work has grown elaborately articulate, almost approaching acute proportions. For years, sociologists have observed an undercurrent of worker discontent in this country. In 1973, a special presidential task force on work in America concluded that significant numbers of Americans were dissatisfied with their working lives. In 1974, Studs Terkel's published text *Working* arrived at the same conclusion through hundreds of interviews with individuals in all arenas of work. Later, Opinion Research Corporation's special report *Managing Human Resources, 1983 and Beyond* once again reinforced the occurrence of a quiet frustration in the collective hearts of America's work force. What emerged from the Opinion Research Corporation study was the finding that, while people generally continued to like their own work, they have become increasingly dissatisfied with the organizational environment in which they are working. As the report states

> Employees are becoming increasingly disenchanted with their companies, and their level of identification will continue to drop unless something is done to arrest the overall decline. It should be noted that managers' attitudes are dropping along with the attitudes of those who report to them. If managers are becoming less loyal to the organization, then the employees who report to these managers cannot be expected to maintain favorable attitudes.[2]

As Robert Henri notes, "There is something in environment which affects all men, causes them to live for a time in a surprising fullness, or, on the other hand, causes them to close up."[3] While we must believe that there are many millions of workers who do in fact like the work they do and are proud of their skills, we must, at the same time, respond with vigor to the imperative of doing something "to arrest the overall decline" of human satisfaction with the environment in which work is performed.

The organizational system is the atelier of "artists" at work. It provides an environmental form that saturates the artisans' awareness of their surroundings as either a creative or restraining force, since it is the steady development of their feelings toward the corporate world around them that gives reality to humanized conceptions of things, places, acts, and facts within the framework of the workplace environment. It is in this environment that "Our thoughts are nourished, our feelings conditioned, and our actions guided by our interpretations of the signals inherent in our surroundings."[4] In actuality, the power of what happens on the job is indeterminable. Potentially, it holds the capability to assault our standards and to abuse and erode the functional system with shoddy work. On the other hand, it can be an open-ended source of prideful attitudes which in turn can bring into being a positive change in individual consciousness and behavior essential to advancing the quality of work itself as well as the quality of the human condition at work.

THE QUALITY OF WORK LIFE

In the mid-sixties, Douglas M. McGregor, in his writing, "New Concepts of Management," voiced the conviction that

> We will witness during the next couple of decades some profound, far- reaching changes in the strategy utilized to manage the human resources of enterprise. The changes will not be superficial modifications in current practice, but basic revisions of certain concepts that have dominated management thinking during the past half century or more.[5]

In the latter part of the sixties, McGregor's astute prediction began to take form as "growing concerns about the effects of employment on the health and well-being of employees and about job satisfaction"[6] surfaced throughout the U.S. world of work. Researchers, along with union and government leaders, became interested in the issue of influencing the quality of work experiences of American jobholders. During the same period, between 1969 and 1973, a series of national attitude surveys were conducted that drew additional attention to what was called "the quality of employment," or the total impact and influences of work-related experiences on the individual.

In 1973, The American Center for Quality of Work Life was founded by Ted Mills, president of TMA, Inc., who viewed quality of work life (QWL) as "an original propelling force in creating the larger contours of the 'future work' phenomenon of the 1980s." Mills recollects that

> Neither he nor the thousands of his coworkers . . . were aware that what they called "QWL" in their earliest 1970 experiments was but a first, formal expression of something considerably larger happening in American society—a quiet, unpublicized transformation of what an increasing majority of Americans wanted out of life, at work as well as at home, and finding ways and means to provide it.[7]

Sociologist Daniel Yankelovich called this transformation a major "value shift" in American society. In the seventies, his studies, like all national surveys, showed an increase in preoccupation with self. By the late seventies, his firm's studies showed "more than seven out of ten Americans (72 percent) spending a great deal of time thinking about themselves and their inner lives—this in a nation once notorious for its impatience with inwardness."[8] Yankelovich's surveys showed that new questions had arisen, questions such as Will I be able to make a good living? Will I be successful? had been replaced by queries such as How can I find self-fulfillment? What does personal success really mean? How can I grow? These more introspective questions mirrored a whole new set of values and expectations that began to enter the American workplace in the seventies.

While many different definitions of the term "quality of work life" have evolved over the past decade, in essence, what it comes down to is what happens *on* the job. Perceiving it more properly in the context of "the quality of life at work," Stanley Peterfreund, president of Stanley Peterfreund Associates, considers it to be "a state of factors on the job," including:

- *Work Itself*, work processing factors
- *Work Environment* (including both the physical surroundings and the managerial style and climate), and
- *Personal* (and personnel) factors."[9]

As Peterfreund views it, the quality of life at work is high when people at work feel that

With regard to *work-related factors*:

- Duties are challenging, interesting, and varied.
- They are expected to meet high (but reasonable) standards of quantity and quality in an achievement-oriented, get-it-done-right atmosphere.
- Work practices, procedures, and methods are sensible and effective.
- Change takes place with a minimum of dislocation and a maximum of personal involvement, and contributes to a sense of improvement.
- Operational information and assistance are available when needed.
- Employees control the technology (rather than being controlled by it).
- They have adequate support resources needed to get the job done.
- There is opportunity to use judgment and job wisdom (as well as skill).
- The job and its outcome are well-defined enough to permit individual responsibility to be clearly assigned.
- Training and preparation are adequate for and relevant to assignments.

With regard to *environmental factors*:

- Their organization is committed to high-quality service or product and succeeds in achieving that objective.
- Open, two-way communication characterizes the climate.
- There is a sense of shared objectives, that one's performance contributes to the organization's success; there is identity with the team.

- They have influence (an adequate amount of say) in decisions that affect how the work is done.
- They are provided with physical comfort appropriate to the task.
- There are opportunities for socialization.
- They work with managers who respect them, encourage them, and reinforce them positively as well as provide constructive criticism.
- They have leadership they can respect; leaders who have a sense of direction, who have a knowledge of what is going on in the workplace, who care about people, who run an organization of worth.

With regard to *personal factors*:

- They are able to utilize their skills and talents in their job assignments.
- They are recognized and rewarded for accomplishment, not just compensated for being there.
- Rules are enforced equitably and fairly.
- They have opportunity to develop talents and to grow personally.
- They are well-informed about job opportunities and benefits.
- All have equal opportunity for financial rewards, work assignments, time off, and promotions.
- Their performance is appraised regularly, and feedback is complete and honest.
- The job provides opportunity to enjoy the work, have fun, feel a sense of satisfaction.

As we peruse these factors, we recognize certain underlying themes running through the listing that communicate these kinds of expectations of people at work today:

- rewards tied to performance
- a job that allows individual judgment
- increasing participation in decision making
- an environment that fosters growth and self-development
- interesting and meaningful work
- being informed about all matters relating to life at work
- work that is challenging
- a job that requires the use of one's mind and one's creativity
- an adequate share of responsibility
- recognition as an individual

Obviously, the above listing of work-, environment-, and personal-related factors are stated in quite general terms, yet they provide direction of thought in the planning and structuring of QWL processes and programs within the contemporary workplace. What needs to be done, of course, is to translate these factors into specific QWL designs fitting to the needs, conditions, and resources of the individual organization, while systematically retaining their original sense.

Since the beginnings of the QWL movement in this country, we have witnessed translations of diverse kinds. For example, the enrichment of work and increasing participation of workers in decision making became a central thrust of union-management collaboration in such industrial giants as General Motors, Ford, and AT&T.

QWL principles were adopted in 1983 by American Airlines and subsequently converted into practice in the form of QWL committees, whose employee members were provided the opportunity to discuss problems and express their concerns about working conditions and job satisfaction.

The ongoing efforts of Procter & Gamble evidence the conversion of QWL precepts to experimental projects emphasizing teamwork and the pushing down of increasing authority to all employee levels.

To sustain interest and support of its QWL process, the Sherwin-Williams plant in Richmond, Kentucky, developed and introduced a productivity-gain sharing program designed to encourage and reward employee suggestions for more efficient performance.

Hundreds of U.S. firms are currently using quality circles, which, in the viewpoint of their managements, capture the essence of the QWL idea. The use of quality circles in recent years has become highly popularized as an effective approach to institutionalizing employee involvement in problem solving.

The reality in all of these happenings is that, irrespective of the QWL-related programs or projects utilized—whether decision-making participation, QWL committee structures, teamwork promotion, gain sharing, or quality circles— these singular approaches are not ends in themselves, but means to achieving a higher purpose. Quality circles, perhaps, offer the most vivid example of this principle. All too many circles today are not racking up success stories for their sponsoring organizations, simply because initially they were created and positioned within corporate environments that had not been put in readiness for their effective integration and management; when activated, they were not organizationally linked with the attainment of a greater end.

THOUGHT BEFORE ACTION

A commitment to improving the QWL can bring with it significant benefits. However, certain fundamental principles of thought need to be considered and subscribed to before determining organizational patterns of

QWL action. Among the more important of these guiding policies are these:

- Fully understand that the chief executive officer (CEO) and members of the top management team are the focal point of leverage and influence in gaining QWL success throughout the enterprise. What is central, of course, is the way the CEO actually behaves that

    is crucial for the survival of organizational renewal and change activities. It is his [or her] behavior (and subsequently that of other officers) that ultimately does or does not confirm the idea that organizational development is necessary, credible, and inexorably linked to his [or her] leadership style.[10]

    This thought does not at all limit the key issue of managerial credibility to the top of the organization. Management in its entirety needs to have had a good track record of worthiness of belief in its discussions, deliberations, and decision making in employee-relations matters.

- Comprehend completely that success depends on commitment to fundamental changes in the environment of the organization, the style of management, and the redesign of work. It is a long-term commitment requiring the exercise of a *process* mentality if these transformations utimately are to be fulfilled.

    QWL needs to be perceived as an objective, not as a program or a technique. The focus of its purpose, as seen by Nadler and Lawler, "is not only on how people can do work better, but on how work may cause people to be better."[11] Such a worthy aim demands the employment of systemic actions that will go beyond the mere appearance of cosmetic value and bring into being essential improvements in the quality of the human experience at work.

- Acknowledge the requisite that the QWL process includes within its bounds the total organization. Drawing on several sources of experience and research, Nadler and Lawler offer this advice:

    . . . it is important that QWL activities not be limited to certain groups in the organization. When only certain levels in the organization or certain groups of employees are involved, projects often fail because a "we/they" relationship develops. When lower-level employees are involved but management isn't, middle management often resists and blocks changes that are initiated by these groups. When some work groups or workers are involved and others at the same organization level are not, counterproductive intergroup rivalry often appears, and it becomes difficult to transfer the new structures and learnings to the rest of the organization. Even though it may be difficult to start everywhere in an organization at once, it is possible and important to put structures in place at startup that will quickly allow everyone to be involved, that will communicate what is occurring, and that will show a commitment to implementing the new practices organizationwide.[12]

As the organizationwide plan and process are followed, it also is important that QWL objectives first be sought at the managerial positions before moving on to improvement efforts at employee work levels.

- Recognize that the shape of work will need to change if it is to better fit the human needs of people at work, resulting in the enhancement of human qualities of life on the job. Alterations in the status quo of the manner in which work is performed will call for strategies for initiating significant organizational changes fashioned to bring into existence fundamental differences in organizational structure and arrangements, in basic relationships between the individual and what he or she does on the job, and in the way in which the growth and learning of people working in the organization are nurtured. All of these conversions underscore the essentiality of *flexibility* as a key cultural value.

- Realize the indispensability of creating a problem-solving environment in which people will be encouraged and given the opportunity to solve new problems, in new settings, and in new relationships. Once again, emphasis is placed on the need for a systematic process that will enable such an environment to be created. Without question, a programmatic approach will not suffice.

- Pay particular attention to communication and cooperation. Faulty communication can hinder the QWL movement in two fundamental ways: it can impede the successful launching of the organizational effort, and subsequently it can cause a continuing lack of understanding of how the QWL concept works on the part of the employees.
  Believed to be a major cause of failure, as reported by Greenberg and Glaser,

  is the reluctance of both employees and management to tear down the barriers to cooperation. . . . All members of the organization must develop a mutual trust based on the concept that each individual is basically honest and wants to do a good job. . . . The biggest problem will always be, who will be the first to tear out a section of their own barrier.[13]

- Enhance the human resource function in response to a changing organizational and cultural environment. In most organizations, personnel or human resource departments were never conceived or organized to become involved in transforming work processes on an organization-wide basis. As Ted Mills puts it, "In most companies today, the emerging field [human resources] still hides behind old, comfortable, and usually wholly inappropriate corporate doors."[14]

If QWL is to have a promising future, human resource departments must be brought out of their traditional hideaway places and moved to positions of responsiveness to the challenges of a modern work force that places new demands on corporate managements; of establishing aggressive employee policies; of addressing the requirements of the organization and its management in placing the quality of human performance at work at a high level of corporate priority; of advancing the effectiveness of training and education by embracing the idea of QWL throughout all elements of the learning process; and of fulfilling the obligation to be creative in formulating guidelines for management and employee expectations, development, accountability, and rewards.

THE KEY ACT OF ASSESSING

Assessment—the act of evaluating the essential dimensions of current conditions and circumstances—is a process that managements must engage in on behalf of their organizations and their people if the culture and character of the enterprise is to be understood and if appropriate direction and approaches toward QWL improvements are to be discerned. It is through the conscientious act of assessing that managements gain a deliberate fix on the state of affairs of the organizational conditions required to accommodate the above-cited principles believed to be crucial to the success of a quality of work life endeavor.

A first step, then, is to examine and evaluate strengths and weaknesses in organizational areas such as mission, philosophy, values, policies, and goals; leadership, commitment, and behavior; structural arrangements, relationships, and flexibility; communication, coordination, and collaboration; management style, and decision making practices; personnel administration, human resource management, and performance management. Naturally aligned with this phase of assessment is the need for a continuing consciousness of the penetrating effects of the external environment on organizational effectiveness.

While the key act of assessing is never a perfect event, "The process of asking critical questions is a prerequisite to improving organizational effectiveness because it helps guard against unsystematic, self-perpetuating, conclusion-confirming evaluations."[15]

Focusing on Management

In addition to its forthright concerns about conditioning and preparing the total organizational environment for the introduction of the QWL concept, top management also needs to achieve early on "a degree of understanding and acceptance of the concept from supervisory personnel and higher managers," according to Peterfreund. "And it means, also, that they must develop a realistic grasp of the consequences and a willingness to adjust to them."[16] This thought returns us to the earlier principle that underscores the importance of implementing QWL objectives before moving on to any new "partnership" approach at the employee work levels. As Peterfreund states it

> Thus, operationally, we envision a period of management make-ready necessary before inviting the employees to join the party in any new capacity at the workplace level. With very few exceptions, it would be premature to leapfrog to the work floor and expect sustained change to occur there as the result of a new employee-management (or union-management) partnership, if the necessary preparatory work has not been done first.[17]

A principal component of the preparatory work that needs doing is believed to be the imperative of assessing the state of mind of managers as affected by a composite of factors related to work itself, the environment in which work is performed, and personal fulfillment on the job. The findings of such an assessment must then lead to "planning and implementing the actions necessary to build a wholesome QWL for the management force."[18]

The QWL assessment being proposed is viewed as possessing purposes, structure, and form different from those expected of the more traditional and typical applications of employee attitude surveys. The more significant variations are these:

- Whereas employee attitude surveys, in most instances, exercise a wide dispersion of inquiry, the thrust of the QWL assessment is directed toward a more clearly delineated purpose and outcome.

- Employee attitude surveys tend to be administered in response to the presence of an adverse organizational climate, causing employees who may view the survey negatively to exhibit a resistance to the survey itself. Contrarily, the QWL evaluation is believed to offer a more positive posture from the viewpoint of employees who are reflecting upon the underlying intent of management.

- While employee attitude surveys generally reach out for the views of the total employee populace concomitantly, the proposed QWL assessment process concentrates on a single organizational level at a time. In a descending, sequential order, the inquiry centers initial attention on top management, then subsequently middle management (department directors), followed by supervisory personnel, and finally the largest population of nonmanagement employees. Each of these hierarchical steps of scrutiny is orchestrated at its own separate time, thus offering the opportunity to modify the questions so that they are most fitting to each organizational segment of respondents. Alterations in the questionnaire instrument at each step also offers the advantage of reworking queries to form linkages in responses received from people at different organizational levels. Employee attitude surveys, as they are commonly designed, do not grant the choice of these optional directions.

- Another beneficial dimension of the descending approach is that, at each stage of the survey, immediate feedback and corrective action occurs, bringing with it a cumulative stream of positive change as the process of surveying proceeds downward through the organization.
- Rather than circumventing management at any level, the proposed QWL assessment positions *all* managers in a partnership role within the mainstream of the survey process.

Let us take a closer look at the participation of managers at various levels as they become respondents in their organization's investigative effort.

At the Top Level. At the top, meaningful results can be obtained through individual interviews—accompanied by the use of a well-designed questionnaire—aimed at gaining opinions and perspectives about what it is like to work for the organization at the top management level. What is sought after are not only the attitudes and feelings of each executive as they pertain to his or her own position of responsibility, but also the thoughts of each individual with respect to the workings of the top management group as a team.

It is believed to be essential to launch the assessment at the top if the QWL effort is to gain success. After all, it is here where we find the focal point of power and responsibility for renewing the organization, and it is here where we need to examine discrepancies between management theory and executive behavior. If indeed there are discrepancies in the CEO's behavior, for example, do "subordinates choose to play it safe, to act as if discrepancies do not exist"?[19] Is there truly a climate at the top that nurtures frankness, trusting, and a willingness to take risks, or are these qualities merely professed to be valued by the CEO, but not practiced? Obviously, there are many questions along these lines that need to be asked at the top if we are to capture a sense of perhaps some of the origins of human behavior further down in the organizational system.

At the Middle Level. At the middle of the organization, the QWL assessment gives us a chance to take a whole new look at many commonly held notions about how managers at the middle (department directors) think and act, and about the values they hold. A picture of what managers consider most important can clearly emerge from information provided by a questionnaire instrument such as that displayed as Exhibit 5-1. As this input information is analyzed and evaluated, questions subsequently asked of people at the supervisory levels can be so fashioned as to provide precise connections with queries responded to by their bosses.

In the opinion of Schlesinger and Oshry, no one seems to be addressing the QWL dilemma faced by middle managers. As they view it:

> In a business environment crying out for creative solutions to significant human resources problems, the consequences of inattention to the middle manager have become quite severe. We simply cannot afford to allow middle managers to believe that QWL is for workers at middle managers' expense. The continued existence of such a belief will certainly hinder our attempts to make U.S. organizations more humane and productive places in which to work.[20]

Only after the QWLs of top management, department directors, and supervisory personnel are evaluated and adequately addressed through appropriate corrective actions are nonmanagement employees invited to "join the party" as the QWL assessment process is extended downward to lower levels of the organization.

All of these evaluations are made in the interest of advancing the cause of quality as the orderly and sequential stages of the QWL assessment process move us closer to a clearer and more proper vision of people and work, of the barriers that need to be removed to promote further the *will to work,* and of the extent of humaneness in the fundamental relationship of our employees and their life at work.

> A person does live to work—in that it is through his or her work if we define that word broadly—that humankind finds the way of expressing individual uniqueness in a creative way. But to do that it must be his or her work, not someone else's. It must also, however, be work that is produced with and for others—people being designed, I think, to live in community. That is to say, an *individual* living and working *with individuals.*[21]

In harmony with the thought that people are designed to live and work in community, this chapter gives voice to the essentiality of directing vigorous attention to the QWL of people at work as an indispensable element of the totality of institutional quality, and of the need for continuing QWL assessment that effectively embraces the individual as well as the community of individuals. Without question, the level of quality attained in the world of work holds a direct relationship to the way people at work feel, act, and think. It is these states of being that, in large measure, represent the worth of the human capital of an organization.

Exhibit 5-1 QWL Assessment Designed for Department Managers

I. *Work-Related Factors*

	Definitely Disagree	Inclined To Disagree	Inclined To Agree	Definitely Agree
1. My management duties are challenging, interesting, varied				
2. I have a great deal of freedom in the way I manage my functional area(s) of responsibility				
3. I have a great deal to say over what changes are made in my functional area(s) of responsibility				
4. I feel I can honestly disagree with my administrative team representative				
5. Work practices, procedures, and methods are sensible, effective				
6. Operational information and assistance are available when needed				
7. There are adequate support resources needed to get the job done				
8. In addition to skill, there is adequate opportunity to use judgment and job wisdom				
9. Expectations and performance criteria related to my job and its outcomes are clearly communicated and understood				
10. Training and preparation are adequate for and relevant to my managerial assignments				
11. I should be allowed to make some decisions that are now made at the administrative team level				
12. There is a high understanding and agreement between myself and my administrative team representative on the goals each is to accomplish				

II. *Environmental Factors*

	Definitely Disagree	Inclined To Disagree	Inclined To Agree	Definitely Agree
13. MC provides an achievement-oriented, get-it-done-right atmosphere				
14. MC is committed to high-quality service or product, and succeeds in achieving that objective				
15. Open, two-way communication characterizes the climate at MC				
16. I feel that my performance contributes to MC's success				
17. I hold a strong identity with the medical center's management team				

Exhibit 5-1 continued

	Definitely Disagree	Inclined To Disagree	Inclined To Agree	Definitely Agree
18. I can influence the decisions that are ultimately arrived at by the Administrative Team				
19. I have respect for the administrative leadership of MC				
20. My boss encourages me, and reinforces me positively				
21. There are sufficient opportunities for socialization within the management ranks				
22. I am provided with physical comfort appropriate to the task I do				
23. I have a good sense of the direction in which MC is headed				
24. My supervisors are viewed, treated, and adequately prepared as members of management				
25. I work with people I like				
26. There is a high level of mutual trust within MC				
27. The department managers and supervisory group at MC work well as a team				
28. There is a high level of commitment on the part of the Administrative Team to goal setting and goal achievement				
29. The Administrative Team evidences a high and consistent level of commitment to cost effectiveness and productivity improvement				
30. I believe that innovation and creative thinking are fostered and encouraged at MC				
31. Using initiative and risk taking are characteristics of MC				
32. I understand the purposes and workings of the Administrative Team				
33. I view the values held by the Administrative Team to be consistent among all its members				
34. I am adequately informed about those things I feel I should know				
35. My boss makes decisions that are adequate and timely				
36. Our organization has high standards of performance				
37. MC is a good organization to work for				
38. The people at my level perform well in their jobs				
39. There are adequate opportunities to discuss operational problems and to exchange views with other department managers				
40. I feel that the present emphasis given to cost effectiveness and productivity improvements are not negatively affecting quality of service				

Exhibit 5-1 continued

III. *Personal Factors*	Definitely Disagree	Inclined To Disagree	Inclined To Agree	Definitely Agree
41. I am able to fully utilize my skills and talents in my management assignments				
42. Rules are enforced equitably and fairly at MC				
43. I have the opportunity to develop my talents, to grow personally				
44. My performance is appraised regularly				
45. The feedback I received regarding my performance is complete and honest				
46. My job provides the opportunity to enjoy work, to have fun				
47. I feel a sense of satisfaction from the job I do				
48. I have been appropriately and equitably recognized and rewarded for my accomplishments				
49. I consider myself to be well-informed about fringe benefits				
50. I consider the "benefit package" provided by MC to be satisfactory				
51. I am experiencing too much stress on the job				
52. My boss often lets me know how pleased he or she is with my work				
53. Other comments you wish to make:				

NOTES

1. Marilyn Ferguson, *The Aquarian Conspiracy* (Los Angeles: J.P. Tarcher, Inc., 1980), p. 345.

2. Opinion Research Corporation, *Managing Human Resources/1983 and Beyond.* (Princeton, NJ: Opinion Research Corporation, 1983), p. 13.

3. Robert Henri, *The Art Spirit,* (New York: Harper & Row, 1984), p. 236.

4. Philip Thiel, *Visual Awareness and Design* (Seattle: University of Washington Press, 1981), p. 26.

5. Douglas M. McGregor, *Leadership and Motivation: Essays of Douglas McGregor,* ed. by Warren G. Bennis and Edgar H. Schein (Cambridge, Mass.: The M.I.T. Press, 1966), pp. 21–9.

6. David A. Nadler and Edward E. Lawler III, "Quality of Work Life: Perspectives and Directions." *Organizational Dynamics,* Winter 1983, p. 20.

7. Ted Mills, "The Participative Revolution," in *Quality of Work Life,* ed. by Kenneth A. Buback and Mary K. Grant (St. Louis: The Catholic Health Association of the United States, 1985), p. 3.

8. Daniel Yankelovich, *New Rules* (New York: Random House, Inc., 1981), p. 4.

9. Stanley Peterfreund, *Managing Change: The Quality of Work Life,* (Englewood Cliffs, NJ: Stanley Peterfreund Associates, 1980), p. 3.

10. Chris Argyris, "The CEO's Behavior: Key to Organizational Development," *Harvard Business Review,* Mar.–Apr., 1973, p. 5.

11. Nadler and Lawler, "Quality of Work Life," p. 20.

12. Nadler and Lawler, "Quality of Work Life," p. 29.

13. Paul D. Greenberg and Edward M. Glaser, *Quality of Worklife Improvement Efforts* (Kalamazoo, Mich.: W.E. UpJohn Institute for Employment Research, 1980), p. 34.

14. Ted Mills, "Human Resources—Why the New Concern?," *Harvard Business Review,* Mar.–Apr., 1975, p. 53.

15. Kim Cameron, "Critical Questions in Assessing Organizational Effectiveness," *Organizational Dynamics,* Autumn, 1980, p. 79.

16. Peterfreund, "Managing Change," p. 3.

17. Peterfreund, "Managing Change," p. 3.

18. Peterfreund, "Managing Change," p. 3.

19. Argyris, "The CEO's Behavior," p. 5.

20. Leonard A. Schlesinger and Barry Oshry, "Quality of Work Life and the Manager: Muddle in the Middle," *Organizational Dynamics,* Summer 1984, p. 4.

21. Charles Handy, "The Changing Shape of Work," *Organizational Dynamics,* Autumn 1980, p. 26.

Chapter 6

The Essentiality
of Human Conduct

The great secret is not having bad manners or good manners or any other particular sort of manners, but having the same manners for all human souls.
—George Bernard Shaw, *Pygmalion V*

The idea of work as a principle of right or good conduct; as a central source of feeling proud and of achieving self-dignity; in fact, as a vigorous, vivid sign of life is an American quality that many find missing in our present day world of work. In the words of Pope John Paul II, "It is always man who is the purpose of the work."[1] Yet, today, excessive numbers of workers are torn between a need to fulfill personal imperatives and a need to submerge themselves in some kind of consuming, constraining function. "The delight of function"[2]—an apt phrase coined by the German psychologist Karl Buehler to suggest the joy that activity can bring with it—is not a pleasurable experience now commonly lived through by people at work. Regrettably, there persists a quiet frustration in the collective hearts of our workplace as a result of the failure of work to express man in a deeper sense by bearing a particular mark of man and of humanity.

This quiet crisis in the workplace is wearing away the *quality* base of human activity, and it is management's increasing obligation to safeguard this foundation. Management at all levels must cultivate the human dimensions of employment that foster and sustain a mark of work characterized by functions that permit people to be fully themselves, to express themselves through independent thought, to utilize their own capabilities, and to make use of their own creative powers; anything less will tend to weaken the very base on which the quality of work itself is supported.

The quality of job performance is joined by the encircling quality of work life as we perceive the concept of quality in its totality. For while the skills and capabilities of the craftsman to do the job are indeed beginning requirements, there is the requisite of the human *will to work*. This essential and activating principle of the individual is reflective of the spirit of the place in which work is performed—the surrounding environment where pleasure from work needs to be derived, dignity valued, and personal fulfillment actualized.

"The formative influence of the environment is commonly so profound"[3] that it causes human behavior patterns and the individual's search for satisfaction of the body and the mind to have a local character. How important it is, then, for organizations in service industries to effect their mission as humanizing forces by providing work environments in which the quality of life at work becomes a positive and satisfying experience for their people, releases their potentialities, and contributes adequately to personal and collective fulfillment. Surely, by the absence of these kinds of conditions, limits to growth, both for the individual and the organization, may very well be the ultimate happening.

In this chapter we arrive at the third element of the human equation of total quality, that of human demeanor at work. As we return once again to basics, focus is given to the increasing need for individuals to conform to the rules and conventions of polite social behavior as they engage in the service and care of others. Attention also is given to the desirable presence of decorum not only in terms of the positive impact of the quality of being proper, but also in terms of the negative outcomes of certain faddish approaches being employed in today's work environment.

HISTORY OF MANNERS

Every civilization has had its own state of quality, and each historic period of the past its own struggle between humanity and bestiality. The awareness of this fundamental conflict and the source of harassment and pain it brings are reflected in the literatures of all ages.

> On a Sumerian clay tablet 5,000 years old, a father laments the behavior of his son who is so much interested in material satisfaction that he fails to cultivate higher qualities—"he neglects his humanity."
>
> Zarathustra taught 2,500 years ago that at the time of creation the twin original spirits had to choose between good and evil. One became associated with truth, justice, and life; the other with lies, destruction, injustice, and death. The struggle between good and evil has continued ever since.[4]

History is abounding with examples of the role of human choices, decisions, and actions that influenced the quality of human life and the relative presence of brutishness and humanity in human affairs. The civilizing process, which has no beginning, cannot in reality be traced back indefinitely. However, in providing a brief account, the medieval standards of the Middle Ages—the period in European history between antiquity and the Renaissance (A.D. 476 to A.D. 1453) is thought to be a reasonable beginning point.

As reported by Norbert Elias, "The Middle Ages have left us an abundance of information of what was considered socially acceptable behavior."[5] Religious leaders during the twelfth and thirteenth centuries set down, in Latin, precepts for behavior that give testimony to the standards of their society. Besides these precepts from the clerical society, there are, from about the thirteenth century on, corresponding documents in the various languages, all of which provide an early framework for the concept of "courtesy" and an introduction to conversation and conviviality. In addition, there surfaced, primarily in the fourteenth and fifteenth centuries, a whole series of poems designed as mnemonics to inculcate table manners.

As Elias writes, "The standard of 'good behavior' in the Middle Ages is, like all later standards, represented by a quite definite concept. . . . It was a different standard from our own—whether better or worse is not here at issue."[6]

Walter Lippmann, the American journalist, once placed these words in print on codes of conduct:

> There is no mechanical gadget by which the moral level of public life can be maintained. There is no spasm of popular righteousness which will raise it much for very long. All depends on the code of conduct which is fashionable. All depends on the working rules of behavior which the leading and conspicuous men and women in a society practice because they believe them, which most of the others conform with as a matter of course. . . .[7]

This principle of thought was exemplified in the Middle Ages. It also proved to hold some truth during the subsequent Renaissance period (fourteenth through sixteenth centuries), when Erasmus of Rotterdam gave meaning to the concept of *civilité* through his short treatise *De civilitate morum puerilium* (on civility in children), which appeared in 1530. Erasmus's text is about something very simple: the behavior of people in society. In many respects, the thoughts he delivered are close to our own today, yet in others still quite remote.

Erasmus's treatise, along with a succession of humanist writings on manners, form a kind of bridge between those of the Middle Ages and modern times. From the sixteenth to the twentieth centuries, books on manners have provided detailed information about the gradual transformation of behavior and emotions. In Elias's view,

They show precisely what we are seeking—namely, the standard of habits and behavior to which society at a given time sought to accustom the individual. These poems and treatises are themselves direct instruments of "conditioning" or "fashioning," of the adaptation of the individual to those modes of behavior which the structure and situation of his society make necessary. And they show at the same time, through what they censure and what they praise, the divergence between what was regarded at different times as good and bad manners.[8]

In each period of history there are *cultural* factors that either sustain the traits of a previous era or cause certain forms of conduct to disappear. Even those characteristics that have persisted over time, according to Jules Henry, "are marked by subtle alterations and have become subject to changing social factors which have distributed them in special ways in the population."[9]

In his writings, Henry expressed much concern with our national character in a culture increasingly feeling the effects of almost two centuries of "lopsided preoccupation with amassing wealth and raising its standard of living."[10] This concern with the character of contemporary America is one shared by a significant segment of our population, which deplores the changing conditions that have played havoc with our culture and values during the more recent decades.

"May you live in interesting times," goes an ancient Chinese curse. These years approaching the twenty-first century in which we live are certainly interesting enough, and if there are any who are bored in the process, one can only conclude that they are not paying attention.

If we are paying attention to our present-day social environment, we are well aware that the change index has been blowing up a storm in many ways.

- There is a general anxiety in the land that something is wrong. "American anxiety is the anxiety of all the modern world," states Marc Ullmann. "It is simply stronger in the United States than elsewhere because this country today is mankind's most advanced social laboratory. Wherever he looks the American cannot find the model for what he will be tomorrow. . . ."[11] What is causing much of this anxiety is the general decline of decency, moral behavior, and trust, and there is evidence that increasing numbers of people are beginning to think seriously about these problems.

- There is a rise in general violence and hate in our society. It has infected friendships; it has replaced sharing with the pleasure of overpowering and manipulating, and it has dimmed the feelings of love. Violence has become an untamed force that continues not only to abuse human life in a society where illegal drugs are readily available, but also to damage precious resources as a result of man's wrongful exercise of power in transforming the face of our planet and its environment.

- There is great uncertainty and fear about the future that pervades many parts of the American society. As a result, there is a growing array of pessimists who look forlornly toward tomorrow. Unquestionably, this sense of hopelessness is a direct result of the pervasiveness of the media. Even in the best of times, good news enjoys scant coverage in the media. Jules Henry adds "technological driveness and dynamic obsolescence"[12] as common elements of the emotional crisis in America.

- There are persistent signs that individualism, which lies at the core of American culture, is out of control. In the opinion of Robert Bellah,

> Some of our deepest problems, both as individuals and as a society, are closely linked to our individualism. If we press our individualism to the point where we forget others, forget how much we need others, forget that as individuals we can only be realized in relationships, community and society, then we find ourselves in trouble—the sort of trouble that has been evident for some time in our society.[13]

What is visible today is the weakening of enduring commitments to marriage, family, community, and the society in which we live.

- There is a living and thinking for immediate utility that brings with it a terrifying impatience among Americans. Instant learning, instant work opportunities, instant success—all are part of an instant culture in which we find a penetrating attitude expressed in the thought: "Today is as important as tomorrow. Why wait for tomorrow when you can have it today?"

- There is unbridled self-interest prevalent throughout our present-day culture. As people act to maximize their self-interest, they subscribe to the growth of philosophies that preach "Look out for number one."

  For decades, too many have been narcissistic, holding onto a grandiose sense of self-importance or uniqueness and spending their lives desperately seeking constant attention and admiration to counteract their feelings of inner emptiness.

- There is a decided shift in motivation at work. Workers today are not necessarily less motivated than before; however, their expectations of work have risen, and work has to compete with other values in their lives more directly than ever before. Not everyone can work in exciting, self-fulfilling jobs; still, the notion of "self-fulfillment" has filtered down to the lower economic levels.

Certainly there is no "gloom and doom" intent to the citing of these current happenings in our society. Rather, the recognition of their presence is meant to convey and underscore their reality, acknowledging the fact that the degree of their gravity is an individualistic point of view. In any event, it would seem logical to conclude that societal characteristics such as increasing violence, anxiety, fear, crassness in relations, and absorption in private achievement are bound to cause widespread injury to the code of human conduct and to mar the quality of the attitudes and behavior of individuals as they exercise their responsibilities within the work environment of health care.

CHARACTERISTICS OF HUMAN BEHAVIOR

> The cave man is in fashion, but for the wrong reasons. His unpleasant characteristics are being publicized and used to explain modern man's misbehavior. He is assumed to have been nasty and brutish, and since we have descended from him, it is claimed that we are condemned to retain the worst aspects of his nature.[14]

Those are the words of René Dubos, but it is an argument that can be countered by the thought that human nature is intrinsically good, but defiled by civilization. The latter view, which holds greater value, requires our increasing attention as we face the challenges of managing people and of advancing the quality of their work performance, all within an external environment of unwholesome conditions of human behavior running rampant in today's society.

Happily, there is a signal of hope. It is the evidence of Americans' growing concern with the misbehavior of people showing itself in print almost daily, and the character of human deportments being written about covers the full range of A to Z. For example, the tendency to be

arrogant	negative
boastful	offensive
cynical	pompous
disagreeable	querulous
egotistical	raffish
fault-finding	surly
gloomy	tacky
humorless	unfriendly
impatient	vindictive
jaundiced	wrongheaded
kindless	xenophobic
lanquid	yahoo
malevolant	zigzagger

Here are a few selected samples of expressions of thought appearing in print pulled from the authors' files:

- *Time* magazine, which itself has contributed a good deal to grossness in our era, speaks out about certain needed improvements in human conduct. An editorial on the magazine's essay makes the statement, "If *Time* is starting to gag at what passes for taste and manners in our society, then a good many other people must have been retching for quite a while."[15]
- In the *Wall Street Journal,* Arthur Witkin, founder of Personnel Sciences Center, says that fresh hires in management training programs have above-average intelligence, but most lack tact, diplomacy, and understanding of people.[16]
- Webster's Unabridged Dictionary devotes sixty-six column-inches to the definition of *take,* and only twenty-two column-inches to *give.* Comments Leo J. Paulin, who made the observation, "There's a clue to our troubled society."[17]
- In *Connoisseur* magazine, Thomas Hoving writes his article on a question of vulgarity just after seeing two movies—*Cobra* and *Caravaggio.*[18]
- Appearing in the *Los Angeles Times* was an article about the San Diego Junior Assembly's teaching 12-year-olds good manners.[19]
- A full-page advertisement on "whatever happened to 'yes, please' " came into view of the public via the *Wall Street Journal.* A reduced reproduction is shown as Exhibit 6-1.[20]
- Irene Gunther, who writes frequently about social issues, wrote an article for the *New York Times,* "New York's New Rudeness," in which she asks, "Can't people answer others decently?"[21]
- Under the headline "Rampart Rudeness," the *Wall Street Journal* published on its front page a three-column article on boorish behavior in the U.S. today.[22]
- For the *New York Times,* the novelist James A. Michener prepared an editorial piece entitled: "You Can Call the 1980's 'The Ugly Decade'."[23]

What is read in print comes alive as we experience day-to-day contacts with individuals whose behavior is expected to meet acceptable standards of courteous conduct because of the very occupation they are engaged in: the provision of service. Yet our encounters prove otherwise as we witness or come face to face with

- the bad manners of a waiter or even the maitre d' in celebrated restaurants whose successes breed disdain

Exhibit 6-1 Example of Concern for Diminishing Manners

Whatever Happened To "Yes, Please"?

It went
the way of
"Thank you,"
"Excuse me,"
"Yes, sir."
Do you know
who just about
killed all those
phrases?
All of us.
We did not use
them enough.
We now get
"Huh?"
"What?"
"Gimme more."
Mannerly responses
are learned at home.
Rude, barbaric
responses also are
learned at home.
William of Wykeham,
who was born in 1324,
said, "Manners
maketh man."
If we're
so smart
in the
20th century,
how come
we're not
as civilized
as William was
in the
14th century?
To the child
who says,
"Huh?"
pass along this page.

Source: A message as published in the *Wall Street Journal* by United Techologies Corporation, Hartford, Connecticut 06101. © 1987 United Technologies Corporation.

- the lack of civil behavior on the part of plumbers, carpenters, and electricians, who, back a few decades ago, would do jobs for householders after-hours or on weekends, and were glad for the work
- the thoughtlessness of a taxi driver who will not even consider getting out from behind the wheel to assist a passenger

- the disappearance of airline attendants, who seem to believe their service assignments terminate after serving the in-flight meal
- the aloofness and abruptness of the individual who registers a guest at a hotel, and ineptly plays out the role of "ambassador-in-charge" of creating first impressions as lasting impressions
- the inhumane act of no eye contact when a customer makes a transaction with a teller at the bank or a cashier in the local grocery store
- the resounding silence—the cutting off of human contact—on the part of a service-station attendant, who is more often not in uniform, whose closed-mouth behavior also excludes a final "thank you" for purchasing a full tank of gas

Such human events are all too familiar and disconcerting to many of us. However, even more disturbing is the behavior of some people not worthy of imitation who are employed in the health care environment, where the human condition is quintessential to the care and well-being of their fellowman. For example

- the ill-mannered switchboard operator—very often the first contact with a hospital—being called by a concerned member of a patient's family
- the polarization between people whose loyalties to their own professional discipline cause conflict and competitiveness between departments, with the patient being the ultimate victim of all-too-frequently-occurring rifts
- the open controversies—in full sight and within hearing range of patients—between the newer, younger nurse who is less inhibited, more demanding of life and therefore more demanding of management, and her nursing supervisor who holds a high sense of organizational loyalty and whose ideological beliefs may be out of step with the current value systems of her subordinates
- ancillary services personnel who display an absence of courtesy, warmth, politeness, and kindness—qualities that true professionals should possess and practice in their interactions with other human beings in need of care
- the embarrassing behavior of an attendant, housekeeper, dietary employee, or cashier who exhibits extraordinary inconsideration or indifference in the presence of patients and their families
- the boorish behavior of physicians in their professional exchanges with employees of the hospital

While we may acknowledge the imperfectness of man, we cannot, in keeping with our own sense of right conduct, condone these kinds of thoughtless occurrences of behavior believed to be most inappropriate within such a deeply human environment as health care.

Irving H. Page, M.D., editor of *Modern Medicine,* in his *Wall Street Journal* writing, gave the warning that health care organizations had better deliver their medical expertness with efficiency and concern for good manners. In his words:

> I am appalled at the number of high level meetings being held throughout the country under the aegis of prestigious organizations concerned with the "delivery of health care." I would even accept this singular inappropriate phrase if some attention were given to simple problems that involve human satisfaction and happiness.
>
> We seem forever concerned with ethics, or organ transplants, cloning, informed consent, and population control—subjects that are either rare or about which we probably can do little. I have yet to hear of a conference on good behavior.[24]

The tension of living in today's society and its culture brings with it behavior all too often incompatible with the intrinsic purposes of any people-serving-people industry or enterprise. Frustration, irritation, alienation, and a growing restiveness among members of America's work force are feelings we find difficult to cope with, but their very existence offers a clear message that in today's human service setting, professional or technological efficiency is not the complete standard, nor should organizational growth by itself be considered as an absolute good. Rather, of precedential concern, established by order of its importance and urgency, is the behavior and performance of people working in service organizations.

In our health care institutions, as in other work environments, there is indeed a proper place for the pronouncement of a code of conduct that is tied closely to the mission and goals of the organization and to its cultural values and that forms the basis of accountability for compliance. There, too, is the imperative of making the quality of human conduct a subject of focus within all elements of the educational system, with managers at all levels taking the lead and setting the model. Above and beyond these given requirements, what is paramount to the human condition at work is a vigilant attentiveness to arresting the harmful force of causing employees to experience estrangement from personal feelings and emotion.

ESTRANGEMENT FROM PERSONAL FEELINGS

Arlie Russell Hochschild, in her book *The Managed Heart* vividly describes from a humanist perspective the process of estrangement from personal feelings and its role as an "occupational hazard" for a large segment of America's work force. This estrangement occurs when workers become alienated from an aspect of *self* as a requirement of the job and as a result of institutional managing of their feelings.

When management exercises control over the feelings of its people, and when private capacities for empathy and warmth are put to corporate use, something is added to physical and mental labor. Hochschild defines that something as "emotional labor," which requires one "to induce or suppress feeling in order to sustain the outward countenance that produces the proper state of mind in others."

Hochschild followed emotional work into the job market by entering the world of a flight attendant at Delta Airlines, about which she wrote this commentary:

> A twenty-year-old flight attendant trainee sat with 122 others listening to a pilot speak in the auditorium of the Delta Airlines Stewardess Training Center. . . . The young trainee sitting next to me wrote on her notebook pad, "Important to smile. Don't forget smile." The admonition came from the speaker in the front of the room, a crewcut pilot in his early fifties, speaking in a Southern drawl: Now girls, I want you to go out there and really *smile.* Your smile is your biggest *asset.* I want you to go out there and use it. Smile. *Really* smile. Really *lay it on.*
>
> The pilot spoke of the smile as the *flight attendant's* asset. But as novices like the one next to me move through training, the value of a personal smile is groomed to reflect the company's disposition. . . . Trainers take it as their job to attach to the trainee's smile an attitude, a viewpoint, a rhythm of feeling that is, as they often say, "professional."[25]

As the Pacific Southwest Airlines (PSA) radio jingle goes,

> On PSA our smiles are not just painted on.
> So smile your way
> From L. A.
> To San Francisco.

Fortunately, few people take literally such messages as "our smiles are not just painted on," "fly the friendly skies" and "we move our tails for you," nor are they expected to. However, what indeed needs to be taken seriously is the core of the problem hidden behind the advertising screen of these simple, repetitious doggerels—namely, the commercial distortion of the trained management of individual personality and feeling at the work place. "It is the rise of the corporate use of guile and the organized training of feeling to sustain it"[26] that we are witnessing, says Ms. Hochschild. Increasing numbers of organizations are replacing actions supportive of natural or spontaneous feelings with institutional mechanisms designed to foster the organization's desired feelings in workers: the "managed heart."

In the health care field, "guest relations" is the catch phrase of the eighties, "something to which hospitals have turned as a way of curbing the exodus of patients in today's competitive environment"[27]—also as a means of shaping the behavior of their people. The descriptions of guest relations programs are as varied as the titles they go by, and while many such programs offer a certain degree of value to the overall quality effort, they tend persistently to evidence a set of fundamental deficiencies generally common to guest relations undertakings. For example:

At the Organizational Level

- The "institutional mechanism" of guest relations programs fits comfortably with the faddish, short-term, programmatic mentality popularized by today's corporate style of managing. As L. Rita Fritz puts it, "Many hospital executives have a false sense of security. They have a program. It exists alongside dozens of other hospital programs. . . . The problem with this approach is that guest relations can't be reduced to a program or technique."[28] In her article, Ms. Fritz makes mention of a survey of 119 nurse executives, 60 of whom said they had guest relations programs in their hospitals. Of these respondents, only three (5 percent) felt that these current efforts would be impacting hospital operations 18 months hence.

- A major flaw is the absence of designing, developing, and implementing the "guest relations" approach as a process (not as a program) and as an integral component of a larger system (not as an isolated effort and an end to itself) that serves the higher purpose of quality enhancement (not merely improved guest relations as a more narrowed outcome).

- The purchase of "canned" or "packaged" guest relations programs from outside sources follows an all-too-familiar pattern of corporate behavior in attempting to fit the disconnected fragments of a manager development effort together. The end results are similar—they are less than effective—because the program "does not take" since it is placed *on top* of the organization, and it initially has not been created as an instrument specifically fitting to the mission, goals, culture, and environment of the particular organization in which it is utilized. There is the failure of suitable modification of what is purchased.

At the Individual Level

- The institution places parameters around the employees' personalities and emotions, as they are required to arrange their acts and actions according to organizational rules and customs, thus showing their feelings in institutionally approved ways. This characteristic of one hospital's program is forcefully expressed as a goal of guest relations: "to establish, communicate and achieve standards of excellent performance with accountability of individuals for program effectiveness."

- Another crack in the wall of guest relations is the preemption of employees' feelings by a prominence of concern for the feelings of others—clients, patients, customers. With the flight attendant in mind, Ms. Hochschild asks these questions:

> When rules about how to feel and how to express feelings are set by management, when workers have weaker rights to courtesy than customers do, when deep and surface acting are forms of labor to be sold, and when private capacities for empathy and warmth are put to corporate uses, what happens to the way a person relates to her feelings or to her face? When worked-up warmth becomes an instrument of service work, what can a person learn about herself from her feelings? And when a worker abandons her work smile, what kind of tie remains between her smile and her self?[29]

Basically, what is in error at both the organizational and individual levels is the singular focus on organizing and engineering the feelings of people at work, rather than placing the center of interest and attention on management actions that can be exercised toward enhancing the overall conditions of work itself and the quality of the work life environment in which work is done, the two areas marked for concentration in Chapters 4 and 5. It is from these intrinsic and indispensable virtues of change that people will feel good about who they are, because they will feel good about what they do and about the organization and its purposes for which they do it. It is management's greatest power to act effectively in curing the maladies of human conduct in the workplace.

Any organizational effort to manage the hearts of its people has a human cost attached to it. It is to be considered an ethical issue if individuals at work are victimized by programmatic endeavors designed by others to establish an institutional "model of an unhealthy false self."

In terms of such estrangement from personal feelings, it is believed that Constantin Stanislavski would voice this warning for all workers to hear:

Always act in your own person, as an artist. You can never get away from yourself. The moment you lose yourself on the stage marks . . . the beginning of exaggerated false acting. For losing yourself in the part, you kill the person whom you portray, for you deprive "him" of the real source of life for a part.[30]

NOTES

1. "Laborem, Exercens," *Third Encyclical of Pope John Paul II,* Sept. 15, 1981.

2. *New York Times,* Sept. 4, 1985, p. 17.

3. René Dubos, *Beast or Angel?* (New York: Charles Scribner's Sons, 1974), p. 177.

4. Dubos, *Beast or Angel?,* p. 61.

5. Elias Norbert, *History of Manners,* (New York: Pantheon Books, 1978), p. 60.

6. Norbert, *History of Manners,* p. 62.

7. *New York Times,* Date unknown.

8. Norbert, *History of Manners,* p. 84.

9. Jules Henry, *Culture against Man* (New York: Vintage Books, 1965), p. 7.

10. Henry, *Culture against Man,* p. 8.

11. Marc Ullmann, "Notable & Quotable," *Wall Street Journal,* date unknown.

12. Henry, *Culture against Man,* p. 22.

13. Robert N. Bellah, "Is Individualism Out of Control in America?" *Los Angeles Times,* Feb. 15, 1985, p. 7.

14. Dubos, *Beast or Angel?,* p. 41.

15. *Sunday Journal and Star,* Lincoln, Nebraska, date unknown.

16. *Wall Street Journal,* Oct. 21, 1986, p. 1.

17. Leo Paulin, *Readers Digest,* date unknown.

18. *Connoisseur,* Sept. 1986, p. 35.

19. *Los Angeles Times,* Dec. 21, 1986, p. 20.

20. *Wall Street Journal,* Jul. 8, 1986.

21. *New York Times,* Dec. 13, 1986, p. 19.

22. *Wall Street Journal,* Mar. 12, 1987, p. 1.

23. *New York Times,* Jan. 1, 1987, p. 31.

24. *Wall Street Journal,* date unknown.

25. Arlie Russell Hochschild, *The Managed Heart* (Berkeley: University of California Press, 1983), p. 4.

26. Hochschild, *The Managed Heart,* p. 5.

27. Kari E. Super, "Memorial Hospital Emphasizes Guest Relations To Attract Patients," *Modern Healthcare,* Aug. 29, 1986, p. 42.

28. L. Rita Fritz, "Developing a Consumer-Driven Hospital: Four Fatal Flaws," *Healthcare Forum,* May/Jun. 1986, p. 39.

29. Hochschild, *The Managed Heart,* p. 89.

30. Constantin Stanislavski, *An Actor Prepares* (New York: Theatre Arts Books, 1965), p. 167.

Part III

Human Affairs

Chapter 7

Quality As the Province of the Human Resources Function

It is not important that you come in early and work late. The important thing is *why*?
—Charlie Brower, Chairman of the Board of Batten, Barton, Durstine, and Osborne

Workers in health care today, like the workers in other fields, want the work they do to be work they like to do. Increasingly they want more variety, more responsibility, and more flexibility, and, true to being artists, they want work that does not prevent them from being themselves. All of these characteristics bear heavily on the quality of work itself. Gaining human will to work, in turn, requires a quality of work life that recognizes the whole system of organizational effort in relation to individual needs and capabilities. There too is the concern for the proper deportment of people at work that befits the environmental needs for human caring and compassion.

This triad of quality elements, which were discussed in Chapters 4, 5, and 6, are human issues that need to be viewed and measured in human terms. They find their origin in people, their advancement or depreciation in people, and their future potential in people. People—their attitudes, feelings, behavior, diligence, and attentiveness toward the human elements of care and service—are indeed the business of the human resources function.

A NEW BREED OF WORKERS

In September 1979, *U.S. News and World Report* proclaimed the presence of a prosperous, restless, demanding, new breed of workers in these words:

As the nation marks Labor Day, 1979, this new breed of worker is fomenting discord in offices and factories across the country. Business, labor, and government are under pressure to devise new ways to manage today's work force.

Unlike their parents, contemporary workers do not view their jobs as a simple contract: A day's work for a day's pay. "Today's workers want much more," says labor-relations analyst John R. Browning. "They want nothing less than 8 hours of meaningful, skillfully guided, personally satisfying work for 8 hours' pay. And that's not easy for most companies to provide."[1]

These dramatic changes in the way workers perceived their job entitlements began to take shape during the sixties and seventies, when the American work force had been transformed by a rapid influx of millions of young workers, including many women and blacks. It was a work force that already had known prosperity. Young, educated, and ambitious, they had come to expect good wages, fringe benefits, and a plentiful supply of job opportunities. The changed social values and high educational levels of this younger labor force as we moved into the eighties, combined with economic strains, put great pressure on the existing obsolete industrial relations system in this country that fostered an adversarial relationship between management and labor. As reported in *Business Week,*

Social cooperation at work surely predates recorded history. But organized labor's growth as a deeply adversarial institution in the U.S. coupled with management's retention of obsolete methods of controlling workers—Frederick Taylor's "scientific management" approach, for example—have blinded both sides to their mutual interests.[2]

During the fifties and sixties, increased research and the development of theories on worker psychology were generated by a host of American psychologists who led the way in research on motivational theory, alienation, the impact of different management styles, and the need for—or lack of—clearly delineated hierarchies to make things work. The recorded contributions of these founding fathers put to rest the common misconception that the theories behind participatory management have been imported from Japan. Some of the theorists who pointed the way toward reshaping relationships with the new breed of worker who arrived on the job with different values, different needs, different awareness, different demands, and different motivation include Douglas McGregor, Frederick Herzberg, Rensis Likert, and Chris Argyris.

THE NATURE OF OUR WORKPLACE

In addition to the complexity of challenges brought to the task of managing the new breed of worker, there also are present certain deficiencies and inconsistencies within the health care workplace that are likely to run contrary to any efforts undertaken on the part of organizations to enhance the quality of work life of their people. In earlier chapters (particularly Chapter 2), attention was directed toward complexities of the internal work environment as the health care organization and the workplace it offers interplay with the values and expectations people bring with them from a societal climate plagued with conditions under which it is difficult to hold fast to a sense of human worth.

Impressions of the health care workplace embrace a whole series of dichotomies and inconsistencies between beliefs and happenings that tend to work against the potential success of creating new processes and mechanisms for solving "people problems." Altogether, the recognized complexities of the workplace, along with the increasingly new and different expectations of the new breed of worker, not only make our times interesting, but difficult and frustrating in terms of exerting a positive impact on human behavior at work.

- *In our time,* there are concerns about a loss of enthusiasm and commitment among managers that is profoundly important. Middle managers, especially, are beginning to look and act dispensable at a time when their roles are changing to those of facilitator, trainer, mentor, and counselor, with more responsibility for their employees' personal growth and development.

- *In our time,* we witness the entry of people into the workplace who have become much better educated and much more sophisticated.

- *In our time,* we are approaching a historical moment in American economic development, when the number of professional, managerial, and technical workers will exceed the number of blue-collar workers. Common to most of these workers of the new economy are the requirements for education and training; a broader latitude for creativity, independent thought, and independent action; career advancement potential; and opportunities for greater recognition. "Their stock in trade is knowledge, their working tools, above all, ideas."[3]

- *In our time,* American jobholders have a great deal of discretion over the quantity and quality of effort they invest in their work, but managerial skills and training have not kept pace with the movement to a high-discretion workplace.

- *In our time,* we find that most employees are not prepared to settle into their jobs for the long haul and to make a real commitment to a given career track. Only about 40 percent say that five years from now they intend to hold the same job they do now. Another 30 percent say they plan to leave their current work; the remaining 30 percent simply do not know what they will be doing in the way of a job five years from now.[4]

- *In our time,* people in professional and executive positions are more likely to be well-satisfied with what they are doing. However, at the bottom of the ladder—in unskilled and service jobs—there are serious signs of dissatisfaction with work.
- *In our time,* turnover and absenteeism persist as major problems. The health care industry experiences the third highest absenteeism rate among nonmanufacturing, finance, and nonbusiness groups, while its turnover is tied with finance for the highest rate.[5]
- *In our time,* we find adult workers reexamining and reappraising the standards and values by which they live. The majority of job-holders feel that, under the right conditions, they could significantly increase their performance.
- *In our time,* the composition and characteristics of the work force continue to undergo significant changes: it is older, more female, more ethnic, growing more slowly, less unionized.
- *In our time,* we will be witness to "the great jobs mismatch," with a growing mismatch between the skills required for work and those the disadvantaged possess. "And that poses the danger that the U.S. will enter the 21st century as a nation of haves and have-nots glaring at each other across a deep divide defined by education and skill."[6]

While there are other signs of our time that could be cited, they all add up to the realization that a different way of managing people has taken shape. The challenges of a new breed of work force place demands on corporate managements to establish policies and processes that will match changing organizational needs with changing employee expectations, all in the interest of increasing the quality of human performance at work.

TRANSFORMING TODAY'S "PERSONNEL" FUNCTION

The focus of this chapter is on the role of the human resources function in advancing the levels of quality within today's and tomorrow's health care organization. As we perceive quality embracing the elements of the quality of work itself, the quality of life at work, and the quality of human conduct, the human resources function takes on a position of centrality.

As a beginning to the discussion that follows, let us consider two known facts:

- First, there is no single answer to the challenges that lie ahead. Changes in the external environment will affect organizations in different ways, as will the internal needs and characteristics of the enterprise. What is certain is that some organizations will correctly identify the requirements for change that the future will impose. Others will not. Those who identify the requirements and respond timely to them will master the movement toward higher levels of quality in human performance.

- Second, the "personnel administration" systems in most health care organizations are not as yet sufficiently equipped to cope with today's "people" problems, much less the problems of tomorrow.

A historical account of the development of the personnel administration activity in health care "shows a degree of stagnancy that has caused this key function to be ill-equipped to deal with many of the current problems of a human service industry."[7] The cause of the failure of sufficiently progressive change in this critical area of endeavor rests at the doorsteps of both top management and the human resource executive. Over the past four decades, there has persisted a lack of commitment and leadership on the part of chief executive officers and their administrative members. At the functional level, there are as yet too few who perceive and understand the long-term, arduous planning, designing, and learning processes *true* human resource management efforts demand. "The traditional human resources department is populated by technical specialists who have narrow expertise in the standard menu of the human resources spectrum—salary, benefit programs, career administration, and so on."[8] Unquestionably, the age of such narrowly based competencies in the human resources function is over.

Within a more recent period, the health care industry witnessed a human resource phenomenon that suddenly took off exponentially. It was the widespread change in the functional designation of *personnel administration* to *human resources*—a change that followed the lead of other industries. This phenomenon neither made "personnel directors" the new corporate heroes nor made the function itself necessarily capable of responding to the needs of the new breed of workers or of giving purpose to their life at work within a highly humane setting.

The future challenges in the arena of human performance at work require more than cosmetic application of functional redesignation. Called for as essentialities are: (1) fresh, innovative thinking and new perspectives about managing human resources in a people-serving-people environment; (2) the making of some difficult choices and decisions; and (3) hard work.

What all of this means is that the traditional bent of the "personnel" function as we have known it in the past must be made subject to a self-renewal that will extend its orientation and activities beyond merely administering time-honored personnel practices. If administrations and their "human resource" staff executives fail to answer this call to action, the result can be nothing more than a continuance of relegating the "personnel" function to the past and familiar status of secondary citizenship within the health care organization, whose mission is uniquely humane in its purposes.

DEVELOPING A HUMAN RESOURCE MANAGEMENT SYSTEM

Required between now and the year two thousand, if the totality of quality within health care organizations is to be served, is a wider range of vision on the part of administrations and their human resource executives that views the function from new and different perspectives oriented toward institutional growth and effectiveness. The aim of this chapter is to assist these key players in advancing their awareness of the requirements called for in redefining and redesigning the "personnel" function, as well as an awareness of the values, contributions, and influences of a *human resources system* within their organizations in terms of institutional outcomes, organization and management development, and economic performance.

This objective is served through the offering of a conceptual model—an ideational structure—designed for the creation of a human resource management plan and process that give consideration to essential program strategies and programs. Naturally, each organization must make adjustments to the model that fit its own peculiar conditions and circumstances.

The plan and process set forth on the following pages provide a recommended framework of a systematic approach toward planning and implementing the conceptual and operational aspects of human resource management. It is believed to be a process that not only is a balanced one in terms of qualitative and quantitative considerations but also is viewed as a future-directed, results-oriented effort with a high level of benefits for both the individual and the organization. Most important, the recommended human resource process is in keeping with the values of today's and tomorrow's workers, and thus gives particular emphasis to the factors essential to the development of a positive quality of work life. Finally, the proposed process is considered to be a meaningful one, since it moves the "personnel" function well beyond the boundaries of its traditional role and extends its activities within the design of a human resource management process linked to the formulation of corporate strategies.

Introduction to the Plan

To minimize the impact of external and internal environmental factors on the ability of an organization to conduct its human resource business in an effective and efficient manner, the need for a planning process is indicated. As with any attempt at strategic planning, the human resource management planning process requires that general statements of mission and purpose be established and then made more specific by developing long-range objectives. Following this task is the development of detailed process elements and program strategies to achieve objectives and purposes.

As a beginning point, an effort has been made to approach the issue of mission/purpose through the development of an overall definition of human resource management. Evolving from this definition is the creation of a number of long-range objectives for a human resource management plan, with accompanying process elements and program strategies.

In giving definition to the concept of human resource management, it is believed appropriate to embrace the ideas of

- defining and expressing corporate commitment
- advancing the effectiveness and responsiveness of management
- identifying human resource needs
- enhancing the value of the employment environment
- maximizing performance contributions
- promoting free and open communication and coordination
- achieving cost effectiveness

The definition of human resource management that follows is offered solely as a framework of thought at the very outset of identifying the overall purposes and scope of the idea of human resource management. It is not intended to provide a common expression for all organizations, since, as subsequently indicated within the process itself, each organization needs to develop its own statement of the meaning of human resource management.

A Definition of Human Resource Management

People at work in the health services environment constitute the greatest contributing force to attaining the overall mission of the individual institution. The total system of selection, placement, utilization, and development of human resources must be the coordinative responsibility of executive leadership at all levels, subject to the elements of the management process, and directed toward the integration and fulfillment of organizational goals and the values, needs, and aspirations of employees. In achieving these ends, the activities of personnel, training and education, and management sciences are integrated to

- *Give attention to the essentiality of defining and expressing corporate commitment to the human affairs of the organization* through incorporating human issues into the institution's strategic planning process. This interfacing of human resource issues with corporate planning is accomplished at the board level through the medium of its mission and philosophical documentation and at the administrative level through its goal-setting process.

- *Advance the overall effectiveness and responsiveness of management* through the development, presentation, and reinforcement of activities that identify and respond to manager needs for increased skills in leadership, direction, and motivation of people; that enhance the ability of managers to understand and share the values of the contemporary worker; and that directly advance the development and outcome of the organization.

- *Identify the human resource needs of the total organization, and recommend plans to meet them* through the employment of processes that translate corporate plans into human resource requirements; the development of short-, medium-, and long-range human resource plans for management and nonmanagement personnel; the assessment and inventorying of existing human skills within the organization; the establishment of plans that define career opportunities for development of potential; the establishment and maintenance of personnel management services that contribute to employment stability; and the provision of employee and management feedback for evaluation and adjustment of plans.

- *Enhance the value of the employment environment through the upgrading of employee attitudes toward the institution and improvement of employee morale within the organization* through a combination of efforts, including those specifically responsive to other purposes identified within this definition, with a focus on the premise that employee attitudes toward the job, and their level of morale, are key components in providing a high level of professional and economical service and in retaining qualified employees. Fundamental to these efforts are programs conducted periodically to solicit employee expressions about organizational capabilities, and designed to translate findings into effective action plans that respond to needs and overcome barriers to employee satisfaction with life at work.

- *Maximize the performance contributions of all employees in attaining optimum productivity and organizational outcomes* through programs and actions intended to change skills and behavior required in the performance of technical and humanistic work, to respond to the needs of employees to understand the larger expectations of the organization and to have a say in how they do their work, and to bring into being organizational changes invented to fit the task and its people.

- *Promote free and open communication and coordination of effort within the organization on a continuing basis* through the development and implementation of comprehensive programs designed to enhance free-flowing, multidirectional exchange of information within management and between management and employees, based on an awareness of peoples' expectations of full disclosure and instant knowledge.

- *Achieve measurable cost effectiveness in the management of human resources* by developing systems and procedures that maximize the utilization of human time, human skills, and human potential. It is advanced in part by the development and application of programs conceived to assess and adjust staffing utilization, to reflect modern methods of balancing workload and available skills, to enhance human productivity and employee self-worth, and to maximize cost effectiveness of work organization and workload. It also is achieved in part by the preparation and execution of activities that audit the cost, administration, and performance of personnel management policies, plans, and programs, and propose improvement and/or corrections as necessary.

Clearly, these elements of action and activity evidence the need to widen the franchise of the personnel administration function in keeping with the administrative imperative of setting into place the qualities of a work environment that is concerned with human beings—their achievements, their interests, and their needs.

With the personnel (human resources) department as the core of the organization's total human resource effort, the movement toward human resource management—and its continued maintenance—is, in the main, the responsibility of management at all levels of the organization. In the process of this movement, the human resources function needs to evolve toward a comprehensive resource system that is based on identified needs of the organization and of the people it employs and that cuts across a wide range of human resource issues.

Human resources management, as defined by Ancilla Systems, Elk Grove Village, Illinois, is presented as Exhibit 7-1.

Long-Term Objectives of a Human Resource Management Plan

The overall desired objective of the plan may be stated as follows:

- to minimize effectively the impact of the identified external and internal environmental factors by having correctly identified and prioritized such factors in terms of importance to the enterprise; then, to design, develop, and implement effective human resource program strategies in response to those factors

Exhibit 7-1 Ancilla Systems' Definition of Human Resources Management

---

HUMAN RESOURCE DEFINITION

Human Resources includes, but is not limited to: auxiliaries, boards, board committees, employees, medical staff, volunteers, and other contributors to Ancilla Systems mission and goals.

Ancilla Systems recognizes its human resources as its most important asset.

We at Ancilla Systems embrace a new systemic concept. We recognize that more traditional basic functions need to be kept up to date. However, we must pay keen attention to a newer, broader definition of Human Resources Management.

Human Resources Management:

- Is the knowledge, skills, creative abilities, talents and aptitudes of an organization's work force, as well as the value, attitudes and beliefs of the individuals in the health care process.

- Is part of the planning process that establishes organizational goals and strategic plans for the system.

- Is the performance of all managerial functions involved in planning for, recruiting and selecting, developing, utilizing, rewarding, and maximizing the potential of the human resources of the organization to assure leadership and management effectiveness.

- Translates organizational goals and strategic business plan into Human Resources objectives.

- Provides a leadership quality of work life which utilizes the full potential of all individuals, advances the quality of work itself and enhances human conduct.

- Believes that performance evaluation and appraisal is a process by which the individual as well as the organization monitors work in a systematic way to provide feedback and improve effectiveness. The appraisal process is concerned not only with the goals and objectives of the organization, but also with the development of the individual.

- Understands that communication of information is the very essence of all organization. Communication is a process that involves the sending and receiving, not only of information, but of attitudes and feelings as well.

- Recognizes that research and planning provide the framework and direction for successful achievement of objectives.

- Is sensitive to the need for cost effective methods and programs and recognizes that productivity can best be improved through the development of a people-oriented quality of work life program.

- Knows that a key ingredient in the success of our health care organization is the effective development of leadership in all our human resources.

- Ensures career opportunities throughout our System and nurtures professional and personal growth.

Source: Courtesy of Ancilla Systems, Inc., Elk Grove Village, Illinois.

Subobjectives of the plan in support of this overall objective include:

- to set forth the human resource management programs and processes requisite for realizing a return on human potential within the organization
- to move management toward the position of maximizing and responding to the human values and needs of the organization and employees alike
- to provide the organization with an operational and educational process that will foster the placement of its position on the leading edge of management technology, and to provide new interpretations to traditionally linked management concepts

Human Resource Management Process Elements and Program Strategies

Figure 7-1 provides an overview of a recommended human resource management (HRM) process embracing eight major elements of action and activity. While each of the eight process elements have been placed purposely within a designed sequence of order, they are not to be viewed as singular and discrete. Each of the elements holds some degree of interdependence and interrelatedness with other elements of the process.

By their description, it becomes obvious that the first five elements influence, and have impact on, the *total* organizational system. Elements 6 through 8, on the other hand, have their primary focus on particular hierarchical levels of organization. Yet, while these last three elements are directed toward the top, middle, and bottom of the organization, their planning and implementation need simultaneously to take into account interlocking issues and considerations at all organizational levels.

Since the process essentially is a management process, it is imperative that high levels of communication and coordination be maintained between and among all levels of management. It also is key that the primary staff service functions of personnel administration, training and education, and management engineering exercise collaborative and harmonious relations as the process elements are designed, developed, implemented, maintained, and monitored.

Step 1. Corporate Commitment and Direction

Underlying this initial phase of the HRM process is the imperative that senior management and its board make dignity and human experience the highest order of corporate policy.

While there may indeed be a high commitment at the top of the organization to the well-being and the quality of life for the people within the enterprise, all too often the opportunity for arousing the consciousness of that

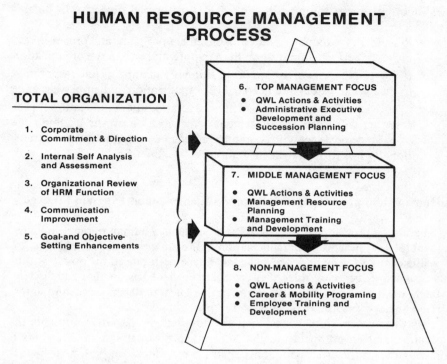

Figure 7-1 Eight Major Elements of Human Resources Management Process

commitment is not fully grasped. It is the intent of this first step to make known the human resource posture of the institutional leadership through the accomplishment of these kinds of actions and activities.

- Adequate discussions at the leadership level (board, administration, medical staff) directed toward arriving at a full, continuing commitment to the concept and process of human resource management. Naturally, the self-assessment findings (Step 2) will be most useful to the conduct of these discussions.

- The development of a set of overriding principles useful in creating and maintaining an organization committed to the enhancement of individual lives at work. Each institutional leadership needs to make explicitly *its own* human resource statement within the context of its mission document; it needs to declare its own set of principles that will characterize the values to which the leadership at the top subscribes and to which the organization as a professional and humanistic entity will devote its efforts and direct its goals.

- Effective communication of this philosophical statement of corporate leadership to all of its constituents. (A statement of human resource philosophy developed by the Inter-Community Medical Center, Covina, California, is included as Exhibit 7-2.)
- Definition of the meaning of HRM as it relates to the individual institution, including the identification of the elements within the process framework that are acceptable to administration and the board.
- Review and determination of the role and responsibilities of the board, with particular attention being given to its membership, committee structure, and agenda coverage.
- Review and determination of the role and responsibilities of the administrative team, with particular attention given to evaluating the performance of its members as it relates to the human affairs of the organization. Accompanying this is the development of needed skills and competencies required within the managerial leadership area of activity.
- Review and determination of the role and responsibilities of the medical staff membership.

What these kinds of actions and activities exhibit is not only a commitment on the part of top management, but an involvement as well.

Step 2. Internal Self-Analysis and -Assessment

The purpose of Step 2 is to gauge the current HRM performance of the organization. In viewing this task systemically, the direction and scope of the analysis and assessment need to encompass all significant elements of the total organization's efforts in HRM.

Step 2 begins with information gathering via the use of questionnaires and interviewing, review of documentation, collection of suitable data, and direct observation. The information gathered will lead to its evaluation and analysis, providing a knowledge base that can be helpful in moving forward within the framework of subsequent steps of the HRM process.

In approaching the assessment of the *total* organization's current performance in HRM from a systems perspective, it would appear appropriate to search out information relating to such areas of consideration as

- corporate strategy, organization structure, and the management process as they relate to the human resources unit
- current goals and objectives as they relate to HRM
- current personnel policies and practices as they tend to induce positive attitudes and behavior
- communication, coordination, and collaboration

Exhibit 7-2 A Statement of Human Resource Philosophy

Inter-Community Medical Center
Covina, California

Beliefs of the Board of Trustees and Administration
Regarding Human Resource Management

As expressed in its statement of purpose, Inter-Community Medical Center has adopted the policy to provide organizational leadership and quality of work life for our employees which will foster skill development, enhance individual dignity, and promote excellence in job performance and patient care.

In keeping with this policy the Board of Trustees and Administration of Inter-Community Medical Center commit to the following beliefs and ideals.

- *We believe* that every effort should be made to enhance individual esteem, integrity, and dignity at all levels during the employee's affiliation with Inter-Community Medical Center.

- *We believe* in the uniqueness of the individual; and, the recognition of differences in employee talents, skills, abilities, and intellect is among the highest in the set of values which our employees regard. Thus, we are committed to human resource management efforts which are aimed at sustaining, fostering, and reinforcing this value.

- *We believe* that a responsiveness to employee expectations in the modern work place is essential to the development of human beings, excellence in job performance and the delivery of quality patient care.

- *We believe* that excellence in management is a goal worthy of continuous attention in order that Inter-Community Medical Center will have sustained health care leadership of the highest quality over time at all levels.

- *We believe* that the work environment at Inter-Community Medical Center must be established and maintained on a foundation of honesty, fair dealing, trust, high levels of cooperation, and openness in communication.

- *We believe* that employee commitment to excellence in job performance is an unending requirement of this Medical Center in order to realize improvements in productivity and cost effectiveness both of which have a direct effect on patient care.

Respectfully Submitted:

The Board of Trustees and Administration of Inter-Community Medical Center

Date: ____July 25, 1983____

Source: Courtesy of Inter-Community Medical Center, Covina, California.

- culture, climate, environment, and problem functional areas as they relate to HRM
- leadership styles and performance
- major processes such as goal setting, performance appraisal, and human resource planning

- management development activities and outcomes
- employee participation programming
- staffing methodologies, resource utilization, and productivity
- organizational arrangements and relationships
- cost effectiveness in HRM
- HRM indicators: turnover, absenteeism, and grievances
- information systems: reports and control
- internal operational effectiveness and efficiency of the HRM function itself

Step 3. Organizational Review of the HRM Function

Step 3 embraces a review and appropriate modification of the existing organizational structure, tasks, and relationships of the function having staff service responsibility for HRM programming.

While structural issues are recognized as results, rather than as starting points, it is important that they be considered at this early stage in light of the organizational requirements of the statements and definitions arrived at in Step 1. Organizational change is a continuing process requiring constant review and refinement as the sequence of the HRM process elements evolve over time.

At this early point, it is believed essential that actions such as these be undertaken.

- Determination of the proper placement of the HRM function within the organizational system.
- Determination of the subfunctional components to be positioned within the framework of the overall HRM function, such as training and education, and management engineering. The boundaries of roles, relationships, and responsibilities of each of these components also need to be fixed.
- Preparation of the statement of mission of the HRM function.
- Identification of the expectations of the HRM executive to be described within a suitably documented position description.
- Identification of the human resource-related expectations of line managers at all levels of the organization.
- Consideration of expectations relating to the involvement of nonmanagement employees in HRM programming activities.
- Determination of relationships of the HRM executive (and his function) with the board, top administration, middle and supervisory management, and nonmanagement employee levels.

- Review for appropriate action the internal organization of the HRM function, including roles, responsibilities, competencies, and potential of its individual members.
- Review for appropriate action other organizational dimensions and mechanisms, such as committees, *ad hoc* groups, or task forces already involved, or to be involved, in HRM matters.

As the total HRM process moves the organization from a personnel administration posture to HRM, it is important that continuing efforts be directed toward the execution of activities designed to audit the basic and more traditional elements of personnel administration (recruitment, selection, orientation, compensation and benefits) for purposes of sustaining a state of enhancement in keeping with the broader conceptual framework of HRM. Surely, research programming is an essential component to gaining new breakthroughs in the various elements of HRM.

Step 4. Communication Improvement

The success of HRM depends on the existence of a climate of openness, trust, and understanding, and on the establishment of channels necessary to maintain a consistent two-way flow of effective communication. Good communication serves as an original and generating source of HRM, and good communication happens only if it is managed.

The self-assessment conducted under Step 2 should offer insight into the extent to which current communication within the organization is in need of repair, and in what particular dimensions. To whatever extent improvement appears to be required, it is advisable that a five-phase approach be undertaken, embracing

- Phase 1. Get feedback, which has, to some extent already been gained through the self-assessment engaged in during Step 2.
- Phase 2. Establish communication objectives that explain, as explicitly as possible, purposes for improving the communication processes within the organization, and specific objectives for achieving these improvements.
- Phase 3. Improve the media as they relate to upward, downward, and horizontal communication. Every medium should have a separate and distinct objective, and in the improvement of each, management must think not only of solving "communication" problems per se, but also of solving specific organizational problems by consciously applying specific communication techniques.
- Phase 4. Improve individual communication performance at all levels, calling not only for formalized training that moves further down into the organization, reaching more and more first-line supervisory person-

nel, but also moving beyond the skills aspects of communication and reaching out to motivation and attitude problems.

- Phase 5. Obtain more feedback to evaluate communication improvement through continuing self-assessment that will provide administration and its key managers the information they need to give direction to the enterprise and to improve organizational performance by having a positive effect on employee attitudes.

Step 5. Goal- and Objective-Setting Enhancements

The assessment engaged in during Step 2 should disclose the degree to which attention needs to be given to the human side of the enterprise within the context of goals and objectives being set by management at all levels. Based on the input provided by Step 2, it is timely under Step 5 to begin building proper balance of qualitative and quantitative considerations in the goal- and objective-setting processes with the introduction of increasing attention to the human affairs of the organization.

Action under Step 5 can have these kinds of effects:

- Position the hospital in relation to the needs of its people.
- Advance the communication of its stance with respect to its human resources.
- Place HRM in a position of higher priority and importance for all levels of management.
- Enhance teamwork and unity of effort among the members of management as objectives are shared.
- Ensure greater integration and coordination of HRM planning.
- Gain and maintain consistency of HRM action throughout the organization.

Step 5 needs to be perceived as the beginning point of purposeful emphasis of the HRM aspects of work, with its genesis being derived from the mission statement prepared under Step 1 of the process. As subsequent steps unfold, it is to be expected that a continuing extension of an emphasis on HRM be maintained over time within the context of the organization's goal- and objective-setting processes.

Step 6. Top Management Focus

A. Quality of Work Life Actions and Activities. There is present on the part of today's work force a psychology of entitlement. It is these expectations (as stated earlier in this chapter) that characterize the environment of future HRM. It is the presence or absence of actions or activities serving these expectations of entitlement that determine the quality of work life (QWL) as perceived by the organizational membership.

As indicated earlier, QWL is, in essence, a state of mind affected by a composite of factors on the job, including

- *work itself,* work processing factors
- *work environment* (including both the physical surroundings and the managerial style and climate)
- *personal* (and personnel) factors

The purpose of Step 6 is to begin translating the above factors into terms and conditions that are specific and applicable to the top management level of the organization. The subsequent Steps 7A and 8A continue the QWL actions and activities processes for the middle management and nonmanagement segments of the employee population. The underlying principle is to "enhance *managerial* job quality first, before turning attention to QWL down the line."

The initial, overall assessment conducted under Step 2 will have provided some early signals about the problems, the needs, the issues, and the concerns impacting on the organization's QWL. Accomplishments under Step 1, on the other hand, will have given direction to the QWL top management wants to achieve. To get a further fix on defining "*where* and *what* we are," further QWL assessment will, at this point, need to take place through personal interviewing and other forms of information gathering.

By knowing where the organization is and where it wants to go, administration then can develop strategies that will move the organization toward its QWL goals and objectives.

B. Administrative Executive Development and Succession Planning. A most important factor in the success of HRM is the strength of top management's commitment to launch and sponsor the process of executive development and succession planning. The commitment, sponsorship, and personal involvement with respect to this process at the very top of the organization sets the tone and pattern that will be followed subsequently at lower levels of management.

Executive development and succession planning must be internalized as a mainstream, day-to-day management responsibility to facilitate the identification and development of management talent in a timely fashion. Essential to the success of HRM is the high-quality planning for management continuity at all levels, beginning at the top.

The cornerstones of the effort at the top include

- setting objectives
- assessing key manager performance

- determining promotability
- establishing individual career development plans
- determining backups for key management positions
- forecasting both short- and long-term management needs

Periodic reviews of these efforts are necessary to evaluate progress and to modify actions as necessary in this crucial area of activity. These reviews must become a fully integrated part of the total management process and must be closely coordinated with organizational strategic planning.

Step 7. Middle Management Focus

A. QWL Actions and Activities. Following the pattern of approach taken under Step 6A, the objective of this current step is to identify the factors on the job that affect the QWL of department managers and supervisory personnel. The aim is to assure *first* an optimum work climate for managers at the middle of the organization, since their needs and desires for a positive QWL at work are no less intense than those expressed by the individuals they supervise.

The sequence of steps, once again, is

- review, analysis, and evaluation of information gathered as a result of the initial self-assessment (Step 2)
- further translation of factors through additional application of interviewing and other feedback techniques (see Chapter 5)
- setting of QWL goals and objectives
- development of program strategies and actions that will move the organization toward the QWL goals and objectives, appropriately integrating plans and objectives at all levels of management
- establishing time frames and responsibilities for implementing, maintaining, and monitoring activities, projects, and other actions within the total QWL process

B. Management Resource Planning. HRM planning is primarily part of the organization's strategic planning process. The objective of the HRM planning process is to assure the right numbers and kinds of people, available at the right time, and with the right skills. It is a process that flows from the overall strategic and operational planning process, and it extends beyond the human resources function to involve managers at all levels.

An effective *management* resource planning process *at the middle* of the organization encompasses five elements.

1. Analyze organizational conditions directed toward answering the question: What is the total corporate setting? Input to this query has already been supplied in large measure by the self-assessment engaged in under Step 2. The totality of the corporate environment embodies the goals of the organization; the communication, coordinative, and control systems of the enterprise; policies and practices; wages; and jobs set by the organizational structure.

2. Forecast future management needs, responding to the question: What are our management needs? The aim here is to develop a "profile" of the ideal set of management personnel relative to long-range goals and institutional needs. The activity within this element must be accomplished systematically, since its purpose is to move the organization from random growth to planned growth with respect to management development.

3. Inventory existing managerial resources directed toward the questions: Where are we now? and What is the gap between what we need and what we have? The purpose here is not only to perform a quantitative audit, but, more important, to evaluate the qualitative dimensions of the current middle management work force in terms of education, proficiency, skills, and promotion potential.

4. Plan for development, seeking the answer to How do we get to where we need to be? Here we activate the movement from planning to action that explores all possible opportunities for mobilizing management personnel, including the possibility of moving managers across departmental lines into more responsible positions, or the redesign of job tasks that would encompass new, additional responsibilities for deserving, competent managers.

5. Review and follow up to respond to the question: How well is our plan working? An appropriate review mechanism should be in place to ensure effective continuity to the HRM planning process through the devotion of time and attention on the part of managers at all levels of organization.

C. Middle Management Training and Development. In concert with the management resource planning process, this step takes the organization to other facets of the overall management development effort covered earlier in Chapter 3.

Step 8. Nonmanagement Focus

A. QWL Actions and Activities. Tied in closely with the QWL processes engaged in earlier, at the management levels, Step 8 extends the effort as it goes "operational" with nonmanagement employees. Following the prescribed series of steps outlined under Step 7A, above, management needs to determine at this point the form of action and activity to be taken to improve the QWL of its employees. While the precise form of activity may vary in each organizational environment, the commitment, essentially, is

- communicating more openly
- broadening participation in decision making and problem solving affecting the conduct of work
- designing "better," more meaningful jobs
- encouraging a greater sense of responsibility at each level
- involving people at every level more in the management of their area of work activity

B. Career and Mobility Programming. The organization, under Steps 6B and 7B, has already moved toward getting a handle on HRM planning. Just as it is initially important that management resources be planned, so too is it essential that other employees be brought into a systematic plan of career and mobility programming.

Nonmanagement employees, with their supervisors, should engage in annual reviews of performance, career plans, and training and development needs. The ability of an organizational system to plan and activate career movement across divisional and departmental boundaries is one of the great values of HRM planning, for both the employee and the organization.

C. Employee Training and Development. The actions and activities of Step 8 follow closely the dimensions presented earlier under Step 7C, which are required to plan for training and development of the employee in order to improve job performance and potential for advancement. They are, essentially, establishing expectations, evaluating results, and developing the individual.

Within this phase of activity, there are various developmental strategies that can be employed beyond the structured and organized teaching/learning experience. Task team participation, job rotation or short-term transfers, committee membership, and continuing manager-employee relations are some of the methodologies available to the organization and its management. Training and development need to be tailored to the institution, whether they be linked to performance improvement or to the needs of employees as participants within the organizational environment of new QWL values and relationships.

The Beginnings of the HRM Process

Innovations in Managing Human Resources is the title of a study report prepared and distributed by The Conference Board in New York. In reading its content, it becomes apparent that traditional assumptions about work, workers, and the workplace are being questioned by increasing numbers of organizations. In the words of James T. Mills, President of the Board, "New management approaches are being tried and evaluated with the expectation of raising productivity, improving product quality, and giving workers a heightened sense of participation in their own work and a closer identification with the company's goals."[9]

The HRM process outlined on the previous pages is believed to be an innovative approach to change. It represents a system of strategies designed to enhance organizational effectiveness through the management of human resources, and its competitive advantages are to be found in the following principles that form its base.

- Human capital is considered to be the greatest asset of any organization.
- HRM is an evolutionary process, demanding a long-term concern and commitment. It excludes the idea of a "quick fix."
- There is only one beginning: total commitment at the top.
- It is imperative that the HRM process be developed and implemented within a systemic framework.
- The idea of "return-on-investment" needs to be an expectation in all HRM activities.
- The unique characteristics of any single institution must be reflected in the ultimate design of the HRM process.
- HRM is a process requiring the effective application of the basic elements of managing: planning, organizing, communicating, motivating, and controlling.
- The HRM process finds its success within the mainstream of management, at all levels of organization.
- HRM is a process that has its roots in strategies to enhance employee participation.
- The HRM process is best served by striking a proper balance between the quantitative and qualitative dimensions of work.
- A key ingredient of the HRM process is innovativeness, not only in the manner in which the overall plan of approach is fashioned, but also in the way all elements of the HRM process are developed.
- The personnel administration unit, as it has traditionally functioned, is no longer an adequate response to the needs of today's and tomorrow's workplace and work force.

RESPONDING TO THE FUTURE WORLD OF WORK

In their book, *Re-Inventing the Corporation,* John Naisbitt and Patricia Aburdene underscore the theme that the basic assumption of a re-invented company is that people—human capital—are its most important resource. What used to be one of the radicals' favorite slogans, "People before Profits," is finding its way into the boardroom and being transformed into a more businesslike but equally humanistic "People and Profits."[10]

From an economist's perspective, Theodore W. Schultz expresses the belief that our most important economic resource is that of "*human capital* which consists of the acquired abilities of people—their education, experience, skills, and health."[11] Indeed, investments in enhancing human capital bring to today's organization inexhaustible contributions to *quality* in the total sense. Unquestionably, there are no permanent limits to the growth of these qualitative achievements.

What is utterly disturbing, however, is that there is probably no other area of modern society that has had less truly professional, scientific, and organized attention than the critical issue of human resources. At the governmental level, securing human well-being receives less-than-adequate attentiveness. At the organizational level, serving people's need to achieve many of their most necessary purposes continues to remain seriously deficient.

The health care industry, like other fields of endeavor, is experiencing the revolutionary impact of changing expectations of people—expectations that mirror the move of America's labor force from living at work to working at living. And as we arrive closer to the twenty-first century, today's and tomorrow's workers will tend to become increasingly attuned to the idea of leading "whole lives," not just a job-consumed existence, and to the idea of useful employment as a "whole person"—the mind as well as the body.

Rensis Likert, in his book, *The Human Organization,* states that "of all the tasks of management, managing the human component is the central and most important task, because all else depends upon how well it is done."[12] The wisdom of this proposition has been captured by many of the Fortune 500 companies that have led the way to dramatic changes in relationships between management and workers by reexamining and modifying human resource policies, strategies, and practices, along with broadening responsibilities of the human resources function; yet evidence remains that, in most organizations today, both health and nonhealth, human resources are underutilized and underemployed. This is due, in the main, to the fact that little or nothing has been done within these contemporary corporate environments to extend innovatively beyond the more traditional personnel administrative activities.

What is perceived as an organizational imperative of the highest order to which boards, administrations, and human resource executives need to address with a sense of urgency is that of "reinventing" the corporate function of HRM so that it will possess the capacity to be fittingly responsive to the future world of work.

By the mid-nineties, a more appropriate designation of the human resources unit might be *department of human affairs,* the reinvention of which will need to bring added dimensions of activity created and designed to advance the quality of people's life at work, the quality of the work they do, their personal demeanor, and any other quantitative or qualitative factors affecting the human affairs of the enterprise. A projective view of some of the areas of focus that need to be introduced within the province of the function include:

- *Human resource planning.* The department of human affairs must be in the business of establishing workable planning systems that will take their rightful place in general corporate planning. Human affairs executives need to be full-fledged participants in planning corporate goals, and be expert in effectively integrating qualitative and quantitative approaches to human resource planning. Specific attention will need to be given to the *management of management* "to ensure a management succession pipeline filled with well-trained, strongly motivated, high-potential individuals to take on the more demanding and more complex problems and positions of the future."[13]

- *Human resource administration.* Policies and practices in the basic areas of human resource administration will need to move away from a traditional stance toward innovation: tailor-made human resource policies; progressive recruitment, selection, and retention programming; and flexible benefits and compensation plans.

- *Quality improvement.* In the future, the department of human affairs will need to have the capacity to carry into effect systemwide interventions aimed at advancing employees' commitment to work and to the organization. Working closely with the organization's quality assurance executive, the director of human affairs must assume a central role in improving the quality of human performance as he or she assists management to build the employees' will to work at superior levels.

- *Leadership development.* The department of human affairs needs to be the center for creating the integrative and sequential elements of a development process designed to bring knowledge, skills, personal characteristics, values, and beliefs into close relationship with human accomplishments in a highly effective and efficient manner.

- *Productivity enhancement.* Establishing and promoting the essentiality of quality in the idea of productivity need to be key tasks of the human affairs department as it directs the activities of the management engineer and designs "a systems approach to productivity enhancement in which all members of the organization are involved in a *partnership* in productivity."[14]

- *Human capital investment.* The focus of tomorrow's human affairs function needs to move from activity to *results* measured in both their qualitative and quantitative dimensions. This new direction is applicable to both process and program levels.

  At the *process* level, a goal of the function is to demonstrate and promote the measurement of the human dimensions of the organization that will cause significant changes in the generally accepted concepts of how a health care organization totally, or a department as a single component of the enterprise, should be managed to be most successful financially.

  At the *program* level, a framework is required for assessing the benefits of human resource programs and for evaluating the likelihood of achieving them, which, in turn, will enable management to allocate resources to those programs that indicate significant outcomes in human and financial performance.

- *Research and development.* Engagement in human resource research needs to be a part of the operational mode of the human affairs department. Areas of future research activity might include organizational research, training and development investigation and evaluation, management appraisal, managerial and technical obsolescence, and turnover—all in the interest of better preparing the organization and its human resources to take on the emerging challenges in the future world of work.

Surely, this is an ambitious agenda for the future, yet if it does not do what is needed, "the HR [human resources] function will probably turn into a dinosaur," says Stephen Drotter, who closes his chapter, "The Human Resources Function," with these thoughts:

> No company should have HR functions that are dinosaurs, for if it does the business is likely to become extinct. The future world of work demands a much more enlightened attitude, philosophy, and role from HR so its contribution can become more valuable. The human resources issues in this volatile business climate may well be the most significant of all business challenges. If HR doesn't contribute it should be abolished. Line managers and employees have a right and a need to expect and get more. If the line is willing to make some changes in the way it approaches its work; and if HR gets its function to perform effectively, the future won't be easy, but it could be much more productive.[15]

NOTES

1. *U.S. News & World Report,* Sept. 3, 1979, p. 35.
2. *Business Week,* May 11, 1981, p. 85.
3. Samual M. Ehrenhalt, "Economic Scene," *New York Times,* Aug. 15, 1985, p. 23.

4. Louis Harris, *Inside America* (New York: Vintage Books, 1987), p. 51.

5. *Hospitals,* May 1, 1982, p. 39.

6. *U.S. News & World Report,* Sept. 7, 1987, p. 42.

7. Addison C. Bennett, "There's More to It than People Shuffling," *Hospitals,* Dec. 1, 1978, p. 95.

8. George Vojta, "Human Resources in the Large Corporation," in *Executive Talent,* ed. Eli Ginzberg (New York: John Wiley & Sons., Inc., 1988), p. 30.

9. Harriet Gorlin and Lawrence Schein, *Innovations in Managing Human Resources* (New York: Conference Board, 1984), p. v.

10. John Naisbitt and Patricia Aburdene, *Re-Inventing the Corporation* (New York: Warner Books, 1985), p. 11.

11. Theodore W. Schultz, *Investing in People: The Economics of Population Quality* (Berkeley, University of California Press, 1981), p. 1.

12. Rensis Likert, *The Human Organization* (New York: McGraw-Hill Book Co., 1967), p. 1.

13. Addison C. Bennett, *Improving Management Performance in Health Care Institutions* (Chicago: American Hospital Association, 1978), p. 123.

14. Addison C. Bennett, *Productivity and the Quality of Work Life in Hospitals* (Chicago: American Hospital Association, 1985), p. viii.

15. Stephen Drotter, "The Human Resources Function," in *Executive Talent,* ed. Eli Ginzberg (New York: John Wiley & Sons, Inc., 1988), p. 76.

Chapter 8

Methods As a Measure
of Quality

Success in your work, the finding of a better method, the better understanding that
insures the better performing, is hat and coat, is food and wine, is fire and horse
and health and holiday. At least, I find that any success in my work has the effect
on my spirits of all these.

—Ralph Waldo Emerson

Here we espouse the credo: Think Small. Our statement of belief is that
well-established health care organizations, often caught in their own
managerial bureaucracy and smugness, can readily settle into an institutional
complacency that supports a custodial role over what is already in place, rather
than an innovative stance that moves them on to something new. We are
subscribing to the notion of getting back to basics; however, the thought is
to move the basics forward, centered in the belief that in today's competitive
world, administrations of health care organizations need to go beyond the
popular idea of "big is better" and find beauty in smallness.

The hierarchical characteristics of the modern organization tend to promote the idea of "thinking big" at the highest point of the organization. It
is quite acceptable that the concept of "thinking small" gains prominence
as we descend to the lower levels of the institution, not "small" in the sense
of narrowness of thinking, "but 'small' in the sense of thinking like a small
entrepreneurial business."[1] That concept means delegating responsibility for
change to those who are closest to the service-link with patients. It means
unshackling the creative talent of middle managers, supervisors, and employees
to seek out opportunities for newness and novelty. Thinking small also means
encouraging the initiative of people at lower levels to advance effectiveness
and efficiency on an operational scale.

Thinking small is an old idea—a bold idea—that does not get the attention it deserves, yet it is an imperative for health care organizations if they
are to be successful and 'big' in meeting patient requirements with products
and services of superior quality.

PERFORMANCE AS THE LARGER PURPOSE

Can smallness solve the problem of bigness? For one to be convinced that smallness is not only beautiful but remarkably sensible, two essentials need to be evident. The first essential is that the components in which smallness occurs be explicitly interrelated and interactive with a larger purpose, thus forming a collective entity or a system of thought and action. The second essential is that the strategies and programs for smallness be designed to serve a designated bigger intent.

The unifying concept of *performance* is viewed as the larger purpose—the bigger intent. It is an idea that already holds a central place of permanency within the organization and represents a most familiar and acceptable notion for employees at all levels.

When viewed within the context of meeting human needs, the concept of performance is not merely doing the right things, but doing things right for the sake of the value, merits, and satisfaction of work itself. Performance is not just how much we do and how we do it, it is how well we do it. Performance, in this context, is not only the exercise of skill and intelligence, it is featured by emergent, powerful expression of energy, enthusiasm, concerns, and creativity of the individual. The presence or absence, in some degree, of quality of individual performance and, cumulatively, organizational performance, characterizes every service and every product the corporate entity provides.

With an acceptance of the principle that "how we perform as individuals will determine how we perform as an organization," initial attention needs to be given to the effectiveness of management at all levels of the enterprise, for the all-important factor underlying the survival and viability of an organization is performance, the major task of today's manager. The organization that will change in terms of advances and improvements that enable it to be of service in new and better ways will be the one whose managers—the new breed—have mastered the skills and techniques of gaining responsibility from people for meaningful contributions and results and who are capable of earning the commitment of people not merely to ordinary performance but to *extraordinary* performance.

The individual who does the most for performance—and is the most gratified—is the one who is not satisfied with things as they are and who finds feelings of satisfaction in trying to improve them. Such an individual is epitomized by the professional athlete on the playing field, the conductor as he stands before his symphonic assemblage, the principal dancer in a corps de ballet, the carpenter who keeps his saw in good order, the physician and the nurse engaged in a surgical procedure. Although their skills and talents may go in many directions, their determination to keep alive the growth of quality in work performance *is not* a random process. These artists, these craftsmen, always demand a lot of themselves and of others.

In reaching for the highest standard of individual performance, the manner in which the organization itself impacts on individual behavior at work, too, cannot be exercised in random fashion. The process must be planned and managed for the best results; only then will the organization be resourceful in the performance of its people; only then will the organization find growth through its investment in the performance "property" inside the heads and hearts of each individual. This is an investment that will bring forth the following kinds of returnable rewards for the organization and its people:

- inquisitive organization
- leading edge
- translation of a philosophy
- higher fulfillment of values
- better use of resources
- new grasp of the nature of performance itself
- rediscovery of the thrill of refining performance
- exceptional and extraordinary achievements
- source of new ideas, new insights, new challenges, new inspirations
- action on the possible, while awaiting perfection
- more effective management at all levels
- discovery of yet unused attributes and strengths
- renewal of the dedication of people to their work
- expansion of peoples' horizons to things they never dreamed that they could do
- greater return-on-investment in people
- problem-solving environment
- focus on measurement and control
- payoff in improved operating results and greater efficiencies; a solid bottom line
- capitalization on opportunities

IT HAPPENS AT THE MIDDLE

The department managers and supervisors at the middle of the organization occupy the leading position in the movement of cost effectiveness and productivity enhancement as these two elements come into a mutual relationship with quality improvement and as they contribute concomitantly to the overall progress of human performance.

The beginnings of this movement rest with executives at the top, who need to provide the role model for the managerial vanguards of effectiveness and efficiency functioning at the middle of the organization. Administration also needs to establish and communicate specific expectations of middle managers and supervisors in these areas of responsibility and to accompany these managerial obligations with suitable accountability and rewards. Expectations should include:

1. perceiving and pursuing improvements in the way things are being done, systemically and perseveringly
2. sustaining a cost/productivity/quality consciousness manifested by diligent assessment and goal setting
3. advancing problem-solving skills and applications of analytical tools and techniques in attacking operational problems
4. maintaining a sensibility to the value of measurement, keeping in fitting balance its qualitative and quantitative dimensions
5. progressing toward developing a work environment conducive to innovative change in which all members of the functional unit can be active contributors to the improvement effort

As we discuss each of these five expectations of managers at the middle, it becomes readily obvious that the delicate art of asking questions is key to getting at the heart of the cost/productivity/quality matter.

1. Perceiving and Pursuing Improvement

Performance is a complex idea, and understanding it is far from simple. It is not just that performance, both individual and organizational, is composed of many elements; the interaction of these elements produces such an unbelievable complexity of interlocked relationships that our familiar ideas of cause and effect are completely overwhelmed. More than that, our common habit of looking at the "bits and pieces" of work and its outcomes often prevents us from looking closely enough at the whole and at the relationships of the parts that make up the whole. Thus, the importance of a *systems perspective* on the part of the managers is highlighted.

A system, in essence, is an array of components that work together for the overall objectives of the whole. A system is

- a unitary whole, with some degree of continuity and boundary
- in most instances, complex
- more than just the simple sum of its parts

- probabilistic in nature
- hierarchical in structure
- controlled by dynamic relations
- made up of a complicated structure of feedback loops
- cunning in its ability to mislead
- sensitive to the processes of learning, development, and evaluation
- totally affected if but "one component is defective, not capable of interacting correctly with the others, not fulfilling its particular function"[2]

To make strikingly important advances in the complex sphere of performance, there is the need to apply a *systems* view—to cause managers to think in different dimensions. For example, the innovative manager can capture the benefits of certain extensions of insight and accomplishment, since systems thinking

- makes sense of complexity and variety through a total, not fragmentary, vision
- leads to rational designs and decisions
- defines the boundaries
- causes one to see the organization in richer terms
- gives insight into the naiveness of our customary concept of control
- translates the unfamiliar into the familiar, as well as the familiar into the unfamiliar
- constantly makes one ask whether or not a "problem" is being specified adequately and whether it is being approached from the right level or viewpoint
- permits a way of asking whether a big change is called for
- helps to tell whether a problem must be taken up right now or may be deferred until other problems have been solved
- offers a sure way to gain significant performance improvements

Virtually all systems in today's world of work are truly complex, consisting of many types of specialized parts or subsystems. Even these subsystems, in turn, may embrace distinguishable components, or subsubsystems.

Beginning with the total organization as a system, it is axiomatic that managers at all levels need to understand not only the organization's role in the health care system, but also the social, political, economic, and educational forces that affect the operation of the health care system. The requirement of viewing the organization as a part of a larger system is essential to developing a posture for positive adaptation based on an understanding of priorities and a capability not only to do things right at any time, but to do the right things at the right time—all in the interest of advancing quality.

Add to the above requirement a second level of consideration: that of viewing the organization itself as a system in which all of its components must interact and interrelate in order to direct effectively the institutional resources to the treatment of the patient. A glaring error on the part of all too many managers today is in viewing the organization not as a system with interacting components, but as an organization comprising separate entities acting independently.

The objectives of this systems requirement are as follows: to promote internal integration and coordination of effort toward organizational goals and purposes; to bring a greater degree of articulation and compatibility between and among the many functional and service components of the institution; and to achieve a high level of wholeness in the organizational system.[3] The importance of these objectives becomes increasingly obvious as we become aware of the fact that as much as fifty percent of quality and other related issues (cost and productivity) are associated with *inter*departmental work flow.

A sensible way for the manager to view his or her functional unit as a subsystem of the organization is displayed as a simple input/output system model in Figure 8-1. The model offers a visual image of the general subsystem with which any operational manager works. It also provides a reference point that makes visible the relationship of each essential element to the others in a single, functional pattern, thus ensuring the manager's consideration of all elements of the functional system as he or she engages in efforts to achieve meaningful change. In Exhibit 8-1 are listings of some of the improvement opportunities under each systems element that need to be looked at in the search for better ways of doing work.

Viewing Performance As a System

Performance is viewed as the all-important concept underlying the survival and viability of an organization in a competitive environment. In whatever manner quality is defined, today's health care organization is clearly ready for more of it, and that quality can come only through the craftsmanship and artistry of people in their pursuit of excellence in performance and in their motivation to provide "the best that can possibly be."

The history of ordinary humans in the environment of the work place abounds with examples of ways in which natural limits of performance have been surpassed by unnatural means resulting from the ingenuity, talents, determination, and energies of the individual. The individuals who constitute the membership of an institutional family are, as a whole, the most important resource we have as we move them forward toward the common purpose of rendering the highest quality product or service.

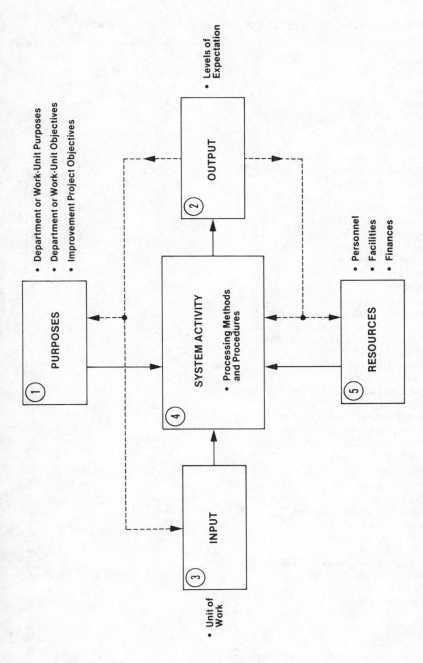

Figure 8-1 Input/Output System Model *Source:* Reprinted by permission from *Hospitals,* Volume 61, No. 18, September 20, 1987, copyright, 1987, American Hospital Publishing, Inc.

Exhibit 8-1 Areas Offering Improvement Opportunities within Operational Units

1. *PURPOSES*
   mission
   goals/objectives
   policies, practices
   rules, regulations

2. *OUTPUT*
   performance standards
   product and service standards
   methodology for measuring output
   monitoring and reporting
   error level
   quality improvement
   delays in completed work
   methods of delivery
   nature of complaints
   lost or delayed charges
   record keeping

3. *INPUT*
   source of incoming work
   changes in "balance" among users
   methods of receiving work
   completeness and accuracy of work
   requests and workload records
   predictability and smoothness of arriving work
   workload changes
   workload patterns and range of variations
   response to overload
   work assignment and control mechanisms
   extent of *stats,* special requests
   future work analyses and projections

4. *SYSTEM ACTIVITY*
   distribution of work
   work processing flow
   backlog methods
   handling of special situations
   chronic trouble spots
   bottlenecks and delays
   sequence of work activity
   make-ready and put-away problems
   work design and work methods
   matching skills to work
   work measurement
   relationship of charges to cost of processing

5. *RESOURCES*
   PERSONNEL
        organizational structure, arrangements, relationships

Exhibit 8-1 continued

availability of needed skills
recruitment and selection
orientation and job instruction
turnover and absenteeism
discipine problems
job descriptions
performance evaluation
training and development
employee suggestions
quality of work life
communication

FACILITIES
physical context of work
productive use of work area
productive use of machines and equipment
quantitative and qualitative levels in materials usage
use of external resources

FINANCE
budgeting process
cost control and reduction
operating cost changes
fixed costs versus variable costs
relationship of amount spent for regular personnel salaries versus
    expense of overtime, sick pay, part-time wages
unit cost analysis
cost of major types of work or procedures
productivity of department or work unit
kinds and quality of needed information
future-directed approaches to cost effectiveness

What is believed central to advancing our total human resources' pursuit of excellence in performance is to ensure that our managers capture the richness of the systems approach to gaining the highest possible levels of performance in all of their endeavors. This approach requires a comprehensive view that will help managers to understand the array of complexities embedded in the overriding idea of performance. Figure 8-2 displays such a design. Simply presented, it embraces the various aspects of performance broken down into manageable components and tied together in an organized, rational scheme. Within an innovative environment, quality is viewed as the core element of this unity of arrangement, impacting and interrelating with the other elements of the system—performance, cost effectiveness, and productivity—and causing them to advance toward their objectives.

To begin with, when we give consideration to the idea of organizational performance, a number of factors come to mind in addition to quality: cost,

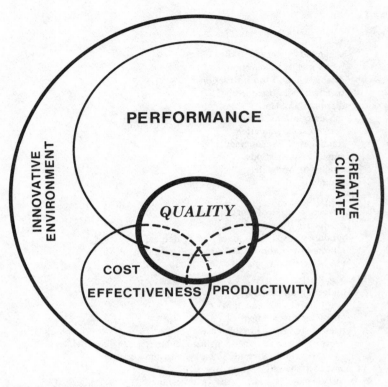

Figure 8-2 Performance As a System

competition, standards, productivity, measurement, values, and vitality. When we focus on individual performance, our attention centers on the following factors.

- *Ability:* the quality of being able to perform a task or set of tasks that find their source in the knowledge, skill, potential, and other characteristics of the individual
- *Motivation:* the desire to perform a job well, which relates to attitudes, feelings, needs, values, goals, motives, behavior, incentives, and job satisfaction
- *Organizational determinants of ability:* the selection and placement, orientation, training and development, instrumentation, information, and physical context of work
- *Organizational determinants of motivation:* the motivational and organizational variables that come into play as performance determinants. All together, the full variety of these variables goes to make

up the quality of human experiences in the workplace—or, the quality of life at work.

Cost Effectiveness. Within the context of the system, cost effectiveness is seen as a contributing force in the movement toward higher levels of human performance. Unfortunately, because economy and performance often appear to be contradictory when examined with a negative attitude of thought, all too frequently the choice comes down to settling for one or the other. In the literature we find many variations on the recurring theme, "Do costs come first—or does quality come first?" We need to replace the idea of "either/or" with the more positive notion of having lower costs and higher quality come together.

This concomitance is more common than one might suspect. A classic example was documented in a story in the *Wall Street Journal:* the Hewlett-Packard Company used a bold approach to convince its people that a quality problem existed and to engage the entire organization in solving it. Its starting place was with a startling goal—one that would get attention—a tenfold reduction in the failure rates of its products during the eighties. Hewlett-Packard's ten-year goal is within grasp, and its people learned not only that much higher quality was attainable but that costs actually could be driven down because of productivity gains associated with doing things right the first time.[4]

In a converse way, many organizations have experienced the positive impact of cost effectiveness and productivity improvement on quality. They have implemented over the years the concept of work simplification as an effective means of motivating employees in the common task of developing and carrying out work improvements. When the goal of "work smarter, not harder" is pursued and success is achieved, the value of the credo Think Small is once again evident.

Productivity. Productivity is a significant constituent of cost effectiveness and a strong contributor to performance improvement. While the cost effectiveness component is directly tied to finance (quantitative), productivity has its roots in the attitudes and behavior of people (qualitative)—in other words, the will to work.[5]

The health care industry gives intermittent attention to productivity. When it is the topic of discussion, it is frequently addressed at a fairly shallow level. Fundamentally, the fault lies in the traditional definition of productivity in terms of efficiencies alone, of meeting narrow technical and monetary criteria. It also lies in the looseness, distortion, and oversimplification that creep into discussions of the subject.

The broadening of our views of productivity to include the query "Productivity for what; for whom?" is demanded by a central characteristic of any work environment: a concern for people. Within this humanistic context, more than anything, productivity is an attitude of mind capable of shattering the scientific knowledge, the logical translations, and the empirical positivism of the high priests of efficiency. While it is humanly imperfect, the proper fitting of technology with the notion of attitudes and values provides the best chance for boosting productivity and for being human at the same time.

In this component of the performance system, a process of redefinition takes place. Within its context, productivity of our human resources is the principal focus, since we recognize that it is not normally the technology that is at fault; rather the real problem most often is traceable directly to people. Thus, as we extend the meaning of quality to embrace quality of work itself, quality of work life, and quality of human conduct, we bring into being an inexorable coupling of quality and productivity.

2. Sustaining a Cost/Productivity/Quality Consciousness

Assessment is a powerful information tool for effective, innovative managers committed to the task of taking their people to where they have not been, in the interest of newness and improvements. It is a tool that rests on the skill of asking the right questions at the right time, at the right place, and of the right people. Add to this skill the enthusiasm of the manager in taking the initiative in posing questions, seeing the importance of asking the right questions, and giving the questions the priority they deserve.[6]

In line with the systemic direction of the previous expectation, there are four hierarchical levels of assessment in which managers need to engage.

- external assessment
- organizational assessment
- functional assessment
- individual assessment

In covering each of these levels, the intent is not to offer an all-inclusive framework of inquiry within which managers should operate. Rather, it is to present a general pattern of thinking and querying that will provide guidance to managers in formulating their own inventory of questions suitable to their knowledge and responsibility and to the situations and circumstances present within their existing environments.

External Assessment

At the external level of assessment, managers not only need to possess a sensitivity to the external forces affecting the total organization, they also need to be conscious of happenings in the outside world that may have a specific bearing on their operational activities. With an eye on the outside world, the attention of the managers should focus on economic, demographic, social, political, and technical areas.

Within the *social* area, for example, managers should ask these kinds of questions relating to human resources.

- Are there any changes in value systems that might be expected in the period ahead?
- What new skills will be needed in managing change and resolving people conflicts?
- In what ways will anticipated legislative decisions affect our personnel practices?
- What new professions will be on the health care scene as a result of new technology?
- Are serious shortages in certain areas of specialization being forecast?
- Will union-organizing efforts tend to increase and be more successful in the future?
- In what ways will management skills become more essential in contract environments?
- What are the chances that increased financial pressures will be a reality in the near future, and what effect would they have on the human resources of the organization?
- Are there to be changes in the industry that will affect education, retraining, and careers?

Organizational Assessment

There are several divisions of questioning that should be embraced by organizational assessment, including

- philosophy, mission, goals, objectives
- programs, product, services
- organizational structure, arrangements, relationships
- communication and coordination
- quality improvement
- management process and practices
- human resource management
- culture, climate, environment
- policies, methods, procedures
- management information systems

- performance management
- financial administration
- materials management
- staffing methodologies and resource utilization
- reports and controls
- training and education
- innovation and change[7]

Add to these categories of inquiry other organizational processes that specifically relate to the work unit for which the questioning manager holds managerial responsibility. Using the above classifications as the assessment's structural form, let us consider a few selected questions that would appear to be proper under the category *communication and coordination.*

- Does the organization hold to the belief that obtaining information is an employee's right rather than a privilege?
- Are organizational communication channels open and free of "noise"?
- Are organizational policies, rules, and regulations clearly and adequately communicated?
- Is information throughout the organization accessible for current decision making?
- Does information flow freely up, down, and across the organization?
- Is goal sharing between and among functional areas characteristic of the organization?
- Are managers provided with the information they need to fulfill their responsibilities?
- Do managers in different operational areas have ample opportunity to interact and discuss common problems? Do they, in fact, do so effectively?

Functional Assessment

Quality levels of human performance are often less than what they could be or should be because of the simple fact that department directors and supervisory managers at the middle of the organization do not make time for the essential task of assessing, analyzing, evaluating, and improving the smallness of the units of daily work—the accumulative elements of single-job activities that relentlessly and invisibly gnaw away at the very fabric of operational effectiveness and efficiency. Managers at the middle also fail to turn their attention to the undisturbed problems lurking in the forgotten areas that lie between departments and work units, where performance, cost effectiveness, productivity, quality improvement, and innovative opportunities remain plentiful but unexplored.

The departmental or functional assessment instrument should be structured along the lines of the elements of the input/output model (Figure 8-1), which contains the general types of questions considered appropriate for challenging the various areas offering improvement opportunities within the operational units (Exhibit 8-1). Naturally, questions need to be designed to address the particular uniqueness of the single department, primarily in terms of the nature of the work performed.

Individual Assessment

At the individual level of inquiry, the objective is to probe the opportunities for advancing the performance effectiveness of oneself as a manager, as well as the performance improvement of one's subordinates. It would seem reasonable to recommend the basic elements of the management process, namely, planning, organizing, communicating, motivating, and controlling, as the structural divisions of inquiry within the format of the individual assessment. Under *motivating,* for example, it is believed that these kinds of questions ought to be asked.

Motivating (for the Manager)

- Do I find my management job to be challenging?
- Do I consider my work to be meaningful?
- Am I enthusiastic about the kind of work I do?
- Am I successful in establishing a climate of trust and confidence?
- Do I apply personnel policies fairly and equitably?
- Do I praise my people openly and frequently for doing good work?
- Do I utilize effectively participative management techniques and approaches?
- Are my own levels of competence in the fundamental areas of managerial performance such that they establish a good model for my employees to follow?
- Do I have in place a personal development plan?

Motivating (for the Employee)

- Are all of the employees reporting to me performing at levels of expectation?
- Does each of my employees exhibit a team attitude?
- Do employees respond in positive ways to growth opportunities?

- Are employees enthusiastic about their involvement in participative management efforts?
- Are there adequate indications that all employees have a high morale level and a willingness to perform?
- Do all employees evidence quality in their performance and conduct?
- Has there been an absence of employee grievances and complaints over the past 12 months?
- Are all departmental employees adequately trained for the jobs they perform?

The total act of assessment, of course, goes beyond the single phase of appraisal, since the final payoff of engaging in evaluation is acting on what has been discovered. This concluding idea encompasses

- defining the problem situation
- setting goals that are measurable, future-directed, specific in their intent, fully documented, appropriate and timely, and results-oriented
- assembling and checking all of the facts surrounding the conditions and circumstances being questioned—all within a reasonable timetable
- generating alternative ideas while maintaining a systems perspective in providing direction to the process
- evaluating the alternatives to arrive at identifying the best idea
- implementing the new idea, based on a plan for carrying it out effectively and efficiently
- assessing the new idea on a continuing basis to ensure that it has lasting value, then moving on to considering further possible improvements

3. Advancing Individual Problem-Solving Skills

"What distinguishes the successes from the failures is a culture of innovation that encourages workers and managers to question all assumptions and to tinker constantly with every piece of the business. . . ."[8] Most health care organizations have barely begun to "tinker" with their old ways of doing things, since the number of managers who have done a major job of changing the ways in which their people do their work is relatively small. Many managers at the operational level fail to get back to basics in terms of analyzing and improving work methods and procedures that tend to become institutionalized, resulting in overmanning, bloated cycle times and *poor quality*.

Technology alone is not the answer to reducing time, waste, and costs of the multitude of labor-intensive methods and procedures characteristic of health care organizations. What needs to be employed on a much broader scale is the human effort required to rout out all that is ineffective and inefficient in work itself, thus reducing each job activity to its lowest terms. As Henry David Thoreau once expressed it, "Simplify, simplify."[9] Such an effort demands a state of mind and involvement on the part of managers at all levels: a willingness to change not just the way their machines operate, but the way their people do their jobs, and to accomplish this change through their own direct and continued analysis, evaluation, and improvement of current work methods and procedures.

If a manager exclaims optimistically that "all is going well," there is a high probability that he or she is skipping over fundamental ideas for cost reduction, productivity, or quality improvement that could be captured through an organized process of work improvement. In business and industry, the name given to this approach to working "smarter, not harder" is *work simplification,* which holds to the proposition that the person doing the job knows far better than anyone else the best way of doing that job and therefore is the one person best fitted to improve it.

All of this says, "we, the human resource, are the answer to the problems we have created."[10] Management at the middle holds a high stake in the continuing solution of organizational and operational problems that are people-connected and that impact, in some direct or indirect way, on the ultimate quality level of services provided.

To fulfill a responsible role in this area of improvement activity, managers need to possess the capacity to apply certain basic tools and techniques of methods and procedural analyses, including the use of the following techniques.

Organizational Charting

Organizational charting is a simple technique designed to display graphically the existing structure of organization. Not only does it enable the manager to visualize easily the relative levels of people and functions within his or her department or work unit, it also provides a clear picture of their true relationships. The value of this type of charting is that it provides a broad, overall view of the functional area so that the presence of any deficiencies in its structure, arrangements, or relationships can be recognized easily and quickly for purposes of moving on to improvement.

Work Distribution Charting

Work distribution charting can lend orderliness and direction to fact finding. It is a useful tool for the manager to use in assembling information about the work of an entire organizational unit such as a department or a small-sized functional area.

The information recorded on the work distribution chart is gathered through the use of "task lists" and an "activity list." The task lists, prepared by the unit supervisor and each employee, are intended to inventory the duties actually performed by each employee, along with the estimated number of hours spent per week on each duty. The activity list, prepared by the unit manager, is used to record the major activities or functions that are or should be performed to fulfill the objectives of the department or work unit. When the activity list is completed, it should be possible to classify each task shown on the individual task lists under one of the activities indicated on the manager's activity list.

With the completion of both the task lists and the activity list, the manager possesses all of the essential information required for a work distribution study. These data then need to be assembled in such a way that they may be analyzed conveniently. This is accomplished by transferring the information found on the activity list and the several task lists onto a work distribution chart. If the chart is properly prepared, the manager can recognize quickly the possibilities for improvement. For example, the work distribution chart

- displays what activities take the most time
- points out the unnecessary work that is being performed
- indicates whether or not skills are used properly and whether or not any employees are doing too many unrelated tasks
- shows whether or not work in the unit is distributed evenly or spread too thinly throughout the functional unit

All in all, the work distribution technique is a valuable tool, yet it continues to be underutilized. It is a tool that managers at the middle need to put to good use at reasonable intervals of time. When deficiencies are found, particularly when it is discovered that an activity is requiring an excessive amount of time, the application of the charting tools that follow will prove helpful.

Flow Process Charting. Flow process charting is a comparatively easy tool to use and is an excellent technique for determining how the step-by-step details of a job are *actually* performed. It provides a simple means of recording a series of events that take place from the start to the completion of a particular process or work activity from the view of one "subject"—a person, material, or paper form. Its value is that it is prepared as the activity or process *is observed,* thereby avoiding wrong assumptions based on memory or recollection.

The flow process chart prepared by Evelyn Cochran, Director of Maternal Child Health and Surgical Services, Inter-Community Medical Center, Covina, California, (Exhibits 8-2 and 8-3) show the benefits of the idea

Exhibit 8-2 Flow Process Chart

PAGE *1* OF *1*

SUMMARY						
	PRESENT		PROPOSED		DIFFERENCE	
	NO.	TIME	NO.	TIME	NO.	TIME
○ OPERATIONS	4					
⇨ TRANSPORTATIONS	6	17				
□ INSPECTIONS	1	MINS				
D DELAYS	5					
▽ STORAGES	0					
DISTANCE TRAVELLED	720 FT.		FT.		FT.	

JOB *TRANSPORTING OUT PATIENTS FOR SURGERY*

☒ MAN OR ☐ MATERIAL *OR TRANSPORTER*
CHART BEGINS *IN O.R.*
CHART ENDS *IN O.R.*
CHARTED BY *EVELYN COCHRAN* DATE *5/6/88*

#	DETAILS OF (PRESENT) METHOD	OPERATION / TRANSPORT / INSPECTION / DELAY / STORAGE	DISTANCE IN FEET	QUANTITY	TIME	WHAT? WHERE? WHEN? WHO? HOW?	NOTES	ELIMINATE / COMBINE / SEQUE. / PLACE / PERSON / IMPROVE
1	TRANSPORTER WITH GURNEY LEAVES O.R. – 1ST FLOOR	Q⇨□D▽					12 PATIENTS PER DAY	
2	TO ELEVATOR	O⇨□D▽						
3	WAIT FOR ELEVATOR	O⇨□D▽						
4	RIDE ELEVATOR TO 2ND FLOOR	O⇨□D▽						
5	GURNEY TO STATION 6	O⇨□D▽	360					
6	LOAD PATIENT ON GURNEY	Q⇨□D▽						
7	WAIT FOR RN CHECK-OUT	O⇨□D▽						
8	CHECK PATIENT	O⇨□D▽					RN/TRANSPORTER	
9	TRANSPORT DOWN HALL	O⇨□D▽						
10	WAIT TO CLEAR OBSTRUCTION	O⇨□D▽					CART IN HALL	
11	WAIT AT ELEVATOR	O⇨□D▽						
12	RIDE ELEVATOR TO 1ST FLOOR	O⇨□D▽						
13	TRANSPORT DOWN HALL	O⇨□D▽						
14	WAIT FOR CLEARANCE	O⇨□D▽					PEOPLE IN HALL	
15	COMMUNICATE W/FAMILY	O⇨□D▽						
16	ARRIVE AT OR	O⇨□D▽	360	17 MINUTES				
17		O⇨□D▽						
18		O⇨□D▽						
19		O⇨□D▽						
20		O⇨□D▽						
21		O⇨□D▽						
22		O⇨□D▽						

Source: Courtesy of Inter-Community Medical Center, Covina, California.

of locating all outpatient surgeries in one centralized area, designated the Ambulatory Care Center (ACC) and staffed as a separate unit. Formerly, outpatient surgeries were scattered on multiple floors as beds were available. The improvement has resulted in better utilization of beds and staff, accompanied by a reduction in cost and time. A simple, singular idea like

Exhibit 8-3 Flow Process Chart

	PAGE _1_ OF _1_
	JOB _TRANSPORTING OUTPATIENTS FOR SURGERY_

SUMMARY

	PRESENT		PROPOSED		DIFFERENCE	
	NO.	TIME	NO.	TIME	NO.	TIME
○ OPERATIONS	4		5		+1	
⇨ TRANSPORTATIONS	6	17	3	6	-3	11
□ INSPECTIONS	1	MINS	1	MINS	0	MINS
D DELAYS	5		2		-3	
▽ STORAGES	0		0		0	
DISTANCE TRAVELLED	720 FT.		320 FT.		400 FT.	

☒ MAN OR ☐ MATERIAL _OR TRANSPORTER_
CHART BEGINS _IN O.R._
CHART ENDS _IN O.R._
CHARTED BY _EVELYN COCHRAN_ DATE _5/6/88_

	DETAILS OF (PRESENT / PROPOSED) METHOD	OPERATION / TRANSPORT / INSPECTION / DELAY / STORAGE	DISTANCE IN FEET	QUANTITY	TIME	WHAT? WHERE? WHEN? WHO? HOW?	NOTES	ELIMINATE / COMBINE / SEQUENCE / PLACE / PERSON / IMPROVE
1	TRANSPORTER WITH GURNEY LEAVES O.R. - 1ST FLOOR	○⇨□D▽				12 PATIENTS PER DAY	
2	TO ACC	○⇨□D▽	160				
3	TO DESK	○⇨□D▽					
4	WAIT FOR R.N.	○⇨□D▽					
5	CHECK PATIENT	○⇨□D▽				RN/TRANSPORTER	
6	COVER PATIENT	○⇨□D▽					
7	LOAD PATIENT ON GURNEY	○⇨□D▽					
8	WAIT TO CLEAR OBSTRUCTION	○⇨□D▽				MOVE BED	
9	LEAVE ROOM WITH PATIENT	○⇨□D▽					
10	COMMUNICATE W/FAMILY	○⇨□D▽					
11	ARRIVE AT O.R.	○⇨□D▽	160		6 MINUTES		
12		○⇨□D▽					
13		○⇨□D▽					
14		○⇨□D▽					
15		○⇨□D▽					
16		○⇨□D▽					
17		○⇨□D▽					
18		○⇨□D▽					
19		○⇨□D▽					
20		○⇨□D▽					
21		○⇨□D▽					
22		○⇨□D▽					

Source: Courtesy of Inter-Community Medical Center, Covina, California.

this, added to the collectiveness of many other contributions to newness, can result totally in offering significant changes affecting the overall quality of patient care and services.

Flow Diagramming. Flow diagramming is a drawing of the work area covered by a process or activity on which are indicated the locations of fixtures and equipment (beds, tables, desks, and files) and the paths of movement between them. In its simplest form, the flow diagram is used to supplement the flow process chart.

In addition to the above charting techniques, there are other data-collecting instruments designed to facilitate the analytical task of the manager.[11,12]

Key to the ultimate success of any kind of investigative work is the skill of the individual manager to ask the right questions within a well-established pattern of questioning designed to examine, in their proper order, purpose, place, sequence, person, and means. Beyond the starting point of asking the Why? What? Where? When? Who? How? in provoking meaningful questions, the problem-solving manager must search for further variations of the basic questions to extend the appropriateness of the inquiry in terms of any given problem under study. Assistance in question asking is contained in Bennett's text.[13]

An example of how one hospital fostered manager understanding and application skills relating to the above techniques, as well as other analytical methodologies, is documented as Exhibit 8-4. The objectives of this particular workshop program were to:

- increase the awareness and consciousness levels of managers in relating their managerial roles and responsibilities to cost effectiveness/productivity/quality issues and problems
- teach managers the tools and techniques of analysis considered appropriate for identifying, examining, evaluating, and improving cost/productivity/quality-related problems
- provide the opportunity for managers to apply analytical thinking and techniques to significant hospital problems
- sensitize managers to the environmental factors that will either enhance or hinder the process of change for improvement
- prepare managers for their role in involving employees in the improvement effort

4. Maintaining a Sensibility to the Value of Measurement

The idea of measurement is present in most activities engaged in by today's manager. Surely, the idea is central to our concern about not only the quantitative side of work but the qualitative side as well.

Today's new breed of manager makes it a ground rule to avoid guessing and making useless and often incorrect assumptions, to avoid phrases such as "I think," "It must have happened this way," or "I guess." Today's manager does not have to guess in most cases, and not guessing provides a much shorter

Exhibit 8-4 Cost Effectiveness/Productivity Workshop

First Day
(9:00–4:30)

Morning

9:00– 9:15	Introductions
9:15– 9:45	Cost effectiveness and productivity—their meaning and their quantitative and qualitative elements; objectives of the Workshop
9:45–10:00	The concept of self-assessment
10:00–10:30	The systems approach
10:30–10:45	Break
10:45–12:00	A systematic approach to solving cost- and productivity-related problems*

  • The overall process
  • Recognition: observation
  • The Flow Process Chart and its principles
  • Q & A discussion
  • Assignment

12:00– 1:00	Lunch

Afternoon

1:00– 1:40	Flow process charting Flow diagramming Procedural flow charting
1:40– 2:15	The questioning process

  • Developing improvements in charted activity

2:15– 3:00	Other analysis techniques

  • Organization charting
  • Work distribution analysis
  • Other guides to developing work improvements

3:00– 3:15	Break
3:15– 4:00	Introducing change in the organizational environment

  • Technical/human balance
  • Expectations of people
  • The complexities of change
  • Selling the idea

4:00– 4:30	Q & A discussion Summary Assignments

*The text *Methods Improvement In Hospitals* by Addison C. Bennett, New York: Preston Publishing Company, Inc., © 1975, is used as a reference throughout the Workshop.

Exhibit 8-4 continued

Second Day	
Morning	
9:00– 9:15	Review of day one
9:15–10:00	The manager as change agent
	• Qualities of managing
	• Problem solving as a responsibility of managing
10:00–10:30	Discussion of assignments
10:30–10:45	Break
10:45–11:00	Discussion of assignments
11:00–11:30	Productivity and the quality of work life
11:30–12:00	Q & A discussion
12:00– 1:00	Lunch
Afternoon	
1:00– 1:30	Productivity of management
1:30– 2:30	Measuring and monitoring productivity
	• Work unit, work measurement
	• Principles of measurement
	• Work sampling, predetermined time standards, time study
	• Staffing methodologies
	• Monitoring criteria
	• The role of the manager in this context
	• Q & A discussion
2:30– 3:00	Break
3:00– 3:30	The integral relationship of goal setting with cost effectiveness and productivity
3:30– 4:00	Involving employees in cost reduction and productivity enhancement
4:00– 4:30	Q & A discussion
	Summary
	Assignments
Third Day	
Morning	
9:00– 9:30	Review of days one and two
9:30–12:00	Presentation and discussion of cost- and productivity-related projects developed by attendees
(Break at 10:30)	
12:00– 1:00	Lunch
Afternoon	
1:00– 3:30	Project presentations and discussions
(Break at 2:30)	

Exhibit 8-4 continued

3:30– 4:00	Problem-solving progress reports by attendees who have not made presentations
4:00– 4:30	Closing discussion Follow-up methodologies Workshop summary and closing

road to the eventual decision for solution. The new breed of manager *insists* on answers that tell how often, how many, or even measured ratios between the troublesome event's frequency and the overall frequency of the daily performance of a given activity.

Often, the ground rule for quantifying measures of effectiveness is a hard prescription, but one that pays the greatest dividends. It calls for getting the numbers whenever possible, and paying attention to them. It is about the only way to move out of the area of opinion and poorly balanced observation and to get onto the firm ground of knowing just what it is that one is trying to do, and where one wants to go. It is the only way to prevent the isolated event from dominating the planning or control process. Even when things are "bad," it is the start of improvement to be able to tell just how "bad" they are, and how often, and in what dimensions specifically.

"Measures of effectiveness" provide certain clearly identified criteria by which the goodness or poorness of a given situation can be judged. They allow managers to recognize a good solution when they see it. Managers can tell whether a requirement is being met and how well it is being met.

What are the key characteristics of good measures of effectiveness?

- The most important characteristic is that the measure chosen *must actually measure* the effectiveness of the system in terms of its objectives.
- Another quality that characterizes good measurement is the selection of criteria that refer to the performance of the *system or process as a whole,* and not just to some of its subobjectives.
- Completeness is another characteristic.
- A good measure of effectiveness is one that is *quantifiable,* thus capable of being expressed as a number. "Good patient care and service in the OPD" does not meet this requirement. "Reduction of average waiting-time by twenty-five percent," or some similar statement, does.
- The measure of effectiveness should be *statistically efficient and simple* to the extent that the measure chosen does not vary widely, and to the extent that the data can be gathered economically.

In general, the "measures of effectiveness" will largely center on the specified dimensions of cost, time, accuracy, capacity, and efficiency—all of which, in varying degree, have the capacity to reveal both the quantitative and qualitative sides of performance.

While it is recognized that too many measures can indeed paralyze action and decision making, it is important that managers take on the responsibility for selecting key criteria to indicate the primary and most important secondary elements to be sought in any organizational or operational process, whether it be in the province of problem-solving, criteria-based job descriptions and performance evaluation, goal setting, labor standards, or quality-of-work-life concerns.

5. Progressing toward Developing a Work Environment Conducive to Innovative Change

To believe that participation in problem solving and decision making is the privilege of but a few is one of the ways that a hospital can imperil its own health and well-being, because this belief does not accommodate the desires of the many who want a say on matters affecting their job and who can bring about change for improvement where change is needed most. It is an accommodation that is in keeping with the values of employees and, as a result, the organization is more likely to keep its valuable employees.[14]

The organization also is more likely to affect quality if it not only moves its managers to reexamining their methods but gets them to communicate effectively with employees to encourage their suggestions and participation, and to train them adequately in problem solving. If circumstances are such that the organizational environment stimulates creative thinking at lower levels without having it discouraged by immediate supervisors, it will be found that employees are eager to solve problems in the workplace.

Bureaucratic management cannot have both the dictatorial, top-down coordination of a strong boss at the top and the distribution of intelligence, communication, and decision-making at all points throughout the organization. It just cannot respond quickly and effectively to countless situations when and where they appear.[15]

As discovered by increasing numbers of corporate managements, the attainment of higher levels of quality comes as a direct result of their responsiveness (through effective employee involvement in problem solving) to the expectations of people in today's work force; namely, using one's mind; the right to know; a voice in decision making; continuing education and self-development, and work that is challenging and meaningful.

> For the majority of people in today's work force, the idea of meaningful work contains two ingredients: 1) the opportunity to identify problems that lie in the way of doing a good job, and 2) positive encouragement to be a part of the improvement process leading to the solution of these problems. Indeed, work simplification serves both of these purposes well.[16]

Structural and content ideas for engaging employees in the search for better ways of doing work and of providing services can be found in two health care-related writings.[17,18]

THE MANAGEMENT ENGINEER IN HEALTH CARE

We cannot speak of the function of management without considering the science and art of management (industrial) engineering. Periodically, members of top management need to renew their acquaintance with the history of industrial engineering. It is interesting to realize how a few men and women introduced ideas that now seem commonplace but that revolutionized old practices of management.

The main lesson of engineering history is simple. Once man began the systematic study of processes used in accomplishing work and began to organize work in logical sequences, he inevitably began to consider the *management* of supervision and managerial behavior. This is when management first became self-aware of how it went about its job. Thus, we find the evidence that justifies the thesis that "management engineering *is* management, and cannot be disassociated from the management process."

Management engineering, in a total sense, is concerned with all phases of accomplishing work, yet, what continues to persist is the apparent narrowness in which the nature and function of management engineering are perceived by top managements in health care as well as by the engineers themselves. If, indeed, we accept the proposition that management engineering *is* management, then the extent of our views regarding this discipline must go beyond the boundary of thought that we have merely the presence of a well-defined body of knowledge and techniques of proved usefulness in very specific categories of application. More appropriate is the thinking that management engineering needs to be employed as an integral part of the whole process of management in order to allow administration and its managers at all levels to respond to the demands of constant change with greater effectiveness and efficiency, and to give due emphasis to problem solving as a way of corporate life designed to achieve quantitative and *qualitative* advancements. Perhaps it is the failure to extend our consciousness into territories beyond current boundaries of attention that has thwarted widespread use of management engineering throughout the health care segment of hospitals of more than 150 to 200 beds.

To bring about greater balance in the quantitative and qualitative dimensions of human performance, today's management engineer will need to identify more fully with the human side of enterprise and to act and reason differently in light of the expectations held by most people employed in our contemporary world of work.

While the engineer's need to explore remains the same, the manner in which exploration occurs will need to be different, since it must move to a system of human values that extends beyond the learning of technical precepts. The engineer's experiences and actions in the decade ahead must embrace a "philosophy of culture" that is the totality of socially transmitted behavior patterns, attitudes, expectations, and all other products of human work and thought characteristic of a humanely based institutional community or population.

Historically, the dominating image of the management engineer in our field has been allied to the outcomes of techniques and scientific exploration, with the prevailing thought of quantitative analysis. Between now and the year 2000, however, the management engineer in health care will need to demand that he or she knows where the technology and the techniques stop and the human affairs and environment of the institution begin, for both belong together as harmonious halves of what is unique in human experience. In essence, the engineer must assume a different posture within the discipline; he or she must make an extraordinary shift from more of the same preoccupation with applications of scientific techniques to functional issues, to a systemic pursuit of a "technology of human affairs and behavior.

In the future, the engineer and management, together, must not allow their amour of the matter of techniques alone to blind their vision of wider concerns about human conditions that ring with greater meaning. Techniques, as they are embodied in the engineer's branch of knowledge, do not exist with disregard for humankind. The engineer is a human being fulfilling his or her human aspirations and finding rewards in the pleasure of his or her work. However, reliance on techniques more for the sake of methods than for the sake of man has inherent limitations for all of us. It needs to be recognized that such dependency, which the management engineer has so expertly evidenced in the past, has inherent limitations. Surely, this more narrowed perception of engineering and its techniques cannot produce the philosophy required to direct our thinking toward such essential questions as these.

- What are the ways in which the analytical observer and the observed interact, and what conditions can the engineer, in the practical application of scientific analysis, bring under control so that human behavior can be predicted?

- How accurate is the notion that an engineer is a cool, impartial, detached individual? How insidious is the emotional attachment to one's own point of view, and what are the ways and means of balancing biases?

- What is the system of values embodied in the technological world of work of the management engineer? What are the social goals the engineer must finally serve? As a licensed specialist and as a human being, how does the engineer address the question of personal and professional responsibility?

- What are the instruments or process that can mitigate the effects of inertia, which, in a specialized, compartmented, and intricate professional organization such as a hospital, makes a mockery of progress?

- Are we being deprived of a certain number of discoveries because our institutional structures are so rigid and our conflicts are so damaging that the environment is not receptive or sensitive to humanistic change?

- How can the health care institution organize itself in an imaginative way to deal with human problems (such as the environmental problems that move people to resist change) through participation of its internal population?

What needs to be done to move in the direction of furthering the quality of individual performance, as the engineer works alongside other members of the organization, both management and nonmanagement alike? Here are some thoughts.

- To begin with, the human element of our technological world is of extreme importance to todays' managements; thus they need to know where is the frontier of our corporate environment. We are no longer principally in the age of scientific management; rather, we find our presence more in the era of the art of managing.

  To work with artists has been the existential pleasure of most engineers, and they are well aware of their reliance on the artists in management. Therefore the engineering discipline needs to be a greater force in aiding and supporting management at all levels of the enterprise. Managements and engineers will be dealing with an imposing set of new demands in managing people who are coming to work with different attitudes and expectations.

- Increasing curriculum enrichment to include the fine arts and other cultural subjects in schools of engineering is an imperative. Many engineering students have traditionally regarded courses in the humanities as educational frills. Fortunately, however, in an effort to prepare engineers to better cope with the social implications of their chosen field, schools such as the Massachusetts Institute of Technology are increasing their emphasis on arts and social sciences.

While renewing curriculum is not easy, it is indeed essential, as it provides the starting gate for lifelong educational experiences along a pathway of broadening one's visions and values.

To make awareness and knowledge whole for engineers, we must take them beyond their own individual areas of expertise, for tunnel vision is a threat to their ultimate effectiveness. Today's and tomorrow's engineer must be skilled in the *art* of managing; he or she needs to be a "technological humanist." This idea finds support in the writing of Samuel C. Florman, who states

> The nation needs engineers who are able to communicate, who are prepared for leadership roles, who are sensitive to the worthy objectives of our civilization and the place of technology within it, and whose creative imaginations are nourished from the richest possible sources—spiritual, intellectual, and artistic. Furthermore, engineers as a group need to preserve their professional self-esteem—and the esteem of the greater community—by guarding against an insensitive mechanical approach to the work they do. And finally, individual engineers deserve the chance to enrich their lives with art, literature, history—the best our civilization has to offer.[19]

- The top managements of health care organizations should take the initiative in forwarding the cause of collaboration among the service disciplines of personnel administration, training and education, and management engineering so as to overcome divisions that have been institutionalized in our health care industry. It would almost appear at times that there exists a widespread assumption that the purposes and methods of these disciplines are as alien as their respective corners of the work world. The isolationism of this particular triad of service functions is unnatural, since, both individually and collectively, they are in the business of "human resource management."

- Research is very important to the engineer, whose very temperament is exploratory. Yet, the national society of management engineering and the managements of our health care institutions generally have not substantiated investigative efforts of the highest consequence through a solid commitment to research and demonstration. Such research will provide a fresh view of the engineer's role in either introducing new patterns of thinking and activity to fit corporate culture or, in fact, to influence change in the culture itself to ensure organizational success or survival.

The overriding thesis of this chapter remains "Think big! But don't belittle small" in the search for quality in human performance at work.

It is a fundamental premise of this writing that organized, intelligent, and continuing investigation of the multitude of diminutive elements of operational methods and procedures offers an almost unparalleled opportunity to improve the quality of services provided by the modern health care organization. The fruits of such improvement efforts on the side of smallness can be extraordinarily abundant and varied, yet such efforts remain a vast, relatively unexploited arena of opportunity throughout our industry.

Good advice for leaders whose attention needs to be on bigness is to consider smallness as well. Chief executive officers and their managers must capture and channel the power of this smallness, for therein lies the potential break from the limits of artificial barriers of current work methods and procedures to a renewal in the way in which things are done.

Small things collectively gained through the energetic efforts of managers, employees, and the management engineer can affect big decisions made by those at the top. But when the smallness of things is overlooked, not only is the point of view from below negated, human conditions within the organization are neutralized as well.

Designing innovatively organizational processes, arrangements, and mechanisms to foster problem solving at *all* levels of the enterprise in the interest of increased efficiency and higher levels of quality can give new direction to technological and human development—a direction that will lead our efforts back to the real needs of man, "and that also means: to *the actual size of man*. Man is small, and, therefore, small is beautiful."[20]

NOTES

1. United Technologies advertisement, *New York Times,* Oct. 23, 1985, p. 29.

2. W.I.B. Beveridge, *Seeds of Discovery* (New York: W.W. Norton & Co. Inc., 1980), p.71.

3. Addison C. Bennett, extracted from *Improving Management Performance in Health Care Institutions* (Chicago: American Hospital Association, 1978), pp. 104–105.

4. John A. Young, "One Company's Quest for Improved Quality," *Wall Street Journal,* Jul. 25, 1983, p. 27.

5. Addison C. Bennett, *Productivity and the Quality of Work Life in Hospitals* (Chicago: American Hospital Association, 1983), p. viii.

6. Addison C. Bennett, portions of this section taken from the article "The Imperative of Assessment," *The Health Care Supervisor*, Jan. 1987. pp. 1–10.

7. "Program for Institutional Effectiveness Review [PIER]," Chicago, American Hospital Association.

8. John M. Broder, "The New Competition: To Make It, Make It Differently," *Los Angeles Times*. Sept. 2, 1987, p. 1.

9. Henry D. Thoreau, *Walden and Other Writings of Henry David Thoreau* (New York: Random House, Inc., 1965).

10. Clair F. Vough, *Tapping the Human Resource* (New York: AMACOM, 1975), p. 1.

11. Addison C. Bennett, *Methods Improvement in Hospitals* (New York: Preston Publishing Co., Inc., 1975).

12. Harold E. Smalley and John R. Freeman, *Hospital Industrial Engineering* (New York: Reinhold Publishing Corporation, 1966).

13. Bennett, *Methods Improvement in Hospitals,* pp. 24, 58.

14. Bennett, *Improving Management Performance in Health Care Institutions,* p. 205.

15. Ernest D. Lieberman, *Unfit to Manage!* (New York: McGraw-Hill Book Co., 1988), p. 208.

16. Addison C. Bennett, "Work Smarter, Not Harder," *The Health Care Supervisor*, Apr., 1988, pp. 1–13.

17. Addison C. Bennett and Samuel J. Tibbitts, *Making Innovation Practical* (Chicago: Pluribus Press, Inc., 1986), chap. 8.

18. Addison C. Bennett, *An Employee Idea Program for Hospitals and Nursing Home Type Facilities* (New York: Preston Publishing, Co., Inc., 1974).

19. Samuel Florman, *The Civilized Engineer* (New York: St. Martin's Press, 1987), p. 195.

20. E.F. Schumacher, *Small Is Beautiful* (New York: Harper & Row, 1973), p. 159.

Chapter 9

Education—The One Great Hope for Achieving Quality

You cannot teach a man anything; you can only help him to find it within himself.
—Galileo

There was a time in the distant past when the quality of our nation's educational system was impregnable to assault. Teachers and professors were held in high esteem and adoration, and the rightness of education was taken for granted. However, the last two to three decades have brought intense criticism upon education, with schools, colleges, and businesses being held increasingly accountable for the unfulfillment of the expectations that our society has for its educational system.

The pace of change to an information-based society and a workplace largely in service industries demands some important reforms both in our educational institutions and in the corporate workplace. As we enter an era of lifelong learning that merges work and education, we become more conscious of the needs of a new generation of workers who will become more directly involved in determining the quality of life in the coming years.

Is it possible for quality to be in jeopardy if, as so many claim, we have the best-educated work force in our history? Quite so, if one supports, for example, the ideas articulated by Edmund Fuller at the commencement exercises of Sewanee Academy—ideas that appear to be as timely today as they were when first delivered. Here is what Fuller had to say:

Some people have said that yours will be the best-educated generation in the history of the world. . . . Unfortunately, it is not true.

It is not so much a lie as an error arising from a confusion of terms. Simply in living, outside of school, you are exposed to more kinds of information, more masses of data, more multimedia stimuli, than any generation that has gone before you. The trouble is, all this that is poured upon you, especially through the potent medium of television, is fragmentary, unorganized, and, worst of all, is

183

unevaluated information. It may have a bearing upon education, but it is not education in itself. It is more likely to hamper than to aid real education. It can lead to the junkyard mind more easily than it can contribute to the comprehensive intelligence. . . .

It is possible that you may become the best-informed generation in history—*quantitatively*. It is also frighteningly possible that you could turn out to be one of the worst-educated generations— qualitatively. There have been times when far few people were educated, but those few received an education in depth unmatched today. You could be cursed with information without wisdom, with data without direction. You could wind up programming machines without knowing the implications of their use, naively handling instruments more sophisticated than yourselves.

There is a problem about man's knowledge and techniques on the one hand and his wisdom on the other. Modern man knows more and can do more than our ancestors. In that kind of knowledge we have advanced. But we are not wiser, or more spiritually perceptive, or more artistically creative than the people of either the far or distant past. It can be argued—I'll grant it's a hot argument—that we are demonstrably less wide, less perceptive spiritually, less artistically creative than those before us.[1]

Whatever our individual stance might be with regard to this "hot argument," it is believed that there is a general accord that the room for improvement in the realm of "education in itself" is considerable in its dimensions.

Education is a crucial instrument of change, yet there persists a lack of clarity about its real purposes. Indeed, "education is in constant process of invention,"[2] as each generation must define afresh the nature, direction, and aims of education to assure such freedom and rationality as can be attained for a future generation. Yet, in spite of these constant refinements, there remain certain fundamental qualities that collectively define the true meaning of "real education." In essence, it is a fostering, nurturing, cultivating process. As Dewey puts it, "All of these words mean that it implies attention to the conditions of growth."[3] It is a lifelong process with the general objective of promoting excellence by helping human beings achieve their optimum intellectual development. Its purpose must be to shape individuals into complete human beings. Above all, "real education" is an art because "it relies upon the combination of know-how and inspiration, of enthusiasm and dedication, of ability and restraint, which the artist has. . . ."[4]

With the guidance of these basic thoughts, let us move on to an examination of the ways in which hospitals and other types of health care organizations can advance the quality of human performance and conduct by responding to the call for reform in the wide range of educational efforts that they sponsor.

CREATING A GROWTH ENVIRONMENT

What needs to be positioned high on our organizational agendas is to bring together more closely education and work. Their separation from each other in the past has been detrimental to the cause of making *total* quality a reality within the work environment of health care.

As stated earlier, quality begins with the performance of people, not things, and it is the quality consciousness and comprehension of the organizational membership that must be gained. This aim can be actualized only if the leadership of the institution clearly perceives and understands the critical flaws embedded in its internal educational system and is willing to work harder, with a deeper sense of urgency, to correct or remove them in the interest of quality improvement. An effective and efficient education and development system in any organization today is not only its greatest weapon against deterioration of quality; it is indispensable to the survival of the enterprise itself.

A growth environment within an organizational framework is not brought into being by what is stated officially and formally; rather, it is recognized by what is done and the way in which it is done. Inexorably linked with the credo, mission, and goals of the organization, the educational system, if it is to manifest a work environment of growth, needs to be

- designed and established as an integral part of the larger purpose of education, that of striving for total human development;
- perceived and established as a network of processes of a continuing nature directed toward serving longer-term outcomes;
- so fashioned as to evidence careful and deliberate thought and worthiness with respect to two essential factors: (1) high levels of quality of all processes within the corporate educational system and (2) the centrality of quality as a pervading value within the content of all learning experiences as it relates to quality of work, quality of work life, and quality of human conduct;
- subject to the basic managerial elements of planning, organizing, communicating, motivating, and controlling, and dependent on the innovative applications of these elements.

A NETWORK OF PROCESSES

If top management is committed to fostering the personal growth of its people as well as enhancing their job satisfaction and helping them become more useful and productive, it must focus on *process*, not programs. Traveling the programmatic route will not lead to quality education because it tends to be fragmentary rather than integral, intermittent rather than ongoing, and casual rather than purposeful in its character.

There are essentially two concepts at play within the organizational system: the idea of *development,* which has as its purpose the expansion or realization of the potentialities of individuals over time, and the narrower notion of *training,* which is directed toward making one proficient with specialized instruction and practice. Both of these growth experiences offer opportunities for gaining new extensions of quality that are not generally being captured in today's health care workplace. Let us examine some of the opportunities available to administrations within the design of these education-directed processes.

- orientation and induction
- development at the top
- development of managers at the middle
- development at the nonmanagement levels

Orientation and Induction

Quality starts with the fundamentals of this beginning phase of employment—fundamentals that evolve from management's understanding of the sociological reality within which it now operates.

Today, individuals are arriving at the doorstep of the human resources department with expectations different from those of their predecessors of but a few years ago. They also bring with them many of society's ills, arriving in a state of emptiness with regard to many of the values that we cherish but that have been diminished by societal corrosiveness. Since it is difficult to maintain high standards of institutional quality without a value system, value focus and clarification need to begin at the initial stage of interviewing a potential candidate for employment.

The selection of the right person for the right job for the right reasons is a management responsibility of no minor magnitude; and as prospective employees arrive at the selection point, one must assume that they possess a sense of motivation to work in an organization that they themselves have sought out and chosen.

> The key task, then, of those engaged in the hospital's selection and placement process is to prevent "demotivation" of the employees, because the evidence continues to show all too many terminations (voluntary and nonvoluntary) occurring during the first year of employment.[5]

The participants in this hiring and placement process also need to avoid making serious mistakes, because errors in decisions at this beginning point can be costly both to the organization and to the individual candidate. Surely, the hiring of people who ultimately fail to measure up to performance expectations can have a cumulative effect on the quality efforts of the institution.

Because the possibilities of committing errors during the selection and placement process can be damaging, the key players in the process need to be professionally trained and well-experienced in this area of activity. Their efforts need to reflect a high level of performance, not merely in a quantitative sense, but, more important, from a qualitative standpoint. Beyond the issues of competence, their performance can be only as effective as the foundation on which it is built; namely, the planning and forecasting of future human resource needs, job analyses and determination, performance definition, established criteria for evaluating performance, and, above all, sound and modern personnel policies, procedures, and practices. The new employee's progress toward achieving high levels of quality work must be guided, assisted, recognized, and rewarded, and the initial step is in proper orientation.

Traditionally, orientation is viewed as the process of guiding new employees toward a clear understanding of the work conditions, policies, requirements, opportunities, benefits, returns, and relationships they should expect from their new employment. Unfortunately, this perception lacks a recognition of the necessity for

- knowledge of the past
- two-way communication
- expression of values
- perceiving orientation as an integral part of a total employee relations process

which, if added to the more traditional mode of orientation, will have the tendency to promote the presence of quality throughout this early period of employment and in the ultimate performance of the new employee.

Knowledge of the Past

History needs to be in fashion when orienting the new employee, for to be ignorant of the history of the organization and the part it has played in the health care arena is to be, in a very fundamental way, unable to understand the workings of the institution itself. History does not get the attention and time it deserves during this initial stage of induction, yet the newly employed person cannot hope to possess essential knowledge about the organization that he or she has recently joined if so little is known of the events that came before.

Two-Way Communication

Merely improving techniques for giving new employees adequate information about their jobs, responsibilities, and entitlements does not reach the basic problem of the induction process today. The traditional definition that emphasizes one-way, downward communication overlooks the reality that employment is a mutual, contractual relationship. It overlooks the knowledge available about employees' motivations, aspirations, perceptions, resistance to change, and the like—and also the effect that these psychological findings have on critical management concerns such as stability, regularity of attendance, morale, and aspiration for growth, all of which are quality-related factors of work. The "one-way" definition misses the important opportunity of orientation—for the manager to find out what is significant and unique about each individual as an employee and as a person while making certain that the new employee has the information needed to begin the job with favorable attitudes, with confidence of success, and with a feeling of wanting and expecting to be a part of a new, exciting, and challenging environment. In short, "orientation should mean an *interchange* of information, impressions, evaluations, and expectations."[6]

Expression of Values

The first weeks of employment are critically important. This is the time when new acquaintances are formed and attitudes about the quality of life at work in a new environment take shape. It is a time when a feeling of anomie is common among new employees who come to a "new world" of work with high hopes, then soon experience a lowering of self-confidence due to feelings of alienation and personal disorganization.

Surely, orientation is not too early a time to rally around a set of beliefs designed to help new employees develop mature values through a positive sense of their own worth. Basic to this process of articulating values such as thoughtfulness, compassion, fidelity, honesty, diligence, fairness, and self-discipline—all of which contribute to *quality*—is the concern for accommodating employees' values as they are brought into harmony with the value system of the organization.

Perceiving Orientation

Orientation cannot be considered as the discrete step that comes after hiring and before placement of the individual in a position of full productiveness. The interchange of information that is orientation begins at the preemployment interviews (both in the human resources department and in the department in which the applicant will be working) and continues to the time when the immediate supervisor begins on-the-job training, which should be designed to start with answering questions developed during orientation. It is important to point out, however, that the same two-way approach, the same sense of a mutual, contractual relationship, should be maintained throughout the full tenure of the employee.

It would appear to be appropriate to refer to this more inclusive approach to orientation, with its consistent, continuing emphasis on frank, adequate interchange of information, attitudes, values, aspirations, expectations, and even doubts, as *co-orientation.*

With a concern for quality, supervisory managers need to be sensitive to the presence of anxiety and uncertainty on the part of the new employee, since it is not uncommon to find many conscientious new employees having doubts about their competence in the new job when they compare themselves with the more experienced co-workers around them. No matter how able, experienced, and concerned new employees may be, they cannot perform at full productivity in a strange work situation until they become familiar with the physical layout, the people, the procedures, the regulations, the channels of communication, and the equipment around them.

To prevent attitudes of discouragement and, often, the early separation of the most conscientious and promising new employees, department managers and supervisors need to

- make it a planned objective of the "co-orientation" effort to assure all new employees that no one expects them to produce at their full capacity at the outset of their assignment in a new work situation, and
- institute a planned procedure for preventing new employees from completing a full day's work initially; this will diminish the opportunity for them to compare their day's output with that of longer-tenured workers.

All too often, work pressure in the department makes for minimal attention to the new employee. The attitude is: "We're too busy right now. We need bodies to get the work done. New employees will do as much as they can now and we'll think about orientation and coaching as soon as we get out of this work pressure." This is too foolhardy and expensive an expedient to continue if management is committed to the task of gaining higher levels of quality performance, of fostering a more satisfying quality of life at work, and of promoting the quality of human conduct within the workplace.

Development at the Top

The Board

To be truly effective, the task of orienting and developing board membership needs to be viewed and exercised through a systems approach, that is, all reasonable elements of the total task must be taken into account; there needs to be a careful selection of the methodologies to be used; and then, most importantly, all of the parts of the development process ultimately adopted need to be properly integrated so that they fit together in an understandable and rational way. At least four major elements are seen as being embraced by the overall process.

Basic Orientation. Basic orientation is initiated at the very outset of new board membership, yet it serves as well as a re-examination of certain basic areas by those trustees who have had some tenure on the board. While it is important not to overload the information-flow system in any of its elements, it is at the same time essential that board members be sufficiently and suitably introduced to a new world of involvement and knowledge. Indeed, trustee orientation offers an initial opportunity to begin focusing on the idea of quality.

Ongoing Educational Programming. Ongoing educational programming within the framework of a trustee development process is a requirement over time for designing a sequential coverage of major issues most pertinent to the health care industry and to the immediate needs of the trustees as identified through an effectively administered self-evaluation procedure. Throughout this integrated series of educational sessions, the subject of the wholeness of quality should be addressed singularly as a significant area of attention; it is also essential that continued reference to its import be made in *all* learning segments of the process.

When engaging the services of outside specialists in the conduct of these trustee programs, it is advisable to avoid "prepackaged" presentations and to insist that the presenters provide meaningful input to the trustee audience by making the contents of their communications fitting to the unique needs and characteristics of the organization.

Certainly, there are sufficient numbers of issue topics to fulfill an ongoing educational process over time, and there are variations for formatting the individual sessions within the process: devoting a brief period of time prior to a regularly scheduled board meeting; gathering the board occasionally on an invitational basis; addressing such issues at a board retreat; and scheduling the attendance of selected trustees at outside conferences and workshops with expected feedback to the entire board. Approaches such as these can be used interchangeably with good effect. The idea is to do it in the most convenient, interesting, and informative way, with the goal of moving the mentality and mood of board membership to the point where they ask for more—a testimony to the *quality* of the process.

Information Flow. Information flow is important, since the trustees' unfamiliarity with the total health care system and its interrelated parts may put them at a disadvantage when it comes to judging the significance of an event and discerning on what they need to devote their time and attention. In addition to arranging for the mailing of selected publications to the homes of trustees, the chief executive officer (CEO) should keep the flow of information moving on a continuing basis as he or she peruses the literature for coverage of key issues and conditions believed appropriate for distribution to the trustees for purposes of keeping them abreast of significant events occurring in the health care field.

Self-Development. The prime responsibility for self-development rests with individual members of the board, but, again, they must look to the CEO for guidance and direction as to what they ought to be reading and retaining. Beyond this kind of assistance, the advancement of trustee skills and knowledge will find its greatest gains in the experience of actively participating in the performance of inquiry and discussion that take place during the board meetings themselves.

The collectiveness of ideas like those above captures the broad view of trustee development considered indispensable to (1) designing a *quality* process of development, (2) advancing the *quality* of trustee performance, and (3) promoting trustee consciousness of the wholeness of *quality*.

The Medical Staff

The task of breaking away from the more traditional view of quality summons certain requirements that bring useful ways of thinking about the education, development, and integration of physicians.

To begin with, the administration can never assume that physicians—or its board—are adequately informed as to "what's really happening here." The administration must serve as the conduit for conveying information that satisfies the knowledge needs of its corporate partners, the board and the medical staff. It is obvious that the physician must have the most complete information and must refer to a clearly defined value system, with the ultimate objective of creating within the organization an environment of unity and reciprocation in which collaboration and integration can flourish for the sake of advancing quality. With the acknowledgment that quality *is* an interchange of sensitivity, responsiveness, and support between management and the medical staff, much attention is given to reciprocal relationships in Chapter 2.

One additional area worthy of consideration is management training, particularly for institutional-based physicians who manage the activities of specialty departments. For physicians, the only sources of practical information about managerial skills have been word of mouth, apprenticeship, or simply trial and error.

The importance of training physicians in the science and arts of managing is emphasized by Dr. Roman L. Yanda in these words: "To be effective leaders, we must deliver the results required and desired by the consumer, rather than just the 'doing our own thing' that is so characteristic of the haughty professional."' In his writing, Yanda cites the management functions demanding attention, including planning and control, concepts of authority and delegation, knowledge of policies, communication and coordination, motivation, and human resource development.

The CEO and Other Members of Top Management

The quality of organizational performance begins at the top. It is the quality of competence, style, practice, and behavior exhibited by the CEO and members of the administrative group that together establishes the model for enhancing the quality of work, the quality of work life, and the quality of human conduct within the entire organizational system. This is indeed an imposing force, yet there is a lack of strong evidence of commitment to planned and organized development of top management executives in health care organizations generally. Rather, when development activities do occur, initiative on the part of the individual executive appears to be the focal point of impetus in all too many instances.

For executive development to bring qualitative returns, a whole system of elements needs to be examined and effectively put into place. The recommended development activities encompass the following elements.

An Organizational Commitment and Policy. The board and the CEO need to commit to establishing an effective process for evaluating and developing their top management cadre. To communicate this commitment with clarity, an overriding policy and set of objectives need to be documented and disseminated to all parties concerned.

Quality Improvement in the Recruitment, Selection, and Placement of Top Level Executives. As an extension of the prior step, the question What kind of manager do we want in our organizational system? needs to be addressed. This, in turn, will affect recruitment, selection, and placement objectives and methodologies employed by the institution.

A close assessment of this key element surfaces certain dissatisfactions with the failure of conventional forms and processes to stay in tune with the transformation of work in the future. The preparatory learning offered by undergraduate curricula, for example, and more specifically by graduate programs, in health services administration, including their residency programs, represent for many aspiring administrative executives a starting point in the real world of work.

Current overall perceptions of residency training call for change. The residency activity must be viewed more as the centrality of graduate education, with classroom learning purposely integrated and tied into this period of work-world experience. This movement away from the converse point of view that places the academic setting as the primary source of knowledge will not only effect a better balance between theory and practice, it also will bring greater worth to the residency training program.

The perceived shortcomings of residency programs become even more disturbing in light of the absence of purposeful *testing* of graduates following their employment in a health care organization. Suitable testing might involve a practice applied by business and industry: positioning potential top executives in various divisions and departments of the enterprise to evaluate further their managerial capacity and competency; the testing might involve the continued assignment of sticky problems to determine the knowledge and intellectual wisdom of the graduates.

This concept of testing, if valid, gives support to the idea of continuous and conscious attention to the potential and planned movement of selected, qualified middle managers into administrative ranks.

The thought that "It is not enough to say that a man has 'arrived.' One must know in what condition,"[8] needs to be recalled in the interest of quality.

Organizational Analysis. Organizational arrangements at the top need to be reviewed in terms of whether or not current structures provide logical stepping stones for advancement and, if not, what alternatives might be feasible and appropriate. As an ongoing policy, attention also needs to be given to the possible introduction of new positions, either permanent or *ad hoc,* to accommodate individual executives within the organizational system. These kinds of actions are tied to an assessment of both short- and long-term business plans and strategies designed to determine the impact on future management resources.

Executive Data Base. An essential element of the development process is an adequate data base on each executive. This profile should be reviewed and updated when the annual performance appraisal is conducted. Also at that time, any changes in the career goals of the individual should be fed into the data base.

Planned Progression. Planned progression of executives resulting from the use of such tools as career planning, performance appraisal, and an informative data base will help in the determination of availability within the organization of backup talent capable of replacing key executives when needed. Planned progression also will help to negate any skepticism about the manner in which replacements and promotions are decided upon.

Performance Evaluation Improvements. A key ingredient to the conduct of a successful development effort is the caliber of the performance appraisal process designed to review and evaluate the strengths, weaknesses, career plans, and development needs of key executives. According to Andrall Pearson, CEOs should try stepping back and asking themselves these questions: "Do you make measurable progress each year in the quality of your senior management group and in the people heading each functional area? Are you generating clearly better quality executives and backups—not just people whose bosses assert are better managers?"[9]

Performance Evaluation of the CEO. The performance evaluation of the CEO yields a solid indication of whether people development is an organization's number one daily priority. It should be conducted by an evaluation committee of the board at the close of each fiscal year. The evaluation of accomplishments and results should be directed toward measurable outcomes based on such performance criteria as:

- Fulfillment of mission and corporate goals. The CEO ultimately is to be held accountable for the overall accomplishments of corporate goals.
- Accomplishment of the CEO's goals as related to organizational progress, including any of the corporate goals, along with his or her own personal development goals as identified by the CEO and/or the evaluation committee of the board.
- Leadership qualities established by the board committee in concert with the CEO. "Different CEOs have different styles of leadership, and there is no way to set forth a model of administration. Nor should the board attempt to impose on the CEO some particular brand of leadership that it favors."[10] Yet, it is considered appropriate to set certain standards believed to be fitting to the unique values, purposes, and needs of the particular institution. The leadership areas of interest at the Bank of America, for example, include the standards of receptivity to change, awareness of people, global outlook, sociopolitical sensitivity, market orientation, congeneric perception, and profit consciousness.[11]
- The elements of activity contained in the CEO's position description.
- Progress in developing members of top management, both individually and as a team. Documented and carried-out action plans would be the measurable evidence available for evaluating this criterion. The objective is not only to build consistency in the competencies of individual team members, but also to develop each beyond his or her own specialty area. Some insightful questions for the CEO to ask are: Does a truly harmonious relationship exist between the financial executive and the human resource executive? Does the financial specialist exhibit a sensibility to the idea that "people are profit?" At the same time, does the human resource executive display a high consciousness of the centrality of cost effectiveness within the organization's human resource system?
- Quality of goals set by the top management members and the extent of goal fulfillment.

At the close of each fiscal year, the CEO should prepare a written report for the board, setting forth contributions and accomplishments. This report should be used as a reference document during the performance evaluation process.

> The question is not whether the CEO is to be evaluated. The importance of the role makes this process inevitable. The real question is whether evaluation can be accomplished in a way that enhances performance of executive leadership and management functions.[12]

Performance Evaluation of Members of Top Management. The performance evaluation of members of top management should embrace the CEO's use of these kinds of performance standards:

- fulfillment of any one or more corporate goals assigned or self-selected
- achievement of individual goals (other than corporate goals) initiated by the administrative member or designated by the CEO
- leadership qualities identified by the CEO
- position description content
- quality of goals (in terms of their substance and contribution to corporate goals) set and accomplished by department directors reporting to the administrative members
- extent and success of efforts directed toward developing managers at the department director and supervisory levels

Each administrative member should prepare an annual report of contributions and accomplishments for the CEO. The report will be useful during the performance evaluation discussion and in developing action plans for future improvements in the quality of performance at the top.

Communication Network. In the broader context, the executive development process needs to include:

- an effective approach to executive orientation
- continuous communication to all individuals involved regarding the various aspects and dimensions of the executive evaluation and development process
- adequate and timely feedback to executives regarding their performance, strengths and weaknesses, and developmental needs

Rewards and Recognition. Reward and recognition practices should be reviewed on a periodic basis for appropriateness relative to the objectives, nature, and characteristics of the executive development process.

Education and Development Planning. Just because the executives at the top have been granted their share of diplomas does not mean that they can take their educations for granted. They need all of the knowledge they can muster to meet today's and tomorrow's technological and scientific problems. They need all of the accumulated experience to tackle economic issues, and all of the understanding of humanity to meet social challenges. Indeed, overeducation for the executive at the top is an idea whose time must never come.

Evolving out of an effectively designed and administered performance evaluation process should follow the planning for continuing executive involvement in new and meaningful learning experiences aimed at moving upward the quality of performance in a formalized and purposeful manner.

Upon return from an external educational event, administrative executives should share any new knowledge gained (preferably in written form) with other members of the top management group as well as with lower levels of management.

Middle Management Identification. There needs to be an effective process for identifying managers at the middle possessing capabilities for potential advancement into higher-level positions. Such a process must give consideration not only to methodologies for their development, but also to supportive incentives and reward systems.

Developing Managers at the Middle

While quality improvement begins at the top, it is the management membership at the middle of the organization—department directors, their assistants, and supervisory personnel—who operate the management systems that make quality improvement happen on a consistent and continuing basis. It is this central group of institutional leaders who hold positional advantage and power to multiply the effectiveness of the entire organization through the quality of their managerial performance.

If this is a believable proposition, it behooves top administration to take full gain of every instrument that will equip the assemblage of middle managers to perform more effectively and willingly, not only as individuals but as a unified and harmonious team. The most effectual instrument for doing all this is training and development—not in the traditional sense, but rather designed with new managerial breakthroughs in mind. This leads us to a key question that administration needs to ask: What must be done to bring about a real and meaningful discovery of what is meant by "effective management," and how do we best go about developing the required competencies throughout the management ranks of *this* organization?

As the members of top management consider the real and absolute problems related to quality with which they are grappling, what will surely come into view, as a response to the above query is being formulated, is the reality that management effectiveness and its development *cannot* be allowed just to happen. Innovative planning, organizing, and control are required. To do less is to deprive the organization of collective skills and capabilities for solving quality-related problems.

Some ideas for action that may stimulate new direction in the thinking of the executives at the top, and potentially may make all the difference in the world of the manager at the middle, were expressed earlier, in Chapter 3. These middle-management-development ideas will not go away. They are ideas that administrations need to subscribe to if there is a desire to change the organizational waistline from fat to muscle, and to advance quality on all fronts.

Development at Nonmanagement Levels

Among many of our present day nonmanagement employees—who represent the best educated and most mature work force in American history—there is much evidence of the absence of a sense of work, a will to work, a satisfaction from work. This disturbing condition prompts the question Are we doing enough of the right things in promoting the growth of our peoples' talents and their capacity for understanding?

If we take stock objectively of what is being programmed for the development of nonmanagement employees in today's health care settings, the response to the above query must be one of denial, for what we find on the development scene are efforts devoid of strategy, process, integration, and continuity—all of which are essential characteristics for achieving advancements in the quality of work, the quality of work life, and the quality of human conduct.

There is strong evidence that, no matter what are the natural or developed skills and characteristics of individuals, unless there is a long and intensive process of support, encouragement, nurturance, education, and training, they will not attain extreme levels of capability, determination, and capacity for contributing qualitative dimensions to organizational outcomes.

When the task of promoting and sustaining quality of human performance at nonmanagement levels is viewed systematically, it is believed that these kinds of ideas need to find a place in our thinking.

Impart Values at the Very Outset. One of the important functions of initial interviewing, orientation, and preparatory training is to pass on organizational history, culture, and values. If this information is imparted in a shallow or trivial way during this beginning stage of employment, a unique opportunity for getting quality consciousness off to an early start is lost.

Position Managers Center Stage. If there is to be a significant change in the education and development of the largest segment of the organizational populace, it would seem reasonable that it begin with management role reform. It would seem equally reasonable that the administration, through its human resources department, determine what kinds of development process elements would suit the needs of a quality-driven environment.

This proposition suggests that the cry be "Forward to Two Fundamentals!" *First,* the idea should be activated that the manager (the boss) holds a major position of influence in the self-development of employees and thus needs aggressively and expertly to carry out the roles of teacher, coach, and counselor. For managers to be effective improvers of performance and developers of people requires the sponsorship of ongoing "train the trainer" and "employee coaching and counseling" programming for department directors, their assistants, and supervisory personnel so that they will become capable of presenting materials competently and smoothly, with full command of the educational content. *Second,* there should be recognition of the "one piece of pedagogical knowledge that is shared by every teacher in the world. We all know it to be true. It is, simply, that the best way to learn is to teach."[13] Yet few managers utilize that very basic piece of knowledge, principally because most managers are not sure how to implement it, since they do not possess adequate skills in the art of teaching to begin with. At any rate, we know the truth of the generalization "the best way to learn *is* to teach," and any attempt to put it into practice will be highly beneficial for members of management at all levels.

Gain Quality through Employee Involvement. Health care organizations need to follow suit in the general upheavals taking place in traditional management-employee roles in other industries. Increasingly, managements are turning to their workers for help with problems formerly handled only by themselves, staff function personnel, or other selected executives. Whether the concept is called "employee involvement" or "worker education," the goals are the same: to improve quality, heighten competitive verve, and open up a new channel for customer relations. Says a senior Aluminum Company of America executive: "It's useless to ask employees to do a better job if they aren't empowered to take steps toward that goal."[14]

The changes are difficult for both management and employee, yet if these things are not done, both the organization and its people will be the losers. Conversely, both will be gainers if a problem-solving climate is created within the workplace, and nonmanagement employees are made part of the solution by being brought into the decision-making mainstream through committee, task force, or quality circle membership.

The dynamics of a task-oriented team are unfamiliar to most people; we are more used to having group functioning controlled by an 'authority' who sets agendas and assigns tasks, and who may at most ask for input from the members. Lacking such an accepted leader, a multilateral setting must work out its own process. Simple techniques for identifying and prioritizing issues have proved effective in moving the process along.[15]

New forms of employee involvement require a great deal of reorganization and experimentation, along with positive motivations. Above all, in fostering the spread of worker participation, the concept must be understood as part of a wider process of change.

Restructure Work. Increasing the level of education and training of non-management employees without also reforming the current structure of work may threaten rather than promote the quality of human performance. Surely, the presence of an imbalance between education and work not only endangers the pursuit of quality improvement, it also puts in peril the achievement of cost effectiveness and productivity. "Research shows that workers become dissatisfied when they work in jobs in which their education and training are underutilized. They are also more prone to turnover and decreased work effort."[16]

The imbalance can be corrected by creating alternative forms of work organization in which employees are accorded greater responsibility through participation in making decisions and sharing work tasks—a concept Scott Myers pronounces in terms of making "every employee a manager." In his writing, Myers states that

Involvement of people in the planning and controlling, as well as the doing of their work, must be understood not as an act of good 'human relations' or as a means of exploitation but, rather, as a sound business practice that benefits both the organization and its members. The supervisor of the future knows he or she is not managing a technique or a program, but a way of life at work that finds expression in all levels of the create, make, and market functions of the organization. Through this way of life, people gradually become more knowledgeable and competent, and migrate and polarize toward a total commitment which leads to continuing growth, success, and self-renewal for both the organization and its members.[17]

Do Things Right in Skill Training. "People will do the right things, and do things right, if they are properly trained to do so," says Robert L. Desatnick, human resource consultant. "Employees who are well-trained produce superior products, which in turn require a minimum of service. And training is continuously repeated to reinforce the learning and maintain the desired behavior."[18] Commitment to this philosophy of training demands major investments—investments health care organizations cannot afford to let go by.

Plan for Development. High-quality performance does not just happen by chance, nor does it happen by holding a loyalty to the practice of conducting occasional "guest relations" programs for nonmanagement members of the organization. When the right things do happen from a quality point of view, more assuredly they will evolve out of a strategic process that embraces a sequential order of integrated segments of subject coverage planned over time. The educational and developmental units of the process are prepared for the instructional conveniences of the *teaching* manager, designed for the active participation of the *student* employees, and invented with a focus of attention on *quality* throughout.

Communicate, Communicate, Communicate. There is a multitude of ways in which administration and its management can capture opportunities for keeping the idea of quality obvious to the eyes and ears of the organizational membership. There are the media of mass meetings, small group meetings, newsletters, television, memoranda, and bulletin boards. Whatever means of communication are employed, they need to be planned in terms of the order of their scheduling, and in terms of the substance of their qualitative coverage.

Make Performance Appraisal Count. The performance appraisal process for nonmanagement employees needs to hold a position of high value and efficacy if it is to give strength to the planning of employee training and development. The essentialities of such a process include clarification of expectations, specific qualitative and quantitative criteria, free and open discussion, complete and timely feedback, concurrence on training and development needs, and appropriate rewards and incentive practices.

Go Beyond Training and Development. If the organization's effort is nothing more than the preparedness of its people for greater competency on the job, it will have failed its purposes, no matter how many of its members have been reached. The true challenge lies in going beyond the traditional confines of training and development to help shape individuals into complete human beings.

GETTING THE QUALITY JOB DONE

As we examine the requirements of newness expressed throughout this chapter, we are impelled to see how important it is to become free in our future thinking, uncoerced by inadequacies of the past. Indeed, the future demands that the ideas of the past be subject to careful analysis and, when warranted, changed or discarded.

Traditionally, the department of training and education has been a reactive function, almost always responding to the demands and pressures constantly being brought to bear upon it. This posture needs to be altered if the department is to do the job of promoting the growth of quality throughout the total organizational system. Education directors who fail to tackle the assignment of moving their units to a new position of strength in terms of their qualitative contributions may well experience further erosion of administrative support of their activities.

The challenge is to advance forward without losing the gains already made, and to envision creatively the new and different ways of attaining higher levels of quality in serving the cause of human development without being shackled by past patterns of thinking. Here are four specific thoughts believed central to the transformation being prompted.

Perceive the Function Differently

The educational scene in health care organizations has changed rapidly in the last decade. Newness in subject coverage, teaching technology, formats and methodologies, and a whole host of other novel dimensions has been introduced and implemented. There is little question that it has been a period of significant change in the ways in which programming activities are carried out within the training and education discipline. Yet there is a question that continues to haunt us: Has this succession of innovations brought about real improvements in the quality of human conduct and performance? A meaningful response to this penetrating question is long overdue, since one gains the impression that it is "anyone's guess" as to whether measurable improvements have actually occurred.

If it is accepted that the principal goal of training and education is to create men and women who are capable of doing things better, as well as capable of discovering and doing *new* things, then we need to transform the purpose and organization of the educational function to fit this goal more closely.

Thomas F. Gilbert gives us a clue for new direction in his book *Human Competence,* in which he strongly states the need to convert the training function into a "performance department" that operates as a profit center. He goes on to say that

> The training staff is probably as good a place as any to get into the performance-engineering business in a systematic way, because few others have as much experience with as wide a variety of perfor-

mance problems. But the performance department must have real responsibility. I suggest that it report directly to the chief officer of the institution and have full power to institute all performance-improvement programs, as long as it could show a measured effect on performance.[19]

The message is clear: we must reassess existing training and educational operations with the conviction that new directions in our thinking and action are essential to the task of closing the gap between the rhetoric and reality of achieving high quality outcomes from our educational efforts within the health care environment.

Put Excellence into the Learning Experience

The essence of quality is captured when the learning experience transcends the single idea of training people *just for jobs,* embracing as well the thought of Ralph Waldo Emerson, who stated that the goal of a good education was to train "man thinking." Writes Baird W. Whitlock,

> What he [Emerson] meant was that we didn't train a man to be a farmer, but a thinking man who farms. We often forget how little of one's life is spent on the job. If we are being 'practical' about training for the real world of the future, we should keep that in mind.[20]

Exposure to true excellence can be placed within the curricula if there is firmly fixed the intent to train, educate, and develop people who will be "thinking persons," people who gain not just *bare* knowledge but *understood* knowledge because what has been imparted combines conceptual enlightenment (the What and the Why) with technique and procedural know-how (the How).

Excellence also finds its source in effective teaching of values indispensable to cultivating potential. Education departments in the health care setting generally have not adequately taken on the task of transmitting values to the organizational membership. They also have fallen down on the job of persistently sharing full insight into the history of the life, development, and past accomplishments of the institution, which inside itself *is* the environment of new learning. All in all, excellence needs to find a suitable foundation not only in the perfection of teaching design and content but, more important, in the pervasiveness of the very subject of quality, and its discussion, throughout all phases and dimensions of the new learning experiences sponsored by the organization.

Demand Artistry in Teaching

To provide excellence in the learning experience of student employees, teachers must avoid the crutch of educational "packages," freeing themselves from outside prescriptions of how and what to teach. "To communicate knowledge and to provide a model of competence," Jerome Bruner contends, "the teacher must be free to teach *and to learn*. . . ."[21] If the teacher is also learning, teaching takes on a new quality—the result being a *partnership* of learning between student *and* teacher.

To instill quality into the educational process, as well as into the student, the teacher must exercise the skills of an artist. Education *is* an art, because it relies on the properties which the artist has and which are awakened in the artist-teacher. "The teacher, like the artist, is in touch with inner sources, with creative imagination, and with the unconscious world of the archetypes."[22]

The teacher's responsibility to provide quality education is also served by

- understanding the values of students that foster their motivation
- exercising intellectual and cultural interests beyond one's own specialty
- using new perspective lenses through which to see familiar ideas and to address current problems differently
- systemically providing a connection of wholeness between students and the world about them, as well as an understanding of the linkage among subject areas within a community of learning, and of the relationship between the learning process and the purpose and nature of work
- supporting the uniquely humanistic nature of the work environment of health care through a spirit of humaneness and humor

Make Return on Educational Investments Certain

The advice of Thomas Gilbert is that, generally, a training and education department (a performance department) should have three areas of responsibility that can be reflected in its own organization:

1. Assessment of performance opportunities.
2. Development of performance systems (including training development).
3. Delivery and implementation of performance systems.[23]

It is through the introduction of this kind of transformational model that two fundamental questions can be responded to more precisely:

- In what identifiable aspects of performance improvement within our organizational system have we invested our dollars this past fiscal year? In what specific amounts?
- To what measurable degree is the quality of our peoples' performance greater this fiscal period as compared with the previous fiscal period? Stated another way, what is the return on our training and educational investments in terms of our peoples' quality of work and quality of human conduct?

The willingness to ask these questions and the ability to answer them will make a difference in our efforts to position the organization's educational system as the one great hope for achieving quality.

NOTES

1. Edmund Fuller, "The Uses of an Education," *Wall Street Journal,* May 25, 1979, p. 31.

2. Jerome S. Bruner, *Toward a Theory of Instruction,* (Cambridge: Harvard University Press, 1966), p. 22.

3. John Dewey, *Democracy and Education* (New York: The Free Press, 1944), p. 10.

4. M.C. Richards, *Toward Wholeness: Rudolph Steiner Education in America* (Middletown, Conn.: Wesleyan University Press, 1980), p. 69.

5. Addison C. Bennett, *Productivity and the Quality of Work Life in Hospitals* (Chicago: American Hospital Association, 1983), p. 5.

6. Addison C. Bennett, ed., *Improving the Effectiveness of Hospital Management* (New York: Preston Publishing Co., 1975), p. 243.

7. Roman L. Yanda, *Doctors As Managers of Health Teams* (New York: AMACOM, 1977), p. vi.

8. Alfred Capus, quoted by Cornelia Otis Skinner, in *Elegant Wits and Grand Horizontals* (Boston: Houghton Mifflin).

9. Andrall E. Pearson, "Muscle-Build the organization," *Harvard Business Review,* Jul.–Aug. 1987, p. 50.

10. Richard P. Moses, *Evaluation of the Hospital Board and the Chief Executive Officer* (Chicago: American Hospital Association, 1986), p. 70.

11. Bank of America document, date unknown.

12. Ad Hoc Committee, *Evaluating the Performance of the Hospital Chief Executive Officer* (Chicago: Foundation of the American College of Hospital Administrators, 1984), p. 18.

13. Baird W. Whitlock, *Educational Myths I Have Known and Loved* (New York: Schocken Books, 1986), p. 3.

14. Terence Roth, "Employee Involvement Gains Support," *Wall Street Journal,* Dec. 12, 1984, p. 33.

15. Charles Heckscher, *The New Unionism* (New York: Basic Books, Inc., 1988), p. 196.

16. Russell W. Rumberger, "Our Work, Not Education Needs the Restructuring." *Los Angeles Times,* Jan. 15, 1984, p. 21.

17. Scott M. Myers, *Every Employee a Manager* (New York: McGraw-Hill Book Co., 1981), p. ix.

18. Robert L. Desatnick, *Managing to Keep the Customer* (San Francisco: Jossey-Bass Publishers, 1987), p. 51.

19. Thomas F. Gilbert, *Human Competence* (New York: McGraw-Hill Book Co., 1978), p. 229.
20. Whitlock, *Educational Myths,* p. 105.
21. Jerome Bruner, *The Process of Education* (Cambridge: Harvard University Press, 1977), p. 90.
22. Richards, *Toward Wholeness,* p. 69.
23. Gilbert, *Human Competence,* p. 230.

Part IV

Models

Chapter 10

Searching into Superiority

Still constant in a wondrous excellence.
—Shakespeare, *Sonnet* CV

These are the words of Harry Mullikin, Chairman and Chief Executive Officer, Westin Hotels and Resorts:

> Our principal value, going back more than 56 years, is *service*. It is the very foundation of our reputation as a company. With superior service, we enhance even further our second value, *quality*. But service and quality are not possible to sustain without our third value, *people*.
>
> Based on these values, our goal is to anticipate every one of your needs and then to deliver them each time you come in contact with us.
>
> When the interrelationship of our three principal values is understood, it leads to yet a fourth value: *value* itself. We believe that when we live up to your expectations for service, quality and good people, you will see Westin as a superior value and prefer to stay in one of our hotels or resorts when you travel.
>
> We are in business to serve you. You can count on it.[1]

A further penetration of Harry Mullikin's thoughts about these values is captured from his "personal note," which appeared in a Westin publication and is included as Exhibit 10-1.

Westin is the oldest hotel company in the United States. Known for its theme—caring, comfortable, civilized—Westin over the years has consistently provided its guests with high levels of quality service.

To gain further insight into how Westin Hotels and Resorts maintain a timely and appropriate response to the quality of the service expectations of their customers, the following interview was engaged in with Robert J. Sed-

Exhibit 10-1 Harry Mullikin's Thoughts about Values

A PERSONAL NOTE
BY HARRY MULLIKIN

Westin People Make the Difference

Our people make the difference. That is an intriguing thought, although the idea is neither novel nor exclusive. It has, however, been our claim for many, many years at Westin Hotels and Resorts. We live by it. We stake our reputation on it.

From the company's standpoint, it means that we nurture and sustain excellence. Our people are carefully chosen, carefully trained, and then rewarded for excellent performance by a strong promotion-from-within procedure that is highly regarded in our industry. As a result, our people tend to stay with us and to grow in their career development.

From your standpoint as our guest, it means that you can expect to be treated with gracious hospitality and attention to detail by people who are confident in taking care of all your needs and who care enough to do so with pride and enthusiasm. There are competent, career professionals at all levels of the company and they're at your service.

Our people are especially sensitive to caring for the frequent traveler, for they know how tough it can be on the road. Some kinds of service can be measured, such as the cleanliness of a guest room or the promptness of a wake-up call. Other kinds of service are intangible and reflect a positive attitude that goes beyond basic expecta-tions, such as the door attendant who addresses you by name or the maitre d' who remembers your favorite table. Often, something as easy as a smile determines a guest's perception of our entire company.

In a very real sense, then, we believe that Westin people set Westin apart from all the others. We know that because time after time in travel industry surveys you tell us so.

As an incentive and a reminder about the importance of this focus, we established an employee award more than 25 years ago. Called the Thurston-Dupar Inspirational Award after two of the company's founders, this award is given annually to the employee who has best demonstrated outstanding qualities of leadership, service, and dedication to his or her work, and whose efforts have helped Westin become a better company in satisfying the needs of the traveling public.

A committee of judges within each hotel selects one person, who then receives the award for that particular hotel. Each hotel's award recipient then becomes a nominee eligible to be chosen as the company-wide winner and representative of the award for the year.

Since the award's inception in 1958, the nominated candidates have exemplified the exceptional "people-make-the-difference" qualities embodied in the award. These candidates are nomi-nated based on significant contributions to their job, their fellow employees' welfare, and their community. Without exception, they portray leadership in the hotel; have an active involvement in community affairs and activities; show dedication to work and improving work methods or services in such a way that the hotel renders better service to the guests; and, as a result, are an inspiration to all.

Those aren't just nice words. They have a deep and profound meaning for us at Westin.

For instance, to our 1985 Thurston-Dupar Inspirational Award winner, Gail Rivera, room service manager at The Westin Hotel, O'Hare, they mean continually volunteering extra time, energy, and creative talents to get the job done—no matter what it is. While she does a superb job for guests in her own area of responsibility, Gail is also a firm believer in interdepartmental cooperation and often volunteers her services in other areas of the hotel as needed.

Gail is an incredibly energetic and giving person. Her volunteer spirit spills over into church, school, and community associations. She works with the needy, the blind, and senior citizens, and participates in various fund-raising events. She is a true inspiration to those around her, and is exemplary of the qualities we look for in recipients of the Thurston-Dupar Award.

Gail also helps create what we like to think of as a distinctive Westin culture. It means that no matter where you go in the world, you can tell when you have checked into a Westin hotel. Regardless of the architecture or the location—whether it's an urban downtown hotel or a world-class resort—Westin hotels all have that same sense of professionalism, of intense interest on the part of the employee for the guest's well-being, and of comfort and understated elegance.

Interestingly enough, the geographical spread of our company-wide winners of the Thurston-Dupar Inspirational Award over the past few years makes this point dramatically. Our recipients have been at hotels widely removed from each other—from Houston, Texas, to Manila, the Philippines.

We have extraordinary people working at our hotels. And they have one goal in mind: a commitment to comfort, care, and civility. This is why our people make the difference.

Harry Mullikin
Chairman and
Chief Executive Officer
Westin Hotels & Resorts
The Westin Building
Seattle, WA 98121

Source: Courtesy of Westin Hotels & Resorts, Seattle, Washington.

delmeyer, General Manager, The Westin South Coast Plaza located in Orange County, California. Mr. Seddelmeyer has been the general manager of the Westin South Coast Plaza Hotel for the past four years. Prior to that, he had worked in seven other Westin hotels over a period of fourteen years. The hotel he now manages has approximately 400 employees, 40 of whom hold management positions.

Q: *The first question relates to whether or not there exists at the corporate or local level a philosophical statement relating to quality?*

RJS: About two years ago, the general managers of Westin Hotels were asked to create a vision statement for our company. While it's a very generalized statement, it does specifically discuss the fact that we want to operate quality hotels which exemplify quality in terms of the service provided our guests as well as our concern with offering our employees a quality environment in which to work.

A vision statement was developed at the corporate level; then in addition to that, all of our hotels have been asked to establish a vision statement. We have one here at the Westin South Coast Plaza. In fact, we have a book that our Hotel's Executive Committee uses. It takes the vision statement for this Hotel, and breaks it down into policies and procedures that we work from.

The vision statement for this hotel states, in part: "It is a first class Hotel providing guests with unparalleled services and products in a comfortable, residence-like environment. The Westin South Coast Plaza provides a safe and secure, professional environment which encourages employee development through personal recognition and financial rewards. The Hotel is a leader in the community, contributing personal and professional resources, all the while providing the corporation and the owner with the highest possible financial returns." We think it's significant that we put that last part at the end even though it is of great concern to us.

Q: *What do you see as the value of this vision statement?*

RJS: The vision statement itself is the basis for the plan of action that we review annually here at the hotel in terms of specific goals created for each year. Our executive committee, comprised of seven of us who manage the hotel, meets every two weeks to go over the specific goals that we have established on an annual basis. This, in essence, is our business plan.

Q: *Does your vision statement tend to change over time?*

RJS: We revised our vision statement about a year ago. The previous vision statement was in existence for about three years. The content has not essentially changed. What has changed is the specific wording and emphasis.

Q: *In what ways do you communicate the vision statement to your employees?*

RJS: We display the document in our employee cafeteria for our people to see and read. At present, we do not display it for our guests to see.

At least once each year, in our employees' newsletter, I will devote my column, the "General Manager's Column," to a reflection of how the vision statement has been tied to our business plan or to our performance plan in each year.

Q: *Have you defined "quality" for your people?*

RJS: Yes we have, without question. As a part of the vision statement there is a need, I believe, for establishing the relationship to quality of each of our employees. So, it is done in a documented form in several different ways. We document what quality means in the employee handbook which all of our employees receive. We address quality specifically in most all of our management's goals—the annual performance goals managers are committed to which are documented.

With regard to our nonmanagement employees, I believe it's pretty clear in all our people's minds what quality means as a result of the various means we use. The real issue, however, is determining and communicating the expectation level in terms of achieving the quality. We need to get down to what it is specifically we're asking our employees to do so that collectively they are delivering "unparalleled service" as expressed in the vision statement.

Q: *More specifically, how do you get at this "expectation" issue?*

RJS: There is a set of specific objectives identified in the employee handbook, several of which deal with quality. In addition, we include our employees in our hotel's goal-setting process. We expect a certain percentage of their goals to be related to quality, which are monitored on an ongoing basis.

Q: *Do you place the responsibility for quality efforts with any single individual?*

RJS: No, not in this hotel. I have had experience in the past in other larger hotels that have had somebody that might specifically deal with it. Normally, someone might be brought in for a prescribed period of time to assist in working up standards and goals. This might be an outside consultant or it could be someone on the hotel staff who would be pulled from other responsibilities to devote their time to our quality effort.

Q: *What is the nature and scope of your human resources function, and what is its role in quality enrichment?*

RJS: Twenty-five years ago the personnel director in our company was probably a clerk from the accounting office who was designated to take care of records. Today, our director of human resources sits on the hotel's executive committee. As recently as two years ago, that was not the case in this hotel. At this hotel the human resources function is comprised of the director and two other individuals who are more specialized in training, since most of the required paperwork has been taken out of their hands by our computers and they don't need to be concerned about health insurance, worker's compensation claims, and many other things.

The director of human resources is a professional—a degree person, if not a degree in that particular field, certainly in a related field such as general business or communication.

The three individuals in the department spend a good deal of time in the area of training, since training is important to us. Our continuing education requirements are quite high. They come from all members of our executive committee, and individual goals are based on these expectations for all of our department heads.

So our human resources function, through the elevation of its position to the Executive Committee level and thanks to the technology available today, can spend its time interacting in the planning process, working on the issues that we feel are very important, and addressing the policies impacting quality.

Q: *What other activities hold high priority in the human resource arena?*

RJS: One of the most significant objectives of the director of human resources is monitoring the quality of work life.

We have always placed quality of work life as a high priority. I believe one of Westin's competitive advantages is offering an unparalleled quality of work life.

Q: *In what way does human resources become involved in quality of work life?*

RJS: They conduct surveys, interview our people, and serve as advisors to an employee committee that basically plans all of the activities the hotel sponsors for employees on an annual basis.

Q: *What can you tell us about recruitment, selection, and orientation of new employees?*

RJS: We are diligent in screening to make sure that the facts presented to us are true. We spend a lot of time training, and the initial orientation is quite important to us.

We believe it important, from the very beginning, to acquaint every employee with the philosophy of our company and our hotel. An important part of our orientation process is encouraging employees to tell us how well we've done in orienting them. There's an initial orientation program that would be common with almost all businesses, then there's the departmental orientation as well. It really goes on for about the first week of the employee's time with us. Subsequently, there's a secondary orientation that comes about a month after the employee has joined us. After we feel that the employee has learned the job pretty well, and the function that's performed, this second orientation is scheduled to cover such areas as fire and life safety. That's when we get into good discussion about quality as opposed to "here it is, folks."

After all this, employees have a chance to give us back in writing their feelings of *us*.

Q: *What are your experiences with turnover and absenteeism?*

RJS: Absenteeism is not too much of a problem. Turnover is a problem for all local hotels based probably on the local economy. In Orange County there has been a very heavy increase in the number of hotel rooms available, and our turnover did not go up very much. We are proud that we did several things to make sure that the employees first had a good place in which to work, and second, they recognized how good it was. So we didn't see an increase in turnover that we had anticipated, but yet it is a problem in our industry. It's always a problem. It is highlighted by the entry level employees in some of the less skilled positions. I would suspect that it would be the same in health care.

We have several people who worked in other Westin hotels and have been here since this hotel opened just about thirteen years ago. One of our banquet servers has thirty-six years with our company. Can you imagine carrying those trays for thirty-six years?

Q: *Do you have an ongoing management development process that reinforces the value of quality?*

RJS: Yes, we do. The backbone of our process is a program that we have purchased, with people throughout the company taking on the role of trainers. The three phases of the development activity, which last about a year, cover such subject areas as interrelationship skills and guest contact skills. And we require everyone to go through the program.

Q: *In health care, there has been an increasing use of so-called "guest relations" programs. Do you have such a program?*

RJS: Yes, we do. Since our company programs are relatively generalized, we tend to purchase more specific type programs from other sources. There are people in the marketplace who have modified training segments to fit a front desk clerk or a food server in a restaurant. Even a food server in an all-day dining room or a coffee shop versus fine dining. They are that fine-tuned.

These modified programs are very important to us, since we can tell the difference when we schedule them on a timely and continuing basis. It also shows when we have a few new employees who have not been through the programs. You can pick out those employees who need training either by guest critiques or by visual experience while utilizing a facility. You can tell who are the most skilled and those who are the most prized of our employees, those who do well in quality of service.

Q: *How do you go about evaluating the individual performance of your people?*

RJS: We evaluate all of our new employees after thirty days of employment, and then they go on the annual schedule of appraisal which falls at a period of time following the completion of our fiscal year, so that numbers relating to operating results can be included in the appraisal process.

Q: *In addition to goals, are there other measurable criteria employed?*

RJS: Indeed. I would say that our appraisal process is ninety percent objective, ten percent subjective. And the objective part of the evaluation includes specific expectations with regard to quality. What's important is that the evaluation is a two-way process in which our employees evaluate us as to how well we oriented them to our expectations.

Q: *Do you practice employee participation?*

RJS: We practice employee participation in all areas of the organization, certainly including quality. We're interested in getting our people to think.

What works well for us are our meetings with all employees, scheduled for one day each quarter. It provides a good forum for discussing quality. Many questions about quality come to us from our employees during these all-employee meetings. And we do not tend to talk about quality in general terms. We get very specific about it, and where we see the need we will establish a task force to deal with specifics, since we need to determine at what level we want to achieve quality. It's nice to have these vision statements about being unparalleled, but we have to establish what we are going to achieve.

One of my own personal philosophies—and I feel it's the company's as well— is the more often and better the communication, the healthier the organization will be. I firmly believe that, because it is surely something I've observed in every hotel. There are several ways in which we try to accomplish effective employee communication, some by spending a great deal of money, some by spending very little. For example, two methods we use are the suggestion box and a telephone hotline, both providing the two-way aspects of communication. And that's very important! In fact, our written suggestion program offers employees several ways to be responded to. They may select a verbal response, or a written response either to their home or at the workplace.

All of the approaches we use bring in questions and comments about quality. How well does it all work? Certainly, there's room for improvement!

Q: *What about coordination—the companion to communication?*

RJS: That, in fact, is a specific subject area in our training program because coordination is of constant concern to us. Obviously, we all need to work together. We're particularly blessed, in a medium-sized hotel like ours, to have good working relationships among our people. It also is fortunate that we don't have such narrow views of one's responsibility in this hotel caused by tradition, as well as caused by, frankly, not having a union, which makes it easier for people to step over and help one another.

Q: *Any other comments regarding employee involvement?*

RJS: Our philosophy is to continuously push down to the lowest levels increasing decision making and participation. Job descriptions for our employees are flexible. They are reviewed annually for opportunities to extend control and responsibilities at the employee level. At the same time, we continue to reinforce the idea of employee involvement with our managers at every level, and we install in them the value of creating an environment in which people doing the work have a chance to recognize the changes that need to be introduced to make their jobs more efficient and more quality-oriented. Along with that, we reinforce the idea of two-way communication when decisions have to be made to change something. We don't want anybody to think that there isn't a forum to respond to changes. That's very important. When I talk with our people about some change that needs to be made, I've got to be big enough to at least listen to the problems that the change has created. I might not be able to do anything about it, but I want to make sure that the employees feel that I *do* want to hear their opinions.

Q: *In what ways do you monitor and measure quality?*

RJS: We're no geniuses at it, but we do talk with our guests to see what they think. We certainly give the employees a chance to talk about both the people who work for them and their superiors in terms of specific issues of quality, as well as other aspects of the organization. We also talk with people who use some of our competition to see what their level of expectation is, and then determine which of these we can match and which we can't.

The problem we fear most—the problem we are most concerned with—is the guest that is not totally satisfied, but decides to go somewhere else and never tells us he doesn't like us and never tells us why. Once again, it's the idea of trying to deliver the expectations the guests hold rather than what we perceive to be the expectations. Of course, a common practice in the hotel industry is the use of evaluation forms placed in the rooms. It is an easy method of soliciting complaints, and we need to know what things went wrong, but like almost all hotel companies, we experience a very low response, particularly positive.

Q: *What about the problem of human conduct on the part of the maid on the floor, the desk clerk, the telephone operator? How do you keep on top of it?*

RJS: We monitor their conduct very carefully, very often. I don't perceive that we have a problem with it. But in our industry, like the hospital industry, there are so many human contacts, you know, and I'm sure that somebody has analyzed how many there are in a 400-room hotel on a given day. It's thousands. And you're dealing with bad days, sickness, and having to be at work with other things on your mind. Since there can be an array of varied problems, a good deal of our training is directed toward helping employees feel better about themselves and their situation. Then there is the training of supervisors in helping them recognize certain signs of problems and in dealing with these problems.

Q: *Would you tell us what you can about the manner in which you reward quality?*

RJS: We utilize many different ways to reward our people, both management and nonmanagement, in addition to salary advancement. And we spend a good deal of money to ensure that there is the ability to recognize the quality of performance. We have incentive programs both for individuals and groups. We establish measurability in several different ways, including talking to our guests. We try to make all of our incentives measurable and we try to make the rewards very good.

Some of the principles under which we operate are these: We recognize employees publicly so that their peers know of their success. Whatever the physical aspects of the recognition, whether it's money, a trip, or a wristwatch, we make certain that its value is properly perceived and that the right reward is going to the right person. We try to establish programs that run for a specific duration and make sure that they are well-publicized so that no one can feel that they've not had equal opportunity to win. Shorter periods seem to work better than annual incentives, so what we are more likely to do is to focus on a special issue for a fixed time and then a month or two later do a different special issue program, again for a fixed period.

Our overall philosophy is to let their peers know about it, let them bask in the glory of their success. We publicize the results very well to all of our employees so that the winners are well-recognized. Nothing so special, but it gets results.

Q: *How do you sustain the quest for quality?*

RJS: Our industry is driven to it for survival. The crux of the hotel industry, which is the same in most industries, is fighting the bottom-line issues and maintaining the quality level that is expected of us. The hotel industry has always lived with an expectation of quality combined with a price-value relationship. Certainly our company is very much driven by the need to sustain a high level. So maintaining constant stimulation regarding quality is a given, not a problem.

Q: *In summary, what elements of a quality-improvement process do you consider to be particularly significant?*

RJS: I would say: selecting the right employees, establishing timely and specific goals, management development, the reward system, and monitoring the standards in the industry as they relate to quality external to our own organization.

Q: *Is this monitoring based on external experiences or comparisons?*

RJS: Both. There are opportunities for exchange within the American Hotel Association and the California Hotel Association. A specific example would be how a plate of food is presented in a banquet room at another hotel versus how we're presenting it.

Q: *Any other elements you wish to add to your list?*

RJS: Surely, the constant task of identifying what the expectation level of the consumer is, because that changes over time. And then redefining and reclarifying over time any changes that are needed regarding any key aspect of our Hotel operations in response to the changing expectations of the consumer.

Then there is internal communication, which I consider to be very important to quality enhancements. We monitor communications rather informally, but we do it pretty frequently. In fact, we've just recently formed a task force to evaluate how well our communications were going in both directions.

I think all through this interview you've not been hearing about many unique processes at work. But what I think sets us apart from the crowd is essentially that we're just diligent in what everybody has the opportunity to do with regard to quality. We are committed to spending time, acting and thinking about it, making certain that quality does enter our thinking in the decisions we make. In the case of communication, for example, while other organizations may not spend the time required, or merely talk about it, we're committed to doing something about it.

Q: *This is my final question: What do you believe still remains to be done in your hotel in connection with your quality improvement efforts?*

RJS: Two things come to mind. First, I believe that we have probably let slip in the last couple of years some of the emphasis that should be placed on our very rich tradition. For instance, all of us in my peer group went through an orientation phase that basically was the history and traditions of Westin Hotels. That program does not exist today; thus there is a generation of management coming up that does not have that rich experience. I think it very important that all of us here at the hotel be exposed to this experience.

Second, I believe we need to continue to work on getting a clear definition for the entry-level employees in the hotel as to how important their every effort is as it relates to the total quality of the hotel. That's our ongoing challenge, and if there is a singular goal in quality in 1989, that will be it, because we all tend to forget how important every act, every transaction we engage in can become. And certainly we see the downside of that if there's been a mistake made. For if there's one mistake during a visit, it may be okay, but if there are two or three, some small things can just bring the issue to a head. If those slight things had not happened, we would probably not have a very dissatisfied guest. We would have one that had not a great experience, but not an experience that was necessarily considered bad either. However, the concern still haunts us as to the perceived degree of damage that was done out there that we don't know about, and the chances that our guest will not come back to stay with us again.

NOTES

1. Westin Hotels and Resorts, Apr. 1987, p. 1.

Chapter 11

Making Total Quality a Reality

Quality is never an accident; it is always the result of intelligent effort.
—John Ruskin

In 1984, with quality at the crux of global competitiveness, an article appeared in an Asian business journal with the provocative title "Japan Does Away with Quality Control." At first, it came as quite a shock to those impressed by Japan's traditional concern with and commitment to manufacturing quality.

Had Japan decided that quality was no longer a priority? Hardly. What it had decided was that traditional quality-control techniques were no longer sufficient and that something beyond these traditional approaches was needed. "A similar realization has taken place at certain companies in the U.S."[1]

The writing of this book, as indicated in the Preface, is centered on the realization that something beyond the essence of "quality assurance," as we have traditionally viewed it within the health care environment, is needed. Even something beyond the more recent surge of new energy and interest in taking on the complex tasks of defining and measuring health care quality with increased precision. That something, as conveyed throughout the discourse of this text, is the formal and explicit embracement of the added human dimensions of quality of work itself, quality of life at work, and the quality of individual demeanor within the mainstream of the health care organization's continuing pursuit of quality enhancement in the broadest sense. To accept this proposition is to take a completely new look at quality. The way in which we perceive and think about quality will make "all the difference in the world" of work.

THE BASIC ELEMENTS OF TOTAL QUALITY ENHANCEMENT

Now is the time to take a completely new *total* look at quality, and to begin drawing a blueprint for quality enhancement that will make a difference in the future, based on a solid belief in the principle that management must

221

lead its health care organization to be all that it can become with respect to the quality of its care and services.

The intent of this chapter is to set forth a proposed blueprint rendered as an ongoing process. "The achievement of quality, the experts will tell you, must be an ongoing process."[2] It must be systemic and innovative in its design. While "making it right the first time" is a tenet to be honored in the world of quality, it is reasonable to expect that the original blueprint will be subject to constant change at a good rate. Each organization needs to be on a fast track in modifying and improving upon not only the various components of its overall quality enhancement process, but also the methodologies for capturing the advantages of new product and service ideas produced as outcomes of the process.

What is to be remembered is that no one holds a monopoly on quality, so the imperative of innovation is evident, even on the part of organizations recognized by *Fortune* as the world's top competitors. Here are just two examples of executing the principle of constant improvement.

- To avoid that fate (of being overtaken) in the midsize part of the copier market where it still leads, Xerox today makes a habit of competitive benchmarking. Company engineers pull apart competing products to see how they are made and then estimate the costs of production in search for new, cheaper, and better ways to make their own copiers.
- Even a product as basic as Levi's jeans has been adapted and improved to stay competitive since its invention in 1853 by a Bavarian immigrant for the miners in the California gold rush. "Over the years we have made in excess of 20 fundamental changes in our basic jeans," says Peter Thigpen, president of the Jean Company, a division of Levi Strauss. "And I don't mean fashion changes. I mean changes like increasing the overlap on the fly from $\frac{3}{8}$ of an inch to $\frac{5}{8}$ of an inch. There is a constant drive around here for self-renewal."[3]

With these opening thoughts in mind, let us move our attention to the following twelve process elements believed essential to a health care organization's efforts to enhance total quality (see Figure 11-1). In the simplest of terms, the elements are these:

1. establish commitment
2. conduct assessment
3. engage in networking
4. set the direction
5. plan strategically
6. create organizational change

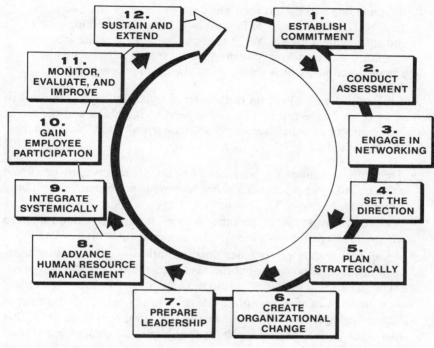

Figure 11-1 Quality Enhancement Process

7. prepare leadership
8. advance human resource management
9. integrate systemically
10. gain employee participation
11. monitor, evaluate, and improve
12. sustain and extend

1. Establish Commitment

This first element of the quality enhancement process, to establish commitment, is a familiar theme, and we most often find it at the top of the list. In writing about the attributes of a quality revolution, Tom Peters says this about commitment:

> I have dwelled on management commitment for the very reason that most experts ignore it. Yes, they put it at the top of their list, in a knee-jerk fashion; but they devote about two paragraphs in a

500-page book to it, and then move on to the nuts and bolts, the "real stuff." They never define precisely what this seemingly soft and squishy item means. Yes, it is about attitudes; but the attitude of abiding and emotional commitment must also be translated into practical actions, which show up on the calendar each day.[4]

At the top is where we look for the genesis of organizational commitment, and as we focus on the proper acts and actions of the board and the senior people in management, this "seemingly soft and squishy item" takes on these kinds of meanings.

- True commitment of the board and its administration must be viewed as an unending engagement; it can neither wane nor be treated with brief popularity.
- A commitment to quality enhancement must embrace commitment to an environment that inspires quality achievement (Chapter 2).
- A call to commitment requires documentation—credo, mission statement, goals, and policies—but there is the caveat of Stanley Peterfreund: "The signals sent out from the top must be consistent with the words."[5]
- The board must give new life to demonstrating active involvement in 'managing' quality. "For most boards, the first step is to agree that managing quality is a new capability they have to develop, with new skills to be learned"[6] (Chapter 3).
- The agenda of the board needs to increase the frequency of quality-related discussions.
- A skill requiring attention by board membership is the ability to ask hard, tough questions about every aspect of quality, not just the quality of the clinical/technological services.
- Organizations still lagging in quality will not regain competitiveness if top management delegates responsibility for quality.
- While top administrative commitment begins with the chief executive officer (CEO), it demands the attributes of solidarity and consistency among *all* members of top management, who need to have strong beliefs and the passion to pursue the goal of quality enhancement.
- True commitment to quality is virtually an obsession with quality that is clearly evident throughout the organization, from the conference rooms, where service ideas are being brainstormed, to bulletin boards that provide up-to-date messages about the progress of quality enhancement.
- Members of senior management, according to Philip Crosby, chairman of Philip Crosby Associates, Inc., have to recognize "that they are the primary cause of the organization's quality status."[7]

- In formulating and promulgating commitment, the leaders' tools are "a clear, concise vision and consummate communication skills—with soul"[8] (Chapter 3).
- To prevent the quality promise from ringing hollow, General Motors' vice-president of manufacturing, Thomas O. Mathues, says, "management must give quality top status, top attention, and top dedication in every decision made, every action taken, and every move made."[9] A study conducted by the American Society for Quality Control (ASQC) surfaced the disturbing finding that "only 56 of the 197 CEOs polled were involved sufficiently in their company's quality operations to even discuss them."[10]
- Real progress toward achieving quality goals will take considerable effort; "there are many problems that will have to be solved, and many chances to be diverted from the path."[11]
- Commitment at the top means personal involvement at the top: fielding customer complaints on hot lines; and personally testing the product or service; meetings at least weekly to address quality issues; and participating in orientation and training.
- Top management must be involved in the management of quality programs, giving visible evidence to the organization's commitment as existing units or new units launch quality activities, and providing positive reinforcement and recognition of quality contributions.
- "Reaching the commitment level is not simply a matter of being a nice thing to do. Quality commitment is a matter of survival in a highly competitive world. Both productivity and customer satisfaction demand it."[12]

A popularized axiom is that the commitment of the senior people to the quality process is unquestioned at the organizations that make the best products and provide the best service. Yet, it is all too easy to become sloppy and comfortable, to retort: "Of course I'm committed to quality! Aren't we all?" There is, of course, a way to test one's individual commitment, as well as to test its reflectivity in the overall commitment of the organization totally, and that is through the investigative process of assessment, which is our next element.

2. Conduct Assessment

In conducting assessment, we are in the zone of inquiry that penetrates the full length of the quality enhancement process. In fact, the idea of assessment runs throughout Chapters 3, 5, 7, and 8, along with scattered queries strategically placed. It is a critical stage of the process, because it has to do with discovery and the opportunity to innovate. Since it has to do with question asking, it seems appropriate to put to use the basic queries of investigation in addressing this activity.

What is assessment? It is an act of evaluation that every effective executive engages in when managing. Most often, however, it is intuitive in nature, rather than planned and organized, thus making the inquisitor vulnerable to conditions in which less than the best questions ultimately are posed. What is desirable is the purposeful design of an information-gathering tool that gives credence to asking the right questions and to giving these questions the priority they deserve. Such an instrument will sharpen the problem-solving mind of the organization, and promote a spirit of inquiry throughout the system.

Why assess? Right at the outset of the quality enhancement process, we are interested in gaining increased knowledge about the organization's current state of affairs with regard to quality strengths, weaknesses, threats, and opportunities for enhancement. A well-thought-through examination of the essential dimensions of present conditions and circumstances is the starting point in moving closer to quality definition, process direction and planning management needs, and environmental improvements.

Where does assessment take place? Internally, it cascades over three hierarchical levels of the organizational system: the organizational level, the functional level, and the individual level. Externally, beyond supplier performance and other factors impacting on the institution's quality of care and service, is the most essential task of unfolding through assessment the customers' definition of quality, of discovering what aspects of quality they expect, and then "designing systems that meet these expectations—or surpass them."[13] As the assessment is made, the organization needs "to examine and reassess how well it manages its relationships with two key groups: internal customers (employees) and external customers (those who purchase its products and services). Both are essential; the two are inseparable."[14] Thus, a key question for management to pose is: Have we identified and met the goal of integrating these two dynamic forces? The competitive edge will not be gained without the support of both groups as creative solutions, not pat answers, are sought, and firming up the customer connection is subject to continued renewal.

When is assessment engaged in? While assessment should be considered as analogous to the idea of "perpetual inventory," at least once annually it needs to be formally instituted to ask customers "How are we doing?" and to gain internal feedback from managers and their people about the quality of organizational performance. Naturally, there still remains the necessity of informal inquiry on a continuing basis.

Who holds primary responsibility for assessment? Of course, responsibility centers on management at all levels. However, to provide the assessment process with the oversight it requires, it is believed prudent to select a member of senior management to take on this important assignment.

How should the assessment be designed?

> Self-assessment, self-discovery, and self-development demand an open-minded inquisitiveness that finds its value in the asking of the right kinds of questions in an objective and insightful manner. In today's competitive world, the questions need to be hard and penetrating. They need to get at what's right and what's wrong, and when necessary must burrow down to the most basic elements of a function that explain what is causing the problem.[15]

For the sake of innovation, the assessment instrument should be invented to embrace two interrelated types of inquiry. The first of these, *response-directed,* is self-assessment aimed at gaining insight into the preparedness of the organization for quality, the responsiveness it has shown in the past to what the customers say they need, and its awareness of the requirements of change. The second dimension, *opportunity-directed,* is that segment of the assessment process targeted toward identifying areas of opportunity for quality improvements needed for the future success of the enterprise (Chapter 8).

3. Engage in Networking

Inside the organization there are departments that serve internal customers: the pharmacy delivers to patient units; the management information systems department serves the members of management; central sterile supply meets the needs of the operating room; and the materials management division responds to the requests of "customers" throughout the system. Each department must determine who its customers are and then network with them to discern what they want, how they can best serve them, and just how well they are doing in responding to their needs. External networks, on the other hand, are ways in which the "mind" of an organization shares its knowledge and experience with other organizations. These networks come in two forms: connections with other organizations within the health field and connections with organizations outside the industry. Both types of networking can be local, national, or international.

Networking, as an alliance that allows organizations to broaden their range of vision, makes all kinds of sense because it offers a high payoff. For example, as a networker we are afforded the opportunity to

- get to know more about the outside world that surrounds us, and as a result, see ourselves and our organization differently
- open up almost limitless possibilities for creative connections with managements external to our own organization

- self-assess ourselves and our organization through comparison
- observe different management styles and different organizational environments
- discover what has been undiscovered
- draw knowledge from the best in any field
- avoid "reinventing the wheel"
- arrive at more meaningful solutions through better understanding of our problems
- increase our ability to perceive newness as we find contrasts occurring in the world around us
- invoke and strengthen values as an inherent quality of association
- expand our vision, thus look more deeply at our problems
- recognize similarities in the world of work that may otherwise escape our senses
- strengthen our capacity for networking as one of our organization's survival strategies.[16]

Through these multiple extensions of sight and insight, managerial thinking is enhanced by a whole new range of possibilities—and that is where the best solutions lie (Chapter 10).

4. Set the Direction

In a three-page advertisement placed by the Chrysler Corporation, Lee Iacocca is quoted as saying, "If you want to be the best, you have to separate yourself from all the talk about quality. And put it in writing."[17] Indeed, turning the corner on quality demands putting in words the organization's thoughts and its purposes. Without a clearly defined purpose, it is difficult to communicate what the institution is doing to meet its quality obligations. Without a purpose, the organization has no single thought to communicate. Without a purpose, there is no convenient way to measure progress (Chapter 2).

In 1912, critics of Woodrow Wilson chided him for engaging in airy rhetoric when he made the remark that "A nation is not made of anything physical. A nation is made of its thoughts and its purposes. Nothing can give it dignity except its thoughts. Nothing can give it impulse except its ideals."[18] Surely, this concluding idea is translatable into organizational language, as the Hewlett-Packard Company (discussed in Chapter 8) discovered when the quality goal it chose was a tenfold reduction in the failure rates of its products during the eighties. The CEO knew this represented a bold approach—a difficult challenge—but he also suspected that anything less dramatic would not convey the importance attached to the issues of quality. In the words of John A. Young, president and CEO, "By establishing a far-reaching goal and getting people to feel in their guts that the goal was reasonable, we felt that some serious movement would begin to occur."[19] It is a startling purpose expressing an ideal that has given the Hewlett-Packard Company the impulse to achieve it.

Other corporations, in both industrial and service sectors, have set bold directions for themselves over the years. To illustrate, the Bell System states its commitment emphatically:

> There is nothing that we know about the increasingly competitive environment we confront that warrants the least compromise of the Bell System's commitment to deliver products and services that are in every respect the best possible. Whether we serve alone or compete with others, our aim is to be best.[20]

In health care, as in other industries, corporate goals that serve lofty purposes such as these must be clear and distinct to the eyes of the organization's constituents, and rousing enough to get their attention. The goals should reach beyond merely acceptable quality levels; they should bring new and different challenges for all concerned in making higher quality the organization's most important end.

Setting a course to meet extraordinary quality standards requires a commitment on the part of the members of top management that all functioning components within the organizational system (including the medical populace) will take the necessary action of creating quality goals; of establishing effective and efficient process and procedural design; of providing products and services at high quality value; of monitoring quality; and of continuing the search for opportunities for further quality improvements. While it may not be possible to achieve an absolute level of zero defects, all quality-related activities should be viewed as moving the organization ever closer to the most desirable goal, a goal that Motorola, Inc., has set for itself, "The pursuit of perfection"[21] (Chapters 2 and 3).

5. Plan Strategically

Having already responded to the question Where are we now? via assessment and networking, and to the question Where should we be going? through the setting of goals and purposes, management is now better poised to take on the query How should we get there? on a planned basis.

On April 8, 1987, the byline appearing in a full-page advertisement of Citicorp offered this message: "We Work Hard To Build Long-Term Customer

Relations. We Won't Sacrifice Them For Short-Term Gains."[22] These seventeen words present two principal thoughts: (1) strategic planning needs to focus on expectations of a new and growing breed of customer: the *strategic* customer, who is more discriminating, strategic-minded, more knowledgeable, and who wants more information on which to base decisions; and (2) techniques to achieve quality improvement in the short term rarely improve quality in the long term. We cannot favor the promises of "crash" programs—which they usually do—to provide fast answers to problems that are solved by slow solutions. What is required is strategic planning—long term—that calls upon management to think through the purpose and business of the organization and its quality enhancement process totally as a complete system, as it provides a road map for its people. Developing a strategy takes time, as does the implemented achievement of quality targets built into the plan.

Top management must be openly and actively committed to improving quality as a strategic necessity."[23] In so doing, it needs to turn to strategic management, a logical outgrowth of its corporate planning process that requires managers well down in the organization, who have to make the plan happen, "to devote time to thinking about the future. . . . Strategic-planning systems have the positive effect of forcing managers to think rigorously about the future of their businesses."[24]

Effective planning also includes within its bounds a more informal kind. It takes place every day in managers' minds, providing a continuing consciousness of quality improvement opportunities in every personal encounter.

6. Create Organizational Change

The quality enhancement process requires an organizational framework that is flexible enough to serve a wide variety of needs, including:

- the appointment of a present member of senior management to take on the task of overseeing the quality effort, in addition to current responsibilities, or the creation of a newly defined position to be filled from within or from outside the organization;
- the formation of a quality enhancement committee at one or more organizational levels, offering the value of (1) providing an organizationwide perspective on opportunities for achieving quality enhancement; (2) engaging dedicated, knowledgeable persons within the institution in a comprehensive attack on quality-related problems; (3) providing a vehicle for instilling quality consciousness at all levels of the organization, and for motivating people to act on quality problems; (4) demonstrating to all involved parties the desire of the organization to provide high-quality care and services; and (5) offering a

voluntary mechanism for assessing and meeting the unique quality requirements of the institution;

- the appropriate and timely accommodation of new organizational mechanisms designed to engage quality problems and their solutions (such as task forces, special *ad hoc* project groups, and quality circles), along with communication networking to link these problem-solving teams and groups within the organizational system;
- the introduction of an adaptable framework that fosters the integration of medical staff members into the overall quality enhancement process;
- the willingness to bring newness to organizational structure and arrangements as may be required by changing reporting relationships, new job designs and placements, and *ad hoc* assignments—all in the interest of quality achievement;
- the need to provide close and continuing liaison between the human resources function and the quality assurance programming unit.

"While the intent is not to create a supernumerary bureaucracy," states Stanley Peterfreund, "it is essential that a workable format, suitable to the particular organizational environment, be carefully planned and introduced"[25] (Chapters 2 and 8).

7. Prepare Leadership

When the act of assessment is engaged in as a task of highest priority, it is essential for the CEO and the senior executive group to look critically into their institutional mirror to make profitable judgments about the quality performance of managers at all levels, and then to move to facilitating a concerted commitment to quality that evidences an imperativeness for building leadership for our time. Unquestionably, this is a difficult assignment if we hold any belief in what Douglas W. Bray tells us about contemporary managers:

Executives now face a host of problems in pursuing the goals of efficient production of quality products, marketing, and profit making. No doubt they could compile quite a list of problems. One suspects, however, that the managerial work force, if mentioned at all, would be restricted to the matter of numbers. Many see the problem of getting rid of the fat in management. There are many more problems than that!

Fat or lean, middle-level managers of the future may be a recalcitrant bunch. The strong tendency of managers to lose motivation as they grow older will be compounded by the initially weak motivation of the current generation of new managers. Both of these trends will be intensified if organizations are seen as cold and un-committed to their managers as they pursue cost containment and rigorous efficiency. Executives may find that corporate goals are elusive when the only ones interested in playing hard are they themselves.

History has moved along. Neither employers nor employees are what they used to be. Things were never utopian, but now utopia seems much farther away.[26]

Effective assessing at the outset of the quality enhancement process (the second element) will indicate just how far managers at both the top *and* middle will need to go in "playing hard" to get their managerial act up to snuff in terms of reaching appropriate levels of quality. No matter how hard the task might be in moving closer to utopia, for certain *it needs doing* if the organization "wants to change quality into an asset rather than a millstone." This is the message of Philip Crosby in his "Reflections on the Management of Quality," which appeared in *Wall Street Journal.* He said that

Quality is a management problem. The work force is not to blame, the public schools are not the villains—management just doesn't understand this complex and subtle concept. . . . Consistent world-class quality is not a matter of luck. It comes only when a management team learns how to deliberately cause it through specific knowledge and action. The traditional methods and systems of quality control and employee motivation just have not been effective in making quality certain."[27]

The subject of managerial leadership is discussed repeatedly throughout the pages of this book, with much emphasis on the need for a new breed of managers

- who must go beyond the normal boundaries of the science of managing to the artistry of managing, which offers the extensiveness of more enlightenment, more sensitivity, and more imagination (Chapters 3 and 4);
- who possess the vision and values of honest inquiry required to facilitate what Michael Maccoby refers to as "strategic dialogue that starts with the leader paying attention to detail and posing a *strategic* question: such as, 'How can we satisfy the customer's needs?' or 'How can we design rewards to improve overall quality and customer satisfaction?', and then moving on to exploring alternatives, engaging in inquiry, and arriving at a decision for action."[28] (Chapter 8);

- who are obsessed with quality—with being the best—and who manifest this obsession by active engagement in a partnership that keeps in constant touch with the needs of their people; that constantly propels them to the forefront of innovation; and that motivates them to deliver unsurpassed services (Chapters 4 and 5);
- who think of their management jobs as *service* jobs, and who strive to instill that same spirit of service in others. "As more and more managers start thinking of their jobs as service jobs, and finding ways to serve the needs of the people in their organizations," state Albrecht and Zemke,

> the factor of service quality will emerge more and more strongly as a competitive weapon. Organizations that have not moved beyond the traditional top-down modes of leadership will be more and more rigid and unable to adapt. Without a believable strategy for service, they will be left behind. We believe that those organizations that succeed in internalizing the philosophy of service management and building customer-driven cultures will flourish[29] (Chapter 2).

8. Advance Human Resource Management

Advancing human resource management to center stage within the institutional setting—from the board room to the employee workplace—is what this process element is all about. Its supreme importance is underscored as we give particular attention to the human side of the quality equation: the quality of work itself (Chapter 4), the quality of life at work (Chapter 5), and the quality of human conduct (Chapter 6). Since the human resources function must be the principal force in making things happen on the human side of the enterprise, nothing less than a *renewal* of the purposes and activities of this function is demanded. The organization capable of this renewal will be the one "that develops to the fullest its human resources, that removes obstacles to individual fulfillment, that emphasizes education, lifelong learning and self-discovery."[30] We in health care are still far from having created such a system.

"Do you really need a human-resource organization?" That is how Andrew Grove, president of Intel Corporation, begins his *Wall Street Journal* article. He then goes on to give his rationale for the question:

> If your managers level with their employees, if they evaluate their performance fairly and set their compensation without prejudice and favoritism, if they know how to handle themselves when their employees gripe and talk about unions, if they fully realize that untrained employees can't possibly be productive and therefore devote

a significant portion of their time to training them, if they talk with and listen to their peers, supervisors and subordinates freely and without rancor, if they tell their supervisors good news as well as bad—you probably would not want to waste your company's money on a human resource organization. Clearly it would be unnecessary and would just add to overhead while compounding bureaucracy.

However, if your company is struggling with strong competition, if it has to change constantly to survive, if the stress generated by the changes permeates its atmosphere, and most of all, if you operate in the real world, with flesh-and-blood managers who are less than perfect, a human-resource organization is vital. What's more, you'd better make sure that it carries weight, makes significant contributions, and adds value to the fullest extent possible. . . .

Our organizations are—and will always be— peopled by imperfect managers who need the contributions of the human resource profession. But we will only truly enjoy the ensuing benefits when our human-resource colleagues accept the inherent element of risk involved in making those contributions and overcome their own fear of that risk.[31]

The "center stage" task of human resource management is far from simple. In fact, it is so difficult that most human resources departments fall quite short of discharging their proper duties. To be successful, any advance in the performance and contributions of the human resources function "must move through a sequence of events and employ a variety of change mechanisms; these are the process factors of change."[32] In Chapters 7 and 9 the reader will find a suitable framework for introducing the process factors of change believed to be essential to the renewal and strengthening of the human resources function—the pulsator of the corporate heart (Chapter 2).

As the CEO and the human resource executive jointly establish goals and strategies for action, they need to be mindful of the principle of thought given primacy by Robert Desatnick: "Managing an organization's human resources equates with managing its customer services. To put it another way, employee relations equals customer relations. The two are inseparable."[33]

Outcomes of studies conducted in 1985 by David E. Bowen, of the University of Southern California's Department of Management and Organization, give support to the notion that taking care of human relations equates with taking care of the customer. Bowen's sample population consisted of two groups of branch banks; one group had twenty-three branches; the other, twenty-eight. Here is what he found:

1. There is a strong correlation between customer and employee views of service quality and the internal climate for service.

2. When employees view favorably an organization's human resource policies, customers view favorably the quality of service they receive.

3. A positive work climate directly affects customer service for the better.

4. Human resources is an excellent vehicle for satisfying both employee and customer needs.[34]

Being aware of the direct link between effective human resource management and excellence in customer service is central to the overall success of the organization's total quality effort and to the consequences of this quality enhancement process, which is both customer-driven and customer-directed.

9. Integrate Systemically

Quality is a question of expectations, a "conformance to requirements," as Philip Crosby defines it.[35] The natural extension of this thought is that "quality is a way of managing an organization,"[36] since if the great, indefinite numbers of day-to-day actions and activities of individuals performed within the organizational system are planned, constructed, and carried out correctly—that is, in line with expectations—then it might be expected that the overall efforts toward attaining high quality of care and service will be successful. If this premise is an acceptable one, it follows that management needs to act out its quality enhancement endeavor in a *systematic* fashion by looking at all of the components in the operational life cycle of the organization, and design the quality-related requirements so that they are linked with the key elements of the chain of organizational and functional events that contribute to institutional performance. This internalized approach is seen as embracing the following three action constituents, each one serving different but interrelated purposes.

Sustaining Quality Awareness. Quality awareness is sustained by integrating the idea of quality on a continuing basis, and in a purposefully designed way, into the context of organizational and operational events that hold a placement of permanency within the institutional system. This is done to keep the notion of quality ever present in the thoughts and actions of people. A high level of quality consciousness can be kept alive through this process of integrating a focus on quality in events such as the expression of corporate values; the documentation of corporate mission, credo, and goals; recruitment notices; employment interviews; orientation and on-the-job instruction; all training and educational programing, and all types of communications media.

Dimensions of Responsibility and Accountability. Responsibility and accountability exist as essential characteristics and obligations of work performed by both management and nonmanagement personnel. It is here that we break down the concept of quality into its manageable parts, where we come closest to giving a definition to "quality."

The *American Heritage Dictionary of the English Language* states the meaning of *define* in these words: "To delineate the outline or form of. . . . To serve to distinguish; characterize." This is exactly what is done at this point. By interlocking quality factors and expectations with the "permanent pillars" of the organization (such as policies and procedures; performance evaluation criteria for board, management, and nonmanagement employees; goal setting; job descriptions; rewards and incentives; standards; quotas; limits; ratios; and percentages), we give shape, contour, and delineation to the meaning of quality that provide guidance and guidelines for all members of the organization in evaluating systemically how well they are doing and how they might do better for the cause of quality.

Developing relevant measures of quality performance also plays an important role in this interlocking process, because health care institutions today are required "not only to provide high quality service, but also to be able to prove that they do."[37] Better ways to measure quality must be high on the agenda of everyone in the organization. To achieve quality goals, management needs a new way of thinking about the principles of measurement—*innovative* thinking that introduces measures where now they do not exist; that replace current measures that are too limited, too shallow, and too subjective with sounder measures that "capture aspects of quality that are important for competitive success"[38] (Chapter 8).

There are three relevant caveats to all of this meshing and measuring, however, that need to be kept continuously before us. The *first* is that the process is vulnerable to being less than the best unless all of the "permanent pillars" to which quality and its measurements are linked are alive and well.

The *second* caveat is that, in light of the potential magnitude and complexities of this process element of systemic integration, careful consideration should be given to approaching the task on a more localized basis; that is, to proceed initially with the identification, placement, and testing of the interlocking quality factors and expectations in two or three selected departments only, aiming to develop a "model" that can then be subsequently extended with appropriate modifications to other operational units of the organization. Very often, this option can prove to be more feasible, manageable, and accommodating for the system, rather than attempting to take on the total organization at one time.

A *third* caution is raised by Tom Peters:

Measurement must be done by the participants; that is, by the natural work group, team, or department itself. It must not be done "to" such groups by the accounting department or by an "audit" or "inspection" brigade. If it is, there is a high risk (1) that the process will become bureaucratic and (2) that turf-fights and squabbles over interpretation of data will break out, setting true involvement back considerably.[39]

Implementation Experiences. Implementation experiences may result from the direct involvement of individuals in various forms of problem-solving mechanisms (such as quality circles, task forces, special assignments, quality-of-work-life surveys and committee work) that are targeted, wholly or in part, toward the objective of improving quality. Personal participation in these kinds of events brings immediate cognizance of the need to position the pursuit of quality high on the activity list of all members of the organizational family.

10. Gain Employee Participation

The quality enhancement process is arduous for organizations "because of the change it implies for all of the individuals involved. One foot in the quality process just isn't enough today; there must be a dramatic change throughout an entire organization."[40] Almost all of the chapters in this book deal with the issues and actions related to unleashing the work force that can begin to forge the cultural changes required in setting the stage for employee participation—the focus of this tenth element of a recommended quality enhancement process.

"During the century management of individuals has become a greater concern as workers have steadily demanded higher levels of meaning and fulfillment in their organizational lives."[41] As recorded by Hickman and Silva, the growth of management of the individual passed through three eras:

- controlling the individual (1910–1960)
- recognizing the individual (1960–1980)
- honoring the individual (1980–late 1990s)

During this history of maturing management of individuals, members of the U.S. work force have progressed from an interchangeable unit of production to the focal point of organizational performance, and it is perceived that this trend will continue in the future.

"Under proper management, the U.S. worker is as good as anyone."[42] To be the best, however, today's worker must experience controlled freedom in workmanship, free play of imagination, and the allowance to invent and to exercise thought—all of which are organizational responses to the needs of the artist at work (Chapter 4). Successful organizations have long recognized that quality suffers when workers are assigned to isolated, narrowed tasks that are void of meaningful challenges. Instead, these organizations are asking their people to think about what they are doing and how it can be done better.

Quality circles gained momentum in the U.S. early in the seventies as a popular mechanism for involving employees in quality and other improvements following General Motors' use of them to help turn around a badly demoralized plant at Tarrytown, New York. More recently, General Motors has turned to the use of quality audit teams, in which each specially chosen member, in addition to having a full-time job in the assembly plant, is also an expert on ensuring quality.

This idea of new sharing of responsibilities among employees also caught fire in other auto-making companies. In sixty-five plants across the country, over one thousand employee involvement groups have been established by Ford Motor Company and the United Auto Workers. These groups of "fault finders" meet regularly in almost all Ford plants and locations and are making significant contributions. As an example, "over 500 employee suggestions were accepted for improving the assembly process and quality of the 1984 Ford Tempo and Mercury Topaz."[43] It is Ford's commitment to excellence and to giving employees an active say in how their jobs are performed.

For Chrysler Corporation, Lee Iacocca has this to say about the relationship between workers and management in Chrysler's system of manufacturing, in which workers speak up and management listens:

> Of course, quality doesn't stop with the engineer. It has to be part of the consciousness of the workers in the plants. Through the establishment of "quality circles," our plant workers have become far more involved than they used to be in the building process. We sit them down in a room and we say: "How about this operation? Can you do it? The engineer says you can, and the manufacturing guy says you can. But you're the ones who have to build the thing. What do you say?"
>
> So off they go to try it for a couple of days. If it doesn't work, they come back and tell us: "That's a bad idea. Here's a better way to do it." The word gets around pretty quickly that management is listening, that we really care about quality, that we're open to new ideas, we're not just a bunch of dummies. That may be the most important consideration of all when it comes to quality—that the worker believes his idea will be heard.[44]

Success stories of employee participation in health care are also making their appearance in print. NKC, of Louisville, Kentucky, for example, has done away with the employee suggestion system. Employees at the NKC system's two hospitals, however, regularly suggest new ideas or service improvements under a new employee quality improvement process. In any given month, since the launching of the new process in 1987, six to ten multidisciplinary groups examine the market, and research new service opportunities. "What we're trying to do," says William G. Galvagni, vice-president of planning and marketing, "is push marketing decision making down to the level where it comes in contact with the customer."[45] Having a system such as this in place can surely be an effective way to respond to both the threat of competitors and the voice of employees.

At Emory University Hospital, Atlanta, as another example, an effective employee involvement technique—the problem-solving group (PSG)—had its beginnings in 1985. The group works to identify, analyze, choose, and implement solutions to various problems that influence the quality of patient care, following these developmental stages:

- gathering data
- identifying problems
- providing feedback
- selecting PSG members
- focusing on problems
- generating solutions
- choosing the best solution
- implementing solutions
- managing successful outcomes

An article in *Health Progress* reports on a PSG project involving a typical paraprofessional unit that "was successful in addressing almost all the 15 identified problems in the department. Involving the staff in the PSG project resulted in higher morale, greater satisfaction with management, and a more favorable attitude toward their jobs."[46]

What these accounts of participative processes (not "programs") evidence is that there is no one right way of getting at effective employee involvement. If there is one right way, it is the approach most fitting to the individual institution in terms of its history of participative management, its current culture and climate, its manager preparedness, and its total resource capacity. Surely, there is no shortage in the number of alternative vehicles from which an organization can choose. As we already have discussed, there are quality circles (or *QCs* as they are often called), that have received mixed reviews over the years. "Proponents say they increase worker productivity and satisfaction. Detractors call them fads, a quick fix for deeper problems."[47] Irrespective of what the ultimate verdict might be, there remain many other organizational mechanisms open for grabs: *ad hoc* or permanent task forces, committee formats, problem-solving groups, audit teams, special assignments, structured employee idea systems, work simplification, and quality improvement workshops—all of which are designed to replace lip service to participative management by bringing democracy into the workplace.

Whatever single or combination of methodologies is preferred and implemented, it is strongly suggested that attention be given to these considerations (Chapters 2 through 9):

At the Organizational Level

- The board and its administration need to create a cultural environment—with a corporate heart—that provides a setting of human conditions conducive to the growth and development of employee involvement in all corners of the institution.
- Top management must continue to think of quality as craftsmanship, to behold its people at all levels of the organization as artists.
- Administration needs to make certain that organizational structure and arrangements are kept flexible and relationships nimble, so that bureaucratic and hierarchical obstacles to effective participative actions will be minimized.
- It is imperative that the selected mechanisms introduced into the organizational system be understood and dealt with as means to an end; that is, integral with, and contributory to, a larger purpose—that of quality enhancement.
- Whatever participative vehicle is utilized, top management must not isolate itself from employee involvement activities, progress, and accomplishments, and must make certain that key organizational elements are well in place and are appropriately accommodating the internal processes of employee participation—elements such as values, goals, policies, procedures, communication and coordination, and reward systems.

At the Manager Level

- Administration needs to be ever conscious of the reality of management attitudes and behavior at the middle and supervisory levels of the organization as related to quality and the idea of involving employees in its improvement, coming out of actual experiences of the past. To be specific:

1. The job of convincing line managers that quality is important to top management should not be taken lightly, since it is not an easy task.
2. Managers at the middle all too often tend to lower their sights on quality improvement, holding to the assumption that a certain rate of failure

is inevitable. Stephen Moss, an Arthur D. Little consultant who has worked with corporations in both the U.S. and Japan, says, "The U.S. manager sets an acceptable level of quality and then sticks to it. The Japanese are constantly upgrading their goals . . . always shooting for perfection and sometimes get close."[48]

3. Serious quality problems arise from managers' common notion that "it's not my responsibility." "The weak links in an organization are usually at the point where departments are supposed to meet. It's at these joints that institutional arthritis attacks. When departments are separated like national frontiers, fully equipped with barbed-wire fences, bristling watchtowers and buried mine fields, serious [quality] losses occur."[49]

4. Managers at the middle very often do not want to undertake the restructuring of relationships with supervisors and workers that may be essential to cooperation in the advancement of quality.

5. Many managers are uncomfortable with ideas from subordinates and reject them out of hand.

6. Top management must be alert to excessive authoritarian practices of managers at lower levels.

- Beyond attitudes, there also is the *skill* of departmental managers and supervisors required to foster employee involvement that demands continuing attention. The process designed for these managers needs to have form and structure, embracing these recommended stages of activity:

1. employee orientation to the process

2. departmental introductory session

3. continuing departmental workshops

4. process maintenance activities.[50]

Certainly, effective train-the-trainer programming would be an essential adjunct to the mainline of the organization's manager development process.

At the Employee Level

- "Building a quality process that produces well-trained employees— workers capable of making greater contributions than we have believed possible—will provide the best departure point."[51]

- Top-level management should rely on "front-line" employees (along with customers) to gauge service quality and corporate image, the key factors in attracting and retaining business, according to a report on consumer attitudes, released March 28, 1988. "The report noted that management constantly must seek comments and advice from front-line employees and customers, who have the best sense of how the company is perceived in the marketplace."[52]

- Administration needs to place high priority on the formation of multifunctional teams to make sure that quality concerns crossing artifical boundaries are addressed.
- A key step in enhancing quality is to look at the way jobs are designed within the organization. In redesigning jobs to meet the demands of today's employees, these factors must be taken into consideration, according to Anthony Di Primio:
  - "Quality control as part of each employee's job
  - Cross-training employees to perform multiskill jobs
  - Worker participation in the design of their jobs
  - Quality assurance and productivity improvement, focused on employee teams that participate in identifying, implementing, and administering remedial strategies."[53]
- Rewards used to control rather than affect movement toward achieving the best "can be demotivating." Reward what is actually wanted, and make it clear what it is that is being asked for.[54]

In establishing the strategies for this tenth element of the quality enhancement process, management, from the start, should consider cultural and developmental goals that go beyond the desired immediate results to be obtained through employee participation in the search for quality advancement. When the management at Southern California Gas Company was asked, "Why do we have Quality Circles?" the response was:

- to increase company efficiency and effectiveness by directly involving employees in problem identification, analysis, and solution implementation
- to develop the problem-solving capability of the work force
- to strengthen management/nonmanagement communications vertically and horizontally in the organization (as well as between staff and line groups)
- to develop the personal and leadership skills of our employees
- to increase employee motivation and job involvement
- to inspire more effective teamwork

"Only one of these objectives relates to the short-term project output of the Quality Circle. The others all relate to the development of organization and people to work more productively with each other in the years ahead."[55]

Obviously, this activity—gaining employee participation—becomes a significant element of the quality process as we give recognition to the fact that the employee, if allowed, can provide extraordinary impetus to the pursuit of quality enhancement. As valuable as this element is, there is much evidence to show that the health care industry is not moving quickly enough, or effectively enough, in the area of employee involvement.

11. Monitor, Evaluate, and Improve

Although quality control was established as an identified discipline in the late forties, managements accustomed to making quantitative-based judgments of their efforts to advance quality entered the fifties with little to go on. "Little would change until several key works were published in the 1950s and early 1960s. These ushered in the next major quality era, that of quality assurance."[56]

In 1951, Joseph Juran authored the first edition of his *Quality Control Handbook*, a publication that became the profession's bible.[57] In that book, Juran regarded failure or avoidable costs as "gold in the mine" because they could be reduced sharply by investing in quality improvement. In 1956, Armand Feigenbaum took industrial managements a step further by proposing "total quality control." High-quality products, he argued, were unlikely to be produced if the manufacturing department was forced to work in isolation.[58] In his words:

> The underlying principle of this total quality view . . . is that, to provide genuine effectiveness, control must start with the design of the product and end only when the product has been placed in the hands of a customer who remains satisfied. . . . The first principle to recognize is that quality is everybody's job.[59]

It is thought that both the notions of quality control and quality assurance might be somewhat susceptive to misinterpretation. For example, the term *control* is believed to be a misnomer, for surely the intent is not to hold quality in restraint, to curb it. As Jane Wagner writes in *The Search for Signs of Intelligent Life in the Universe,* "I worry whoever thought up the term 'quality control' thought if we didn't control it, it would get out of hand."[60] On the other hand, the idea of *assurance* alone is considered a mistakable expression, because while it does mean to make secure or certain, it fails to offer a sense of the adequacy of the quality level being ensured. It also neglects to reflect any intended design to move progressively forward to even higher levels of quality attainment; thus, the preference of the thought of *quality enhancement,* which goes beyond the presence of statical connotations and suggests adding to something already worthy, thus increasing its value. In any event, by whatever name, the effort must be founded on Feigenbaum's initial principle: "that quality is everybody's job."

The job that needs doing during this stage of the quality enhancement process entails (1) keeping watch over, and keeping track of, all of the quality factors and expectations that were interlocked with the permanent pillars of the organization (the ninth element); (2) examining and judging the extent or measure of the fulfillment of the previously established expectations; and (3) expediting the move toward the changes for improvement deemed required or desirable based on the preceding evaluative outcomes. And these tasks are *everybody's job:*

- *The board,* as it insistently engages in continuous examination and discussion of all aspects of *total* quality (Chapter 3).
- *Top management,* as it monitors the progress and success of the quality enhancement plan and process to which it is committed, with all of its members checking outcomes systematically with a view to gaining valuable feedback from lower levels of the organization. Among the main concerns of executives at the top are corporate culture and environment, management roles and preparedness, employee involvement and contributions, and customer satisfaction. With regard to the latter interest, Philip Crosby gives us this thought about customers: "The senior managers of any organization have to continually be forced to keep up. Perhaps they should have to find a customer and spend time with him or her each month. Marketing can't do it all by itself, and sometimes the professionals get so close to the trees that they don't know the woods are all around them"[61] (Chapters 2, 3, 5, 6, and 7).
- *The medical component,* as its members regulate their own conduct in the interest of higher standards, and scrutinize the quality performance of supportive staff within the context of the total organizational system (Chapters 1, 2, 3, 5, and 6).
- *Operational managers and supervisors,* who, on a day-to-day basis, need to be on the alert for recurring lapses from expected performance, putting to use key questions such as these:
  1. What is giving trouble? How can we tell?
  2. Why are we trying to change this procedure, this standard?
  3. How can we tell whether something is "better"?

The success of this eleventh element of the process requires the cooperation of multiple departments.

> To make the system work, many companies developed elaborate matrices . . . listing departmental responsibilities across the top and required activities down the left-hand side. The matrices typically showed considerable overlap among functions, for few activities

were likely to be error-free if they were assigned to a single department or were pursued seriatim. Interfunctional teams therefore became essential: they ensured that diverse viewpoints were represented and that otherwise autonomous departments worked together. Top management was ultimately responsible for the effectiveness of the system"[62] (Chapters 2 to 6, and 8).

- *Service functions,* such as human resources, financial management, data processing, education, management engineering, and materials management, are key to the success of this element of the quality enhancement process. As comprehensive and careful surveyors and appraisers of their role and achievements in the quality effort, as well as of their working relationships with various operational segments of the organization, they can be instrumental in introducing enhancements on a broad and significant scale.

- The multitude of nonmanagement employees, as they serve as "sensors" through personal observation and reporting, become involved in goal setting and in the evaluation of performance against goals, understand and appreciate the value of measurement, and participate in the activation of quality teams that ultimately are the experts on what to change.

    The Bureau of National Affairs, Inc., states that its data show that "giving workers a voice in management of work promises to increase the individual's concern for the product and the process and to generate higher productivity and quality"[63] (Chapters 2 through 9).

Obviously, what is required in this eleventh process element is the return to the act of assessment (element two), with specific focus on the *response-directed* dimension of inquiry. Having a sensible array of good, solid, tough questions offers the opportunity one needs to establish measures of effectiveness; to keep on track of human performance; and to proceed with swiftness and confidence toward breaking new ground in quality enhancement. A basic principle worth remembering is that *you can't recognize a good solution until you have a sharply defined question.*

12. Sustain and Extend

There are two energetic activities at work here: (1) to continue newness in generating and sustaining momentum of the total quality effort; and (2) to remain on a fast track, constantly improving the quality enhancement plan, process, and outcomes. In both areas, all chapters of the text will be helpful.

Continued success in the achievement of total quality enhancement cannot be assured unless management is productive in its ongoing efforts to introduce and implement novel ways of sustaining the interest, motivation, involvement, support, and contributions of its organizational membership. Just as new standards of quality keep surfacing in the functioning of today's health care institution, so is there the need for the constant emergence of new ideas and techniques aimed at sustaining stimulation. There is, in fact, an indefinite number of additive dimensions extending over a broad spectrum of worthy possibilities, ranging from the use of employee newsletters to engagement in corporate research and development. A substantial number of these sustaining practices are covered in the author's earlier writings.[64,65]

The second aspect of this process element, which in part interrelates with the first, calls for reentry into the assessment and networking phases of the quality enhancement process (elements two and three). As in the very beginning of the process, administration and its management enter once again into the acts of assessment and networking at their own appropriate entrance points, depending on where the organization is with regard to its overall quality effort and accomplishments. At this time, principal attention is given to the *opportunity-directed* dimension of inquiry (see element two), in the interest of extending the organization's capacity to advance further the state of quality.

Quality enhancement is an ongoing process; thus it is always ready for more sustenance and extension. Perhaps the greatest threat to its continuing vital existence is the superficial appearance of conditions, circumstances, or events that smack of corporate fadism. To prevent this common organizational malady from creeping in, holding to these principles should prove to be an effective antidote:

- The total effort must be committed to by senior management as an evolutionary process with long-term purposes. A renewal of this commitment should be reaffirmed formally and articulated each succeeding year.
- No enterprise has a corner on quality enhancement. It is an attainable goal for every management, but it truly belongs to those managements who understand that there are no shortcuts and who believe there are no limitations to the quality of human performance.
- Advancements in quality demand that the organizational environment in which the quality enhancement process operates reflects the integrity of the process and the values of what is being sought.
- Achieving quality enhancement finds its main dependency on the task of managing—managing the technology, the work force, and the managers themselves. It must be made an integral part of the management process, utilizing the elements of that process, namely, planning, organizing, communicating, motivating, and controlling.
- To ensure success, it is essential that the quality process be systemic in its design, since the enhancement of quality—which needs to be

customer-driven and -directed —is the business of everyone within the organization.

- The attainment of higher quality, and its rewards, deserve high visibility at all times.
- Innovation must be evident. While newness and novelty can occur by serendipity, they must be arrived at through determined searching and discovery.
- Quality is *not* free. It requires investments of time, dollars, materials, technology, and spatial needs. More important, it demands effective utilization of human capital—the experience, creativity, intellect, health, and energies of people. If these imperatives are prudently met, the return on these investments can be extremely high.
- Above all, quality must be perceived in its totality, extending our view beyond science and technology to embrace the human condition, since the realization of quality enhancement, in essence, is a human accomplishment.

NOTES

1. John Mayo, "Process Design as Important as Product Design," *Wall Street Journal,* Oct. 29, 1984, p. 18.

2. Christopher Knowlton, "What America Makes Best," *Fortune,* Mar. 28, 1988, p. 48.

3. Knowlton, "What America Makes Best," pp. 48–49.

4. Tom Peters, *Thriving On Chaos* (New York: Alfred A. Knopf, Inc., 1987), p. 73.

5. Stanley Peterfreund, "Managing Change: QWL/EI—From Launch to Orbit, Issues and Concerns," Feb. 1983, p. 3.

6. David J. Jones, M.D., "Learning How To 'Manage' Quality," *Trustee,* Jan. 1988, p. 14.

7. "America's Revitalization," *Quality and Productivity,* date unknown, p. 26.

8. Jan Carlzon, *Moments of Truth* (Cambridge, Mass.: Ballinger Publishing Company, 1987), p. x.

9-12. "America's Revitalization," pp. 19–30.

13. Linda Perry, "The Quality Process," *Modern Healthcare,* Apr. 1, 1988, pp. 30–34.

14. Robert L. Desatnick, *Managing to Keep the Customer* (San Francisco: Jossey-Bass Publishers, 1987), p. 1.

15. Addison C. Bennett and Samuel J. Tibbitts, *Making Innovation Practical* (Chicago: Pluribus Press, Inc., 1986), p. 46.

16. Bennett and Tibbitts, *Making Innovation Practical,* chap. 4.

17. *Business Week,* Aug. 26, 1985, pp. 21–23.

18. Frank K. Kellog, "Lesson of '74: Ideals are Essential," *Los Angeles Times,* date unknown, p. 1.

19. John A. Young, "One Company's Quest for Improved Quality," *Wall Street Journal,* Jul. 25, 1983, p. 14.

20. "A Statement of Policy," New York, NY: American Telephone and Telegraph Company, 1981, p. 3.

21. "Viewpoint on Quality" document, Schaumburg, Ill.: Motorola, Inc., p. 3.

22. *Wall Street Journal*, Apr. 8, 1987, p. 9.

23. Frank S. Leonard and W. Earl Sasser, "The Incline of Quality," *Harvard Business Review*, Sept.–Oct , 1982, p. 168.

24. John M. Stengrevics, "Corporate Planning Needn't Be an Executive Straitjacket," *Wall Street Journal*, date unknown.

25. Peterfreund, "Managing Change," p. 5.

26. Douglas W. Bray, "Managers through Time," *Executive Talent*, ed. Eli Ginzberg (New York: John Wiley & Sons, Inc., 1988), pp. 115–16.

27. *Wall Street Journal*, Jan. 4, 1988, p. 24B.

28. Michael Maccoby, *Why Work: Leading the New Generation* (New York: Simon and Schuster, 1988), p. 227.

29. Karl Albrecht and Ron Zemke, *Service America!* (Homewood, Ill.: Dow Jones-Irwin, 1985), p. 191.

30. John W. Gardner, "Toward a Self-Renewing Society," *Time*, Apr. 11, 1969, p. 40.

31. Andrew S. Grove, "Is Anyone Minding the Monitors?" *Wall Street Journal*, Sept. 30, 1985, p. 24.

32. Michael Beer, et al., *Managing Human Assets* (New York: The Free Press, 1984), p. 194.

33. Desatnick, *Managing To Keep the Customer*, p. 15.

34. David E. Bowen, "Taking Care of Human Relations Equals Taking Care of the Business," *Human Resource Reporter*, Nov. 1985.

35. Philip B. Crosby, *Quality Is Free* (New York: McGraw-Hill Book Co. 1979), p. 17.

36. Sandra Blakeslee, *The Changing Technology*, date unknown.

37. Bruce C. Vladeck, "Sharpening the Focus on the Quality of Care 'Crisis'," *President's Letter*, United Hospital Fund, Jun. 1986, p. 4.

38. David A. Garvin, "Competing on the Eight Dimensions of Quality," *Harvard Business Review*, Nov.–Dec. 1987, p. 101.

39. Peters, *Thriving on Chaos*, p. 75.

40. James Houghton, "For Better Quality, Listen to the Workers," *New York Times*, Oct. 18, 1987, p. 19.

41. Craig R. Hickman and Michael A. Silva, *The Future 500: Creating Tomorrow's Organizations Today* (New York: Nal Penquin, Inc., 1987), pp. 246–63.

42. Jeremy Main, "The Battle for Quality Begins," *Fortune*, Dec. 29, 1980, p. 31.

43. *Sports Illustrated*, Ford Advertisement, date unknown, p. 48.

44. Lee Iacocca, *Iacocca: An Autobiography* (New York: Bantam Books, 1984), p. 175.

45. Kari E. Super, "Improving an Old Idea," *Modern Healthcare*, Jul. 3, 1987, p. 184.

46. Gene Barger, et al., "Improving Patient Care through Problem-Solving Groups," *Health Progress*, Sept. 1987, pp. 42–5.

47. Mitchell Lee Marks, "The Question of Quality Circles," *Psychology Today*, Mar. 1986, pp. 36–46.

48. Main, "The Battle for Quality Begins," 33.

49. Mortimer R. Feinberg and Aaron Levenstein, "Silencing the Refrain, 'It's Not My Job, Man'," *Wall Street Journal*, Nov. 11, 1985, p. 22.

50. Addison C. Bennett, *Productivity and the Quality of Work Life in Hospitals* (Chicago: American Hospital Association, 1983), p. 46.

51. Houghton, "For Better Quality, Listen," p. 19.

52. "Report: Let 'Front-Line' Workers, Public Judge Quality," *Los Angeles Times,* Mar. 29, 1988, part IV, p. 2.

53. Anthony Di Primio, *Quality Assurance in Service Organizations* (Radnor, Pa.: Chilton Book Co., 1987), p. 166.

54. Sharon Nelton, "Motivating for Success," *Nation's Business,* Mar. 1988, pp. 18–26.

55. Jack C. Green, "Inculcation of Quality Circles," *Computer Network* (Houston: American Productivity Center, Nov. 21, 1985), L:62.

56. David A. Garvin, *Managing Quality* (New York: The Free Press, 1988), p. 12.

57. Joseph M. Juran, *Quality Control Handbook* (New York: McGraw-Hill Book Co., 1951)

58. Garvin, *Managing Quality,* p. 13.

59. Armand V. Feigenbaum, "Total Quality Control," *Harvard Business Review,* Nov.–Dec. 1956, pp. 94, 98. See also Feigenbaum, *Total Quality Control* (New York: McGraw-Hill Book Co., 1961).

60. Jane Wagner, *The Search for Signs of Intelligent Life in the Universe* (New York: Harper & Row, 1986), p. 26.

61. Philip B. Crosby, *The Eternally Successful Organization* (New York: McGraw-Hill Book Co., 1988), p. 59.

62. Garvin, *Managing Quality,* pp. 13, 14.

63. Patrick L. Townsend, *Commit to Quality* (New York: John Wiley & Sons, Inc., 1986), p. 75.

64. Addison C. Bennett, *An Employee Idea Program for Hospitals and Nursing Home Type Facilities* (New York: Preston Publishing Co., Inc., 1974), pp. 118–40.

65. Bennett, *Making Innovation Practical,* pp. 176–94.

The Quality of Being Individual

The race advances only by the extra achievements of the individual. You are the individual.

—Charles Towne

Quality! The sound of the word is emphatic. It gives rise not only to a boldness in its action, but to sharply delineated expressions of those who experience it. Quality is rare, but it is all around us, and wherever it appears, it makes its presence felt. It is elegant, pure, and delicate; yet its presence, or its absence, "can pierce like a knife."[1]

In whatever ways we may give meaning to the idea of quality, the one overriding characteristic that maintains its firmness is that *quality is individual.* The condition of "quality" is in the eye of the beholder. It is looked at, and reacted to, differently by each single human being whose discrete judgment gives way to personal preferences and appreciation of new values. With certainty, this holds particularly true within the health care environment, where individual judgment is subjective but the condition is not.

Quality in health care is unparalleled elsewhere, because it is a deep sensory experience. "To see, hear or taste quality is to discover something that has been fashioned with love."[2] Indeed, the essential of compassion coupled with the paradox that quality depends on *many* qualities (which is inherent in caring) give true uniqueness to the meaning of quality in delivering health care services.

Several initiatives under way in the health care industry are intended

to improve an understanding of how quality is perceived by the various participants in the health care system, including patients, payers, physicians, and other staff members in health care institutions. In particular, many providers are using patient satisfaction surveys to learn more about what patients want from health care providers and what they recognize as quality problems.[3]

251

The most dramatic quality assessment initiative is that of the Joint Commission on Accreditation of Healthcare Organizations (Joint Commission). The Joint Commission plan focuses the hospital accreditation process on clinical performance measures and outcomes. It involves systematizing information about medical practices in health care facilities and developing meaningful measures of clinical performance adjusted for the severity of patients' illnesses. While the Joint Commission ultimately envisions a full array of measures across clinical medicine, there persists the validity of the thought expressed by Bruce C. Vladeck, president, United Hospital Fund, New York:

> Efforts to improve the quality of health care encounters two of the major generic problems bedeviling those who would make health care more systematic. First, it is often externally hard to move from the statistical aggregate to the individual case. Excess mortality rates may very well indicate a bad hospital or physician, but one can draw a fair conclusion only after substantial further investigation. For example, the patients may have been sicker to start with, or otherwise more at risk; or the data may not have been good from the outset, and, in a normal statistical distribution, 5 percent of the cases will be outliers anyway.
>
> Closely related to the difficulty of drawing conclusions from aggregated information is the underlying fact that clinical medicine is still characterized by considerable uncertainty. Although a lot of progress has been made in the last decade or so in systematizing norms of optimal practice, the realm of the unknown remains extremely wide. The technology and its science base keep changing with remarkable rapidity, so that what seems optimal today is unacceptable tomorrow.[4]

This declaration of concern gives emphasis to the complexities of changing practices and technologies, and substantiates the notion that quality is individual. These difficulties notwithstanding, finding better ways of achieving advancements in quality needs to be high on the agenda of today's health care institutions as they take on the formidable task of refining the meaning and measurement of quality through innovative applications of quality enhancement techniques and processes.

BEYOND QUALITY ASSURANCE

The central intent of this book is to take health care managements beyond the essential core of quality assurance programming, to extend their perception and concentration to a broader, systemic vision of the *totality of quality* that embraces not only quality assurance but also the interrelated elements of quality of work, quality of work life, and quality of human conduct. As these added components are positioned in their rightful place within the wholeness of quality, the function of managing quality moves beyond the sole aspect of clinical/technological services, bringing into being a balanced unity between these scientific services and the factors of the human condition. As we expand our sights in this way, and thus grasp the true completeness of quality, we become even more conscious of the essential thought that quality is individual.

The purposeful design of this writing is to restore human beings to the center of our attention. Its content was developed at a high vantage point from which multitudes of human beings were watched as they worked in the departments and moved through the corridors of different health care organizations. What one is struck by as the observations are made is the verity of the human condition: people are at once much the same, yet altogether different. One is impressed not so much by commonality as by variation—the individuality of each human being within the total organizational populace who is constantly reminded that

> however numerically great mankind is, it is ultimately a collection
> of individuals like himself, each one concentrated on his own destiny,
> bearing his personal perceptions and preoccupations, impelled by
> a vivid, unique sense of private personality that may be submerged
> by the crowd but is never lost in it.[5]

Not only are individual human beings never lost in the crowd; they, too, are never fixed, for they are constantly enlarged by their own experiences.

The dichotomy that becomes evident here is that human individuality brings with it the benefits of individual differences, yet at the same time it causes further obstacles to the quest for quality; for while advancement in quality is to be found in the differing skills, abilities, experience, creativity, and energies of people, the dissimilarities of their individual perceptions and understanding of what quality is can detrimentally affect the cause of quality enhancement. Likened to the patient, the meaning of quality to each member of the organizational family is individual.

THE ARTIST AT WORK

The future of quality rests in the hands of the unique individual who will not be ashamed of his or her originality. "No intentional culture can destroy that uniqueness . . . and any effort to do so would be bad design."[6]

To the contrary, organizational culture must nurture the freedom and uniqueness of the individual so that he or she can in fact make a difference.

No one realizes the importance of freedom more than the artist, and it is through the artistry of workmanship that the future advancement of quality is assured. Taking the role of art in its widest possible sense, the authors hold little patience with the belief that art is the restricted province of those who paint, sculpt, or make music or verse. It is our hope, as it is the desire expressed by Robert Henri (Chapter 4) that *"there is artist in every man."*[7]

To promote the freedom of individuals within the organization—artists in their own right who have an ability to use themselves to the fullest and to become everything they were capable of becoming—is to promote the goals and principles of quality. This is thought to be true whether it is through the artistry of management; the attention of physicians not only to the science of their profession, but also to its art; or the arts of engagement, of concern, and of human perspective on the part of employees. To advance these aesthetic faculties is to increase the depth of individuality.

ORGANIZATIONAL FRAMEWORK FOR QUALITY

Preventing the decline of human individuality within the workplace is complicated by the bigness and complexity of today's health care organizations, yet it is paramount that this individuality be preserved if quality is to improve steadily. Any organization, large or small, needs "to strive continuously for the orderliness of *order* and the disorderliness of creative *freedom*."[8] However, it is more the nature of organizational behavior, in terms of its natural bias, to favor order at the expense of creative freedom. This preference of an organization swings the pendulum toward centralization, which tends to put distance between itself and its people. The fundamental task, then, is to strike a proper balance between the opposites of order and freedom so that quality enhancement finds its true source in the human individuality of the collective corporate membership working well within the context of the systematic order and arrangements of organization.

An attempt toward a discernment of such a balance flows throughout all divisions of this book. Looking back on its content, four principal ideas emerge: environment, leadership, humanism, and process.

Environment

A major threat to individual uniqueness and freedom is an organization without a telltale heart. Besides being thought as the vital center of one's being, the heart is a metaphor for so many sensibilities. It stands for love and affection; it means inner strength or character; it denotes conscious sympathy.

Heart is at the root of almost every emotion, every feeling. With it, all things are possible. Without it, the human spirit fades.

The organization that wears both its heart and head on its sleeve creates a cultural environment capable of fostering the human endowment by causing its corporate membership to live in a surprising fullness—a cultural environment embracing a value system that provides a sense of common direction for all employees, and guidelines for their day-to-day behavior as it commands everyone's attention to the central idea that "what people really care about around here is quality."[9]

People are the product of their environment. Give them the right environment and they will become true artists who feel they are part of a cause they believe in, to which they can dedicate their individual talents and creativity. If the corporate heart is young and vital, the organization will withdraw from a traditional mindset and bring renewal to its present arrangements and processes. It will not be blinded to the idea that "small is beautiful" as it leads science "to the actual size of man"[10] by giving technology a human face. It too will give rise to a spirited citizenry of a corporate community that holds to a higher sense of belonging, participation, and responsibility—a community that offers the cause of quality a network of people who are optimistic about their chances to move ever closer to perfection.

Leadership

A main theme running throughout the book is that high-quality service is the product of high-quality management. Underlying this idea is the call for a new breed of managers who are not merely "managers" in the traditional sense but, more important, who are *leaders* in a new qualitative sense. Surely, management competency is fundamental to the task of quality enhancement; but traditional management theory and practice—even when effective—are not enough, since by themselves, the pursuit of quality and efficiency may very well result in steady deterioration. It is not enough to know how without knowing why; to utilize people without caring for people; to manage daily functions without setting future direction; to exercise power over others without empowering others—all of which are extensions characteristic of effective leadership.

What concerns James MacGregor Burns, whose studies of leadership are extensive, is the concept of "moral leadership." By this term, Burns means

> that leaders and led have a relationship not only of power, but of mutual needs, aspirations, and values. . . . Moral leadership emerges from, and always returns to, the fundamental wants and needs, aspirations and values of the followers . . . the kind of leadership that can produce social change that will satisfy followers' authentic needs.[11]

Viewing relationships as the true nature of leadership brings us back to the notion of the humanist art of managing that embraces these distinctive qualities:

- a *global consciousness* that helps raise individuals from an isolated state into that of whole, integrated beings
- a *vision of newness* that enables the leader to understand and interpret complex relationships, and to be effective in the "continual reconsideration of assumptions underlying old and familiar networks . . . as well as the gathering and sorting of new information"[12]
- a *positive attitude* upon which all things depend, particularly the quality of work
- the *presence of humanism* as practiced by the artist who knows what human beings are like, and who understands with certainty that human beings live far within their limits
- a *quality of growth* that reaches beyond oneself to the wisdom of others, which is then shared to help others to experiment, to be different, and to do something intelligent
- a *desire for qualitative results,* which, in essence, is found in the pursuit of excellence as an expectation of the artistic individual

As David E. Lilienthal conducted his lecture series based on his book *Management: A Humanist Art,* he spoke these words:

> One man sees in a block of stone an inert piece of rock. A sculptor sees in that stone a figure that he can shape from the stone, into what may become an immortal object. The sculptor's act is creative. No less an act of creation is that of the manager, who sees in human desires, loves, hates, aspirations, the materials from which to create something that did not exist before . . .[13]

Humanism

In the province of quality, a most important task that lies before the members of top management today is that of honoring in their behavior the human values that they profess. What is evidenced widely is an all-too-narrow interest in the human condition within the health care workplace. This opinion is substantiated by the prevailing second-rate organizational standing or status of human resources (personnel) functions that is sanctioned by their senior managements.

If there is a beginning point in the renaissance of quality, it is here. We will never get on course until we take some tough, realistic, and innovative steps to renew and revitalize the human resources departments of our present-day health care organizations. And we had better get on with the job of doing just that if we are truly serious about making significant strides in quality enhancement.

The imperative is to establish a new direction in our thinking about the meaning of human resource management and its emerging significance in the nineties. The task ahead is not merely to identify and explore ideas that will affect organizational procedures and practices purely within a personnel administrative context; rather, it is to effect a whole different set of ideas at quite a different level that will bring meaningful and observable gains in the quality of the *total* human effort within the enterprise. For example, as one looks across the full extent of the health care industry, it becomes quite apparent that there is less-than-adequate attention currently being given to such essential activities as:

- human resource planning, with the initial focus on management, as an important determinant of organizational effectiveness
- putting excellence in management as it affects both the operational components and the human resources function of the institution
- proactively reaching out to yet-unrealized dimensions of effectiveness in the performance of the organization, with the realization that the human performance of its individual members suggests a lack of limitation
- activating and maintaining a solid concern about the quality of work life the organization provides its people, which, if directed toward positive actions, can create the human conditions they have long been seeking
- adapting work to the needs of the individual rather than demanding that the individual adapt himself or herself to the needs of the work and to the formalities of the institution
- embracing the concept of "human capital" as an investment, and acting upon those things that will bring returns on the investment, rather than staying with the traditional and all-too-narrow view of "personnel" as an expense
- engaging in research and demonstration, which, if conducted in a continuing and systematic manner, can take the act of creating new ideas from conception through experimentation, development, marketing, and implementation—a route that is not an easy one, but one that needs to be taken if we are aiming at a rebirth of the human resources function in health care

It is clear that the solutions we have at hand will not necessarily work in tomorrow's world of work. We will be confronted with difficult questions for which we cannot find answers in conventional practices. Since doing the same things over and over surely is not the answer—besides, it just is not exciting—it is important that the human resource executive and other members of top management set the kinds of goals that will cause them to give some hard thought to the development of newness as they give increasing attention to the human condition.

Process

A heightened seriousness and intensity of purpose about quality are being exhibited by top managements of health care organizations. Chapter 11 displays the outline of what is believed to be required to transfer this seriousness of intent into action. It is a strategically planned *process*—not a fortuitous succession of programs or "packages"—that needs commitment to as an unending engagement, a process that is:

- in touch with the environment and with the customer
- designed to embrace all dimensions of quality, all operational levels, and all people of the organization
- made whole by unifying the human side of quality with the scientific aspects of providing care and services
- structured in its organization and orderly in its arrangements, yet marked by flexibility in terms of its receptiveness to change and modification
- focused on measurement, and directed toward results
- future-oriented in its purpose and conduct
- fitting to the uniqueness of the individual organization—its philosophy, mission, values, goals, resources, strengths, and constraints
- capable of taking the organization beyond process boundaries to that of "a way of life" which makes quality part of everyday thinking in all corners of the enterprise

Each of the four central ideas—environment, leadership, humanism, and process—has a quality of being individual. When brought together within any one organization, collectively they convey a singular distinctiveness to solving quality problems and to capturing competitive opportunities. *What each organization makes of its individuality is what it makes of its quality.* This is true not only in terms of differences in the ways in which the organization exercises strategic quality management but, more important, in terms of the ways in which it summons up the human characteristics and abilities that differ in each employee.

During the years ahead, as the individual members of the health care work force explore themselves—their goals, aspirations, and values—and attempt to change the world around them, health care managements will need to parallel these individual explorations by improving the quality-of-work-life environment in which their people work. These forward movements on the part of managements will come forth from the understanding that the individual *artist* is aware that sensitivity, feelings, thought, skill, invention, risk, and development are critical to his or her quality of work.

Managements' progressive actions toward the enhancement of quality also will evolve out of their continuing search of the *individual*—a search that will lead finally to the discovery of the

> natural desire in all people: to strive during their lifetimes to develop fully the potential that is born in them; to experience all the emotions that the range of human existence has to offer; and always, above all else, to be permitted to become the individual that *their* hearts and minds tell them they should be.[14]

In all that he or she does, the individual is the quintessential quality of quality. As Irwin Edman put it, "The individual, the summit of human endeavor!"

NOTES

1. Edward Tenner, "The Meaning of Quality," *Quality,* Winter 1987, p. 30.

2. Tenner, "The Meaning of Quality," p. 31.

3. Judith Graham, "Quality Gets a Closer Look," *Modern Healthcare,* Feb. 27, 1987, p. 20.

4. Bruce C. Vladeck, "Sharpening the Focus on the Quality of Care 'Crisis'," in *Presidents Letter* (New York: United Hospital Fund, June 1986).

5. Paul Good and the Editors of Time-Life Books, *The Individual* (New York: Time-Life Books, 1974), p. 7.

6. B.F. Skinner, *Beyond Freedom & Dignity* (New York: Bantam Books, 1975), p. 200.

7. Robert Henri, *The Art Spirit* (New York: Harper & Row, 1958), p. 225.

8. E.F. Schumacher, *Small Is Beautiful* (New York: Harper & Row, 1973), p. 243.

9. Terence E. Deal and Allan A. Kennedy, *Corporate Cultures* (Reading, Mass.: Addison-Wesley Publishing Co., Inc., 1982), p. 21.

10. Schumacher, *Small Is Beautiful,* p. 147.

11. James MacGregor Burns, *Leadership* (New York: Harper & Row, 1978), p. 4.

12. Thomas H. Wyman, *Wall Street Journal,* Apr. 30, 1986, p. 24.

13. David E. Lilienthal, *Management: A Humanistic Art* (New York: Columbia University Press, 1967), p. 35.

14. Good, *The Individual,* p. 171.

Index

About the Authors

ADDISON C. BENNETT, nationally recognized as an authority on organization and management, maintains an independent management consulting practice in Los Angeles, California. His return to consulting in 1984 followed a ten-year association with the Lutheran Hospital Society of Southern California as its vice-president and as senior vice-president of Pacific Health Resources, the wholly-owned subsidary of the Society. Mr. Bennett is a member of the systems board of Ancilla Systems, Inc., Chicago, Illinois, and serves as chairperson of the Systems' Quality Assurance Committee.

The author of 10 books and more than 125 articles on management theory and practice, Mr. Bennett holds the appointment of Clinical Professor, Health Services Administration, University of Southern California. His display of global vision and innovative thinking, spanning over a period of more than three decades in health care, has placed Mr. Bennett on the speaking platform of numerous national and regional conferences, and at institutions of higher learning across the country.

SAMUEL J. TIBBITTS, former president of the Lutheran Hospital Society (LHS) of Southern California, has become chairman of a newly merged company called UniHealth America (an equal merger of LHS and HealthWest). He is also chairman of PacifiCare, a highly successful Health Maintenance Organization (HMO).

During four decades of national leadership in the health care field, Mr. Tibbitts has earned a reputation for vision and innovative action. He was instrumental in pioneering a preferred provider organization (PPO) for employees of LHS and its affiliates, and is co-author of *PPOs: An Executive's Guide* (1983). He founded PacifiCare, an HMO serving 300,000 members, which is now 70% owned by UniHealth America.

A fellow of the American College of Healthcare Executives, Mr. Tibbitts is also past chairman of the board of trustees and past speaker of the house of delegates of the American Hospital Association, from whom he has received the Citation for Meritorious Service. He also served as a commissioner on the Joint Commission on Accreditation of Healthcare Organizations and was recently the recipient of the highest honor given by his peers, the Gold Medal Award of the American College of Healthcare Executives.